KU-016-850

THE HIDDEN PLACES OF THE
LAKE DISTRICT
AND CUMBRIA

By Peter Long

© Travel Publishing Ltd.

Regional Hidden Places

Cambs & Lincolnshire
Chilterns
Cornwall
Derbyshire
Devon
Dorset, Hants & Isle of Wight
East Anglia
Gloucs, Wiltshire & Somerset
Heart of England
Hereford, Worcs & Shropshire
Highlands & Islands
Lake District & Cumbria
Lancashire & Cheshire
Lincolnshire & Nottinghamshire
Northumberland & Durham
Sussex
Thames Valley
Yorkshire

National Hidden Places

England
Ireland
Scotland
Wales

Hidden Inns

East Anglia
Heart of England
Lancashire & Cheshire
North of England
South
South East
South and Central Scotland
Wales
Welsh Borders
West Country
Yorkshire
Wales

Country Living Rural Guides

East Anglia
Heart of England
Ireland
North East of England
North West of England
Scotland
South
South East
Wales
West Country

Published by: Travel Publishing Ltd, 7a Apollo House, Calleva Park, Aldermaston, Berkshire RG7 8TN

ISBN 1·902·00793·X

© Travel Publishing Ltd

First published 1990, second edition 1993, third edition 1996, fourth edition 1998, fifth edition 2001, sixth edition 2003

Printing by: Scotprint, Haddington

Maps by: © Maps in Minutes ™ (2003)
© Crown Copyright, Ordnance Survey 2003

Editor: Peter Long

Cover Design: Lines & Words, Aldermaston

Cover Photograph: Wast Water Lake, Cumbria
© www.britainonview.com

Text Photographs: © www.britainonview.com

Foreword

The *Hidden Places* is a collection of easy to use travel guides taking you in this instance on a relaxed but informative tour of *Cumbria* and "the jewel in its crown", *The Lake District*. The delightful county of *Cumbria* in which the Lakes reside is England's second largest county, but surprisingly has a relatively small population of only 490,000 people which is only slightly more numerous than the city of Leeds. The *Lake District* is most famous for its impressive mountain scenery but also encompasses green rolling hills, fast flowing rivers, deep lush forests and of course the enchanting and languid lakes. Below the fells, peaceful country lanes meander through beautiful little hamlets and tiny rural villages, many steeped in history. This wonderful scenery is of course celebrated by the "Lake Poets" · Wordswoth, Coleridge and Southey. Apart from the Lake District, Cumbria offers the visitor gentle moorland, craggy coastal headlands, scattered woodlands and a fascinating history and cultural heritage.

The covers and pages of the *Hidden Places* series have been comprehensively redesigned and this edition of *The Hidden Places of The Lake District & Cumbria* is the fifth title to be published in the new format. All *Hidden Places* titles will now be published in this new style which ensures that readers can properly appreciate the attractive scenery and impressive places of interest in Cumbria and, of course, throughout the rest of the British Isles.

Our books contain a wealth of interesting information on the history, the countryside, the towns and villages and the more established places of interest. But they also promote the more secluded and little known visitor attractions and places to stay, eat and drink many of which are easy to miss unless you know exactly where you are going.

We include hotels, inns, restaurants, public houses, teashops, various types of accommodation, historic houses, museums, gardens, and many other attractions throughout the area, all of which are comprehensively indexed. Most places are accompanied by an attractive photograph and are easily located by using the map at the beginning of each chapter. We do not award merit marks or rankings but concentrate on describing the more interesting, unusual or unique features of each place with the aim of making the reader's stay in the local area an enjoyable and stimulating experience. In this respect we would like to thank the Tourist Information Centres in Cumbria for helping us update the editorial content.

Whether you are visiting the area for business or pleasure or in fact are living in the counties we do hope that you enjoy reading and using this book. We are always interested in what readers think of places covered (or not covered) in our guides so please do not hesitate to use the reader reaction forms provided to give us your considered comments. We also welcome any general comments which will help us improve the guides themselves. Finally if you are planning to visit any other corner of the British Isles we would like to refer you to the list of other *Hidden Places* titles to be found at the rear of the book and to the Travel Publishing website at www.travelpublishing.co.uk.

Travel Publishing

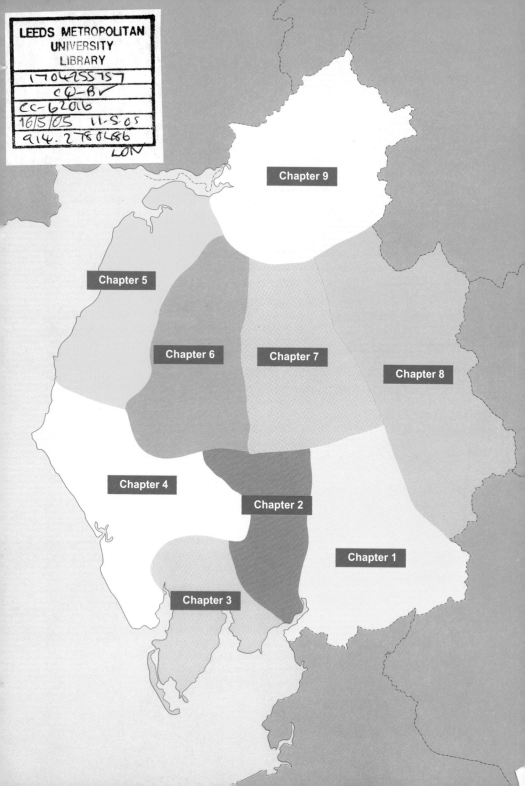

Chapter 9

Chapter 5

Chapter 6

Chapter 7

Chapter 8

Chapter 4

Chapter 2

Chapter 1

Chapter 3

Contents

PLACES TO STAY, EAT AND DRINK

Denotes entries in other chapters

1 Gateway to the Lakes

Visitors from all over the world are drawn in their millions to the Lake District, with its irresistible combination of enchanting lakes, picturesque villages and some of the most dramatic scenery in England. The highest mountain in the country, Scafell Pike (3,205ft), the largest and deepest lakes, Windermere and Wast Water respectively, are all found here, along with hundreds of other mountains, another 14 lakes (but apart from Bassenthwaite they are called 'meres' or 'waters'), challenging crags and lovely wooded valleys.

Despite the huge influx of visitors, most do not venture far from the main tourist 'honey-pots' so it's still easy to find the peaceful glades and windswept, isolated fells celebrated by the Lake Poets, Wordsworth, Coleridge and Southey. Between them, this lyrical trio transformed the pervading 18th century perception of the most northwesterly corner of England as an intimidating wilderness into an appreciation of its majestic scenery.

Cumbria is England's second largest county but with a population (under half a million) only slightly more than that of the City of Leeds. Almost exactly one third of the county's 2,636 square miles lies within the boundaries of the Lake District National Park, created in 1951 to protect the area from "inappropriate development and to provide access to the land for public enjoyment". Its 22,292 square kilometres include a wonderfully varied landscape, and the opportunities for enjoying the great outdoors are almost boundless. Not a single mile of motorway has penetrated its borders and only the very occasional stretch of dual-carriageway, but access to

Levens Hall, Levens

the area is very easy, with the M6 running right along its eastern edge. For many people travelling from the south into Cumbria, their first experience of the county is the area around Kendal and Kirkby Lonsdale. These ancient settlements both provide an excellent introduction to the history, people, and economy of Cumbria. Ideally placed for the Lake District National Park and the south Cumbrian coast, it is easy to forget that this area is also close to the northern Pennines and the Yorkshire Dales National Park.

Devil's Bridge, Kirkby Lonsdale

Kirkby Lonsdale

One fine day in 1875 John Ruskin came to Kirkby Lonsdale and stood on the stone terrace overlooking the valley of the River Lune. It was, he declared, "one of the loveliest scenes in England, therefore in the world". He was equally enthusiastic about the busy little market town - "I do not know in all my country", he continued, "a place more naturally divine than Kirkby Lonsdale".

Ruskin had been inspired to visit the town after seeing Turner's painting of that view, and Turner himself had come in 1816 on the recommendation of William Wordsworth. All three of them made a point of going to see the **Devil's Bridge** over the Lune, a handsome, lofty

structure of three fluted arches reputedly built by Satan himself in three days. According to legend an old woman, unable to cross the deep river with her cattle, had asked the Devil to build her a bridge. He agreed but demanded in return the soul of the first creature to cross but his evil plan was thwarted by Cumbrian cunning. The old woman threw a bun across the bridge which was retrieved by her dog and thus she cheated the Devil of a human soul.

The bridge is at least 700 years old and although its exact age is a mystery we do know that some repairs were carried out in 1275, making it certainly the oldest surviving bridge in Westmorland. By the 1920s, this narrow bridge originally designed for pack-horses was quite inadequate for the growth in motor traffic. A new bridge was built and this, together with one of the country's first by-pass roads, has saved the lovely old town from further destructive road-widening schemes.

Kirkby's Main Street is a picturesque jumble of houses spanning several

Kirkby Lonsdale

centuries, with intriguing passages and alleyways skittering off in all directions, all of them worth exploring. It's still a pleasure to stroll along the narrow streets bearing names such as Jingling Lane, past the 16th century weavers' cottages in Fairbank, across the **Swine**

THE MEWS COFFEE HOUSE & LICENSED RESTAURANT

64a Main Street, Kirkby Lonsdale, Cumbria LA6 2AJ Tel: 015242 71007

An archway off Kirkby Lonsdale's main street leads to **The Mews Coffee House & Licensed Restaurant**. Run by Roselynne Adkinson and her daughter Stephanie, it is open from 10 to 5 every day except Wednesday. Stephanie's cakes, pastries and desserts are renowned in the area, but everything on the menu is well worth trying, from baps and baguettes to traditional English breakfast, afternoon cream teas and a hearty full meal with wine. Originally the stables of a large Georgian

house, The Mews has a bright, traditional look, and the courtyard is ablaze with flowers throughout the year. No smoking inside.

THE SWAN INN

Middleton, Nr Kirkby Lonsdale,
Cumbria LA6 2NB
Tel/Fax: 01524 276223

The Swan Inn voted Camra Pub of the
Season Spring 2002, is a magnificent old-
world village hostelry standing just off the
A683 Kirkby Lonsdale-Sedbergh road. The
premises date back to the last years of the
16th century and started life as a home farm
called Slaters; there was also a blacksmith's
shop on the site. As the years went by, the
farmer began to supplement his income by
brewing his own beer, and later the farm
developed into a coaching inn with stabling
for teams of horses. Richard and Lynne
Lappin became the owners of The Swan in
April 2002 having spent 20 years in the

licensed and related trades, mainly in
neighbouring Lancashire.

The little wood-panelled bar is particularly
well stocked, with a minimum of four ales
(Black Sheep is a resident), draught and
bottle beers, lagers, stout and cider, and an
impressive collection of three dozen malt
whiskies. Food is available from opening
time right through to last orders at 9
o'clock each evening. Richard is a trained,
talented chef and offers an extensive range
of home-cooked dishes for the regular
printed menu and for the long list of daily
specials, which runs to some 20 main
courses alone! The Traditional Farmhouse
Menu tempts the hungry with a
mouthwatering selection of pub classics
such as a 16oz horseshoe gammon steak
served with two eggs; a foot of Cumberland

sausage; liver & onions; deep-fried Whitby
scampi; fish & chips; lamb in a creamy, minty
sauce. There's always a good choice of
vegetarian main courses, with some
delectable desserts to round off a meal
in style.

The separate non-smoking restaurant has
seats for 30, but meals can also be
taken in the bar, or on warmer days in
the beer garden. The garden includes an
area with equipment to keep the children
amused. Friday night brings live music
to The Swan, when all and sundry are
invited to bring along their own
instruments and join in the fun. In
summer the inn is open all day seven
days a week; in winter it's open Tuesday
to Friday evenings and all day Saturday
and Sunday. The village of Middleton is
surrounded by thousands of acres of
picturesque countryside, and the inn
looks towards the imposing Middleton
Fell. The A683 provides easy access
south towards Kirkby Lonsdale, a busy little
market town beloved of John Ruskin, and
north to Sedbergh, beyond which the
Yorkshire Dales National Park stretches up to
the Pennines.

Market with its 600-year-old cross where traders have displayed their wares every Thursday for more than 700 years, past ancient hostelries to the even more venerable **St Mary's Church** with its noble Norman doorway and massive pillars. In the churchyard, a late Georgian gazebo looks across to the enchanting view of the Lune Valley painted by Turner.

The town has three times been national winner of the "Britain in Bloom" competition and also attracts thousands of visitors for its **Victorian** Fair, held on the first full weekend in September, and again in December for the Yuletide procession through streets ablaze with coloured lights and decorated Christmas trees.

Around Kirkby Lonsdale

Hale

7 miles W of Kirkby Lonsdale off the A6

This tiny village surrounded by woodland and close to the Lancashire border is home to the **Lakeland Wildlife Oasis** (see panel) where a wide range of animals and birds can be seen and a hands-on exhibition tells the evolutionary story. Visitors can drape a snake around their neck, exchange inquisitive glances with a ruffled lemur or a meerkat squatting on its haunches, and

LAKELAND WILDLIFE OASIS

Hale, Milnthorpe, Cumbria LA7 7BW
Tel: 015395 63027
e-mail: mail@wildlifeoasis.co.uk
website: www.wildlifeoasis.co.uk

Opened in 1991, **Lakeland Wildlife Oasis** quickly established itself as one of the Lake District's premier visitor attractions. "Half Zoo, half Museum, and totally fascinating" the Oasis takes visitors on an amazing journey through the world of wildlife using a unique combination of live animals and imaginative "hands-on" computer displays. Visitors can drape a snake around their neck, exchange inquisitive glances with a Ruffled Lemur or a beautifully poised Meerkat squatting on its haunches, and admire creatures rarely seen in captivity such as Flying Foxes and Poison Arrow Frogs. Or you can just relax in the tropical hall, colourful with free-flying birds, bats and butterflies. Many rare species have found a secure home here, amongst them the fossa, of which there are only 44 in captivity.

Friendly staff are always on hand to answer questions and let you meet some of the inhabitants face to face! The Oasis was established by Dave and Jo Marsden, both of whom were animal keepers at Chester Zoo before setting up this popular family attraction. It is open every day of the year, (except for Christmas Day and Boxing Day), there is access throughout for the disabled, and other amenities include picnic areas, a snack bar and a gift shop. For parties of more than 30 people, it is advisable to book ahead and the Oasis will then provide a tour guide.

THE KINGS ARMS

Hale, Nr Milnthorpe, Cumbria LA7 7BH
Tel: 015395 63202

The Kings Arms is a handsome hostelry built in 1810 as a coaching inn to serve the then new turnpike (now the A6) that linked Kendal and Lancaster. The tradition of hospitality is being continued in splendid style by landlords Rosalynd and Stanford Robinson, who brought many years experience in the licensed trade with them when they took over the reins in 1994. A fine selection of cask ales, bottled and draught beers, lagers, stout and cider is served in the bar, and the outstanding food for which the inn has become renowned takes its inspiration from near and far. Salads and sandwiches make ideal lighter meals, while main courses offer a great choice that might include steak & kidney pie, griddled steaks, lamb tagine, pepperpot pork, salmon and prawn au gratin and vegetable jambalaya.

The owners are always looking for ways to make their excellent enterprise even better, and the conservatory added at Eastertime 2001 increased the dining space and provided a section for non-smokers. They have also provided ramp access and toilet facilities for visitors in wheelchairs. Two well-appointed double rooms are available for letting on a Bed & Breakfast basis all year round, making the Kings Arms a very comfortable and civilised base from which to tour a part of the country with many and varied visitor attractions. The inn has a beer garden, a bowling green and a private room for meetings, functions or other special occasions.

admire creatures rarely seen in captivity such as flying foxes or poison arrow frogs. The tropical hall is the home of numerous free-flying birds, bats and butterflies, and other exhibits range from leaf-cutter ants to pygmy marmosets. The Oasis was established in 1991 by Dave and Jo Marsden, who were keepers at Chester Zoo before setting up this popular family attraction, which is open throughout the year.

About 3 miles south of the town, **Leighton Hall** is actually in Lancashire but well worth a short diversion. Famed for its collection of Gillow furniture, the Hall has been described as the most beautifully situated house in the British Isles, with the dramatic panorama of the Lakeland Fells providing a striking

backdrop. The elaborate neo-Gothic façade cloaks an 18th century mansion which in turn stands on the site of the original medieval house built in 1246 by Adam d'Avranches, whose descendants still live here.

Arnside
10 miles W of Kirkby Lonsdale off the B5282

This quiet town on the Kent Estuary, with its short but elegant promenade, was once a busy port with its own shipbuilding and sea-salt refining industry. As the estuary silted up during the 19th century, a process accelerated by the construction of the striking 50-arch railway viaduct, so the port declined. Today, it is a favourite retirement destination and a peaceful holiday resort.

Around Arnside itself there is a wonderful choice of country walks, particularly over and around **Arnside Knott**. This limestone headland, now a nature reserve rich in old woods and wild flowers, is part of the Arnside and Silverdale Area of Outstanding Natural Beauty. Knott comes from the Saxon word meaning 'rounded hill', which, in this case, rises 521 feet above sea level and gives extensive views of the Lakeland fells, the Pennines, and the southern Cumbrian coast. There is a beautiful path around the headland and along the shoreline past Blackstone Point.

Inland, and found down a quiet lane, is **Arnside Tower**, one of the many pele towers that were built in the area in the 14th century. This particular tower dates from the 1370s and it may have been part of the chain of towers designed to form a ring of protection around Morecambe Bay.

Beetham

8 miles W of Kirkby Lonsdale on the A6

Approached through a pergola of rambling roses, the **Church of St Michael and All Angels** dates from Saxon times and, during restoration work in the 1830s, a hoard of around a hundred coins, minted in Norman times, was discovered inside the building at the base of a pillar. Although badly damaged during the Civil War, when its windows were smashed and effigies broken, a glass fragment of Henry IV in an ermine robe has survived the centuries. The village is also home to an unusual 19th century **Post Office** with a distinctive black and white studded door.

Just outside the village lies **Heron Corn Mill**, a restored and working waterfall with fully operational grinding machinery. A fine example of a traditional corn mill which operated for trade in the Westmorland farming area, the mill ceased trading as recently as the 1950s. The situation of Heron Mill is ideal as a natural shelf of rock in the River Bela forms a waterfall, providing the necessary head of water to drive the waterwheel. This made the site an obvious one when, in 1220, the Lords of the Manor of Haverback granted lands to the Canons of Coningshead for the construction of a mill. Referred to several times in archives from the Middle Ages, the land was transferred to Sir William Thorneburghe when Coningshead was destroyed in 1538. Visitors to the mill can see an exhibition about its history and view the milling process. Also here is the **Museum of Paper Making**, which was established in 1988 to commemorate 500 years of papermaking in England.

Milnthorpe

8 miles W of Kirkby Lonsdale on A6

Just north of the Lancashire border, Milnthorpe has been a market town since the 14th century. It originally

THE BULLS HEAD

5 Beetham Road, Milnthorpe,
Cumbria LA7 7QL
Tel: 015395 62133
e-mail: joe@bullshead.co.uk
web: www.bullsheadcumbria.co.uk

When local couple Joe and Margaret Waters took over as tenants at the **Bulls Head**, they were inheriting a tradition of hospitality that dates back several centuries. Behind the white-painted frontage on a corner site in the heart of Milnthorpe, the ground-floor area is divided into a quartet of cosy, inviting rooms – three lounge bars and a convivial public bar with a pool table, juke box and other catering facilities. It also makes an agreeably different choice for a corporate meeting, with accommodation at tables for up to 60. For private visitors it's a very agreeable base to choose as a base for exploring the area known as the Gateway to the Lakes. Two family-size letting bedrooms are located on the first floor, and the very reasonable tariff includes a full English breakfast. Milnthorpe has been a market town since the 14th century and once flourished as a port on the banks of the River Bela. The river silted up long ago, but water is close by in abundance with the Kent Estuary and the vast expanse of Morecambe Bay just minutes away. An interesting place to visit on the estuary is Arnside, a peaceful holiday resort around which there's a splendid choice of country and coastal walks. For motorists wanting to venture further afield, the A6 runs south towards Lancaster and north to Kendal; the M6 is also very near.

diversions. The pub is open all day, every day for drinks, which include a wide variety of keg bitters, bottled beers, lagers, cider and both regular and extra-cold Guinness. Food is served from midday to 7 o'clock daily, and later by arrangement for special bookings. Joe and a chef share the cooking, and diners can choose between the printed menu and the daily changing specials board. The choice is abundant, and everything is cooked fresh on the premises – no frozen chips here! Children are always very welcome, and some of the tables are designated non-smoking. It's usually a full house for the weekly quiz, which starts at 8.30 every Tuesday. The Bulls Head is a popular venue for a small party, wedding reception or other special occasion, and the staff can provide a full range of

flourished as a port on the banks of the River Bela but the harbour has long since silted up. The mill of the town's name refers to the waterfalls that once stood alongside the river. A small folly tower on **St Andrew's Hill** was built in the 1830s by the architect George Webster as a means of occupying his idle hours while restoring the town's church.

Sandside

9 miles W of Kirkby Lonsdale on the B5282

From this small village situated on the banks of the Kent Estuary, pack horses and drovers during the Middle Ages together with their sheep and cattle would set off across the treacherous sands into Cumbria rather than take the longer, inland route. Consequently, many lives were unnecessarily lost and the route remains as dangerous today as it was then.

Kendal High Street

Kendal

A survey a few years back by Strathclyde University revealed that the highest quality of life of any town in England was to be found in Kendal, the 'capital' of South Lakeland. That assessment came as no surprise to the residents of this lively, bustling town which was once one of the most important woollen

FLIPPIN FLUKE

Sandside, Nr Milnthorpe, Cumbria LA7 7HW
Tel: 01539563243

Overlooking the vast expanse of Morecambe Bay, **Flippin Fluke** is a very friendly restaurant with family owners Allan and Pauline Syme. Excellent food in pleasant surroundings is what visitors can look forward to, and in the non-smoking rooms Pauline prepares a wide range of dishes for her various menus. She offers something for everyone, from breaded Brie wedges and the famous Morecambe Bay potted shrimps among the starters to traditional English main courses and specialities such as honey-roast duck and slow-roast lamb, and meals end with

some really delicious desserts. This fine food is complemented by well-priced wines. Booking is essential for Sunday lunch.

THE CASTLE INN

13 Castle Street, Kendal,
Cumbria LA9 7AA
Tel: 01539 729983

Behind the welcoming white-painted frontage with its colourful hanging baskets and window boxes, the **Castle Inn** has a delightfully traditional look and feel. Hosts Christine and Geoff have made it a very popular meeting place, both with the local community and with the many visitors who come to see the nearby castle and Kendal's numerous other attractions.

A good choice of real ales, including brews from Tetley and Jennings and four Dent ales, is always on tap, and Christine's home cooking is guaranteed to bring in an eager lunchtime crowd - everything is good, but their all-time favourite is her fish cooked in batter made to her own secret recipe. In the same street and just a short walk from its namesake, the Castle Inn dates back to the early 1700s, and a directory of 1834 lists it as a 'beer house'. By 1870 it had been elevated to the status of an inn, in which role it has been successful ever since.

It's a very sociable and sporting place: it has its own darts, pool and quiz teams, and the local hockey team have made it their favoured watering hole after matches. The inn is open all day every day, so it's always ready to cope with thirsts generated by a walk round historic Kendal. Children are welcome until 6.30pm.

textile centres of northern England. The Kendal woollen industry was founded in 1331 by John Kemp, a Flemish weaver, and it flourished and sustained the town for almost 600 years until the development of competition from the huge West Riding of Yorkshire mills during the Industrial Revolution of the 19th century. The town's motto 'Wool is my Bread' reveals the extent to which the economy of Kendal depended on the wool from the flocks of Herdwick sheep

Kendal Castle

that roamed the surrounding fells. The fame of the cloth was so great that Shakespeare refers to archers clad in Kendal Green cloth in his play *Henry IV*. These archers were the famous **Kendal Bowmen** whose lethal longbows were made from local yew trees culled from the nearby limestone crags. It was these men who clinched the English victories at Agincourt and Crécy and fought so decisively against the Scots at the Battle of Flodden Field in 1513.

Kendal has royal connections too. The Parr family lived at **Kendal Castle** until 1483 - their most famous descendant was Catherine Parr, the last of Henry VIII's six wives. Today, the castle's gaunt ruins stand high on a hill overlooking the town, with most of the castle wall and one of the towers still standing, and two underground vaults still complete. Castle Hill is a popular place for walking and

picnicing and in summer the hillside is smothered with wild flowers. From the hilltop there are spectacular views and a panorama panel here assists in identifying the distant fells.

The largest settlement in the old county of Westmorland, Kendal has always been a bustling town, from the days when it was on the main route to Scotland. Nowadays the M6 and a by-pass divert much of the traffic away from the town centre, but its narrow main streets, Highgate, Stramongate, and Stricklandgate, are always busy during the season. The fine coaching inns of the 17th and 18th centuries, to which Prince Charles Edward is said to have retreated after his abortive 1745 rebellion, still line these streets.

Anyone wandering around the town cannot help but notice the numerous alleyways, locally known as yards, that

ABBOT HALL ART GALLERY AND MUSEUM

Kendal, Cumbria LA9 5AL
Tel: 01539 722464 Fax: 01539 722494

Abbot Hall Art Gallery forms part of a complex within Abbot Hall park and includes work by John Ruskin and the celebrated portrait painter, George Romney, who was born nearby at Dalton-in-Furness in 1734. The permanent collection also includes a wide range of 18th, 19th and 20th century British paintings and watercolours, and the Gallery hosts regular touring exhibitions.

are such a distinctive feature of Kendal. An integral part of the old town, they are a reminder that the people of Kendal used to live under a constant threat of raids by the Scots. The yards were a line of defence against these attacks, an area that could be secured by sealing the one small entrance, with the families and livestock safe inside.

Shoppers are spoilt for choice in Kendal. In addition to all the familiar High Street names, the **Westmorland Shopping Centre**, **Blackhall Yard** and **Elephant Yard**, all in the heart of the town, and the **K Village Factory Shopping** complex on the outskirts,

make it easy to shop until you drop. One local product well worth sampling is **Kendal Mint Cake**, a tasty, sugary confection which is cherished by climbers and walkers for its instant infusion of energy. Another once-popular local medication, **Kendal Black Drop**, is sadly no longer available. 'A more than commonly strong mixture of opium and alcohol', Kendal Black Drop was a favourite tipple of the poets Samuel Taylor Coleridge and Thomas de Quincey.

Kendal's excellent sporting facilities include the **Kendal Leisure Centre**, which offers a one-week tourist pass,

MUSEUM OF LAKELAND LIFE

Kendal, Cumbria LA9 5AL
Tel: 01539 722464 Fax: 01539 722494

A short walk from the Brewery Arts Centre is the **Museum of Lakeland Life and Industry** which is themed around traditional rural trades of the region, such as blacksmithing, wheelwrighting, agricultural activities, weaving, and printing. Here, too, are re-created cottage interiors, elegantly furnished period rooms, a Postman Pat room for younger visitors and a reconstruction of the study in which the celebrated author, Arthur Ransome, wrote the children's classic *Swallows and Amazons*.

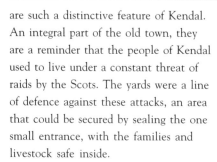

Kendal Wall, which is one of the highest indoor climbing facilities in the country, Kendal ski slope, two local golf courses and a driving range. Drama, music and the visual arts are presented in a regularly changing programme of exhibitions, live music, theatre productions and craft workshops at the **Brewery Arts Centre**. The Centre also houses Kendal's cinema which presents a mixture of mainstream, classic and art house films.

A number of interesting museums and galleries are also located in Kendal. The **Museum of Lakeland Life and Industry** (see panel opposite) which is themed around traditional rural trades of the region, and **Abbot Hall Art Gallery** (see panel opposite) form part of a complex within Abbot Hall park. The museum, in re-created farmhouse rooms, contains a wide variety of exhibits, including Arthur Ransome memorabilia, craft workshops, a Victorian street scene, artefacts from the Arts and Crafts movement, nautical displays and Captain Flint's Locker, a pirates activity area for children and families. The gallery, in an elegant Georgian villa, houses a collection of society portraits by the locally born George Romney and watercolour scenes by Ruskin and Turner, while the 20th century and contemporary scene is represented by Walter Sickert, Ben Nicholson, Lucien Freud and Bridget Riley. The **Museum of Natural History and Archaeology**, founded in 1796, is one of the oldest museums in the country. Based on the

collection first exhibited by William Todhunter in the late 18th century, the Museum takes visitors on a journey from prehistoric times, a trip which includes an interactive exhibit which tells the story of Kendal Castle.

The famous fellwalker and writer, Alfred Wainwright, whose handwritten guides to the Lakeland hills will be found in the backpack of any serious walker, was honorary clerk here between 1945 and 1974. Many of his original drawings are on display. In the summer of 2004 a small exhibition will open chronicling the life of a local eccentric called Millican Dalton. Affectionately known as the **Cave Man of Borrowdale**, he lived for 50 years in a cave blasted from the slate of Castle Crag near Keswick and propounded his views on Quaker pacifism, vegetarianism and the outdoor life. He achieved notoriety between the two World Wars by offering women the chance to go on expeditions involving camping, river crafting and shooting rapids.

Adjacent to the elegant Georgian Abbot Hall and Museum is the 13th century **Parish Church** of Kendal, 'the Church of the Angels', one of the widest in England, with five aisles and a peal of 10 bells. Among the many interesting things to see are the carved reredos of the Parr Chapel, the stained glass windows, and the sculpture *The Family of Man* by Josephina de Vasconcellos. The church also contains a sword thought to have belonged to Robert Philipson, a Cavalier during the Civil War. While away fighting in Carlisle, Cromwell's supporters laid siege to Philipson's house at Windermere. On his return, the Cavalier attacked the Kendal church when he thought the Roundheads would be at prayer. Riding his horse right into the church, he found it empty save for one innocent man whom he ran through with this very sword.

Perhaps the most unusual attraction in Kendal is the **Quaker Tapestry Exhibition** at the Friends Meeting House in the centre of the town. This unique exhibition of 77 panels of community embroidery explores Quaker history from the 17th century to the present day. These colourful, beautifully crafted tapestries are the work of some 4,000 people, aged between 4 and 90, from 15 countries. A Quaker costume display, embroidery demonstrations, workshops and courses, and a large screen colour video combine to provide a fascinating insight into the Quaker movement and its development.

Around Kendal

Levens

5 miles S of Kendal off the A590

At the southern tip of Scout Scar, overlooking the Lyth Valley and the lower reaches of the River Kent, stands **Levens Hall** with its unique topiary gardens. The superb Elizabethan mansion (described as 'one of the wonders of Lakeland') developed from a 14th century pele tower and the gardens were first laid out in 1694. They were the work of Colonel James Grahme, a keen gardener, who purchased the hall in 1688 and employed a Frenchman, Guillaume Beaumont, to create the amazing topiary work (Beaumont also redesigned the gardens at Hampton Court for James II). The fame of the Levens Hall gardens spread quickly and ever since they have been a popular attraction. Today, there are more 90 individual pieces, some almost 20ft high, with the ancient yew trees cut into often surreal shapes. The topiary is by no means the only attraction in the grounds, which also include a Fountain Garden created in 1994 to mark the tercentary of the gardens. The interior of the house is equally rewarding - a wealth of period furniture, fine panelling and plasterwork, a dining room with walls covered in goatskin, and

Topiary Gardens of Levens Hall

Levens Hall Gardens

paintings by Rubens, Lely and Cuyp. The Hall is said to be haunted by three ghosts: a black dog, a lady in pink, and a gypsy woman who, legend has it, put a curse on the family saying that they would have no heir until the River Kent ceased to flow and a white fawn was born in the park. In fact, after many years without a direct heir, in 1896 the River Kent froze over, a white fawn was seen, and a son and heir was born. A major location for the BBC-TV serial *Wives and Daughters*, the Hall's other attractions include a collection of working steam engines, a tea room, gift shop and plant centre.

Only a couple of miles north of Levens Hall, just off the A591, is another stately old residence, **Sizergh Castle**, the impressive home of the Strickland family since 1239 although the property is now administered by the National Trust. Originally a pele tower built to withstand border raiders, the house has been added to and altered over the intervening centuries to provide the family, as times became less violent, with a more comfortable home. Now boasting intricately carved chimney mantels, fine oak panelling, and a collection of portraits of the Stuart royal family, the castle offers an additional 'attraction' in the form of the ghost of a medieval lady. She is said to haunt the castle, screaming to be released from the room in which she had been locked by her fiercely jealous husband. It was here that she starved to death while he was away in battle. More reliable attractions at Sizergh are the well laid out gardens and 1500 acres of grounds which provide superb views over the Lakeland fells.

Brigsteer
3 miles SW of Kendal off A591

This tiny hamlet lies under the limestone escarpment of Scout Scar. From this pretty settlement, the road leads into the National Trust property of **Brigsteer Woods** where, as the climate is milder here due to its sheltered position, there are wild daffodils in the spring.

Burneside
2 miles N of Kendal off the A591

There has been a settlement here since the Stone Age and the remains of a stone circle can be seen close by on **Potter Fell**. By the 15th century Burneside was a settled agricultural area and a rich variety of mills sprang up

Four miles northeast of Kendal off the A685 Tebay road, **Field End Barns & Shaw End Mansion** enjoy an idyllic setting on the edge of the Lake District National Park. Two stone and slate barns at Field End, a former Lakeland farm, have been converted to provide five outstandingly comfortable three- and four-bedroom cottages with separate bath and shower rooms, an open fire, tv, video, many original features and private gardens. The kitchens are equipped with all the expected up-to-date facilities, and central heating keeps the cottage cosy even in the chilliest weather.

The crystal clear River Mint flows through the grounds, and fishing is available on a stretch of the river and on a nearby tarn. Ten minutes walk away, owners Edward and Karlyn Robinson run another holiday complex at Shaw End. This imposing Georgian mansion stands on a 200-acre estate and has been skilfully and sympathetically converted to provide four luxury apartments with two or three bedrooms and everything needed for a really comfortable self-catering holiday – with the bonus of great views across the Cumbrian countryside. With easy access to the M6, the National Parks, Windermere and the attractive market town of Kendal, Field End Barns and Shaw End Mansion provide a perfect base for a touring holiday.

along the River Sprint - fulling, corn, cotton, wool, bobbin, and the original rag paper mill at **Cowan Head.**

The River Sprint, which meets the River Kent just south of the village, has its own remarkably beautiful Longsleddale Valley which curves past Garnett Bridge deep into the high fell country. A bridle path climbs from the head of the valley into Kentmere, another spectacularly beautiful walk.

Grayrigg
5 miles NE of Kendal on the A685

This is a fine village with a cluster of alms houses, cottages, and a simple church found in a lovely rural setting. It was the birthplace of Francis Howgill (1610-69), who was responsible for introducing George Fox to the **Westmorland Seekers**, a group of radical Christians from the area.

Sedbergh

In 1974 Sedbergh was brusquely removed from the West Riding of Yorkshire and became part of Cumbria. However, it still lies within the Yorkshire Dales National Park and the surrounding scenery certainly belongs to the Dales with the mighty **Howgill Hills** - great pear-shaped drumlins shaped by glaciers - soaring to more than 2200ft (670m). **Winder Hill**, which provides a dramatic backdrop to the little market town, is half that height, but with its sleek grassy flanks and domed top, seems much loftier. Four valleys and four mountain streams meet here and for centuries Sedbergh (pronounced Sedber) has been an important centre for cross-Pennine travellers. During the golden age of stage coach travel, the town became a staging post on the route between Lancaster and Newcastle-upon-Tyne. The complete journey between Lancaster and Newcastle took from 4 o'clock in the morning to 7 o'clock at night: 15 hours to cover a distance of about 120 miles, an average speed of 8 miles per hour. At the **King's Arms Hotel**, the four horses would be swiftly changed before the equipage rattled off again across the moors to Teesdale, Durham and Newcastle.

In those days, the stage-coach would have been used frequently by the boys attending Sedbergh's famous **Public School**. Its founder was Roger Lupton, a Howgill boy who rose to become Provost of Eton: he established the school because he felt that one was desperately needed "in the north country amongst the people rude in knowledge". In later years, Wordsworth's son studied here and

Coleridge's son, Hartley, became a master. The school's extensive grounds, through which visitors are welcome to wander, seem to place the old-world town within a park.

That impression is reinforced if you follow the path beside the River Rawthay to **Brigflatts**. Close to where George Fox stayed overnight with his friend Richard Robinson is the oldest **Quaker Meeting House** in the north of England. Built in 1675, and still with its original oak interior, this beautiful, simple building has changed little over the years.

This area is filled with Quaker history and **Firbank Knott**, on nearby Firbank Fell, can be said to be the birthplace of Quakerism for it was here, in 1652, that the visionary George Fox gave his great sermon to inspire a huge gathering from the whole of the north of England. This meeting was to lead to the development of the **Quaker Movement**. The simple boulder on the fell, from which Fox delivered his momentous words, is

THE RED LION

Finkle Street, Sedbergh, Cumbria LA10 5BZ
Tel: 01539 620433
e-mail: geofhailey@aol.com
website: www.theredlionsedbergh.co.uk

In the heart of Sedbergh, opposite St Andrew's Church, the 17th century **Red Lion** is a family-friendly pub with small, cosy rooms and ancient oak beams. Licensee Carole Hailey has established a fine reputation with her home cooking, and her printed menu and specials board provide plenty of choice, from baguettes and omelettes to lasagne, steak pie, battered haddock and giant Yorkshire pudding filled with roast beef, vegetables and gravy. Cumberland Ale and a guest ale from

the Jennings brewery head the drinks list. No food on Monday (except Bank Holidays) or Sunday evening.

marked by a plaque and is now known as **Fox's Pulpit**.

Sedbergh seems a very friendly town. At **St Andrew's Church**, for example, Protestants and Roman Catholics take turns to use the building for their own services, an arrangement believed to be rare in England.

Much of the heart of the town has been deemed a Conservation Area and fortunately many of the older buildings have survived. In particular, the stone-built cottages on both sides of the cobbled yard, known as **The Folly**, just off Main Street, have not only survived unscathed but remain dwellings and have not had the misfortune to be converted to other uses.

To the east of the town, on a small wooded hill top, lies **Castlehaw**, the remains of an ancient motte and bailey castle. Built by the Normans in the 11th century, the castle guarded the valleys of the River Rawthey and the River Lune against the marauding Scots. Also just outside town, on the A683 Garsdale road, is **Farfield Mill** Heritage and Arts Centre, where spinners, weavers, potters, woodcarvers and other craftspeople use traditional skills to produce high-quality goods, all of it for sale in the shop. Also on site are an arts and crafts gallery, a heritage display depicting the history of the mill, and a riverside

restaurant. The mill is accessible to all visitors, with disabled facilities and a lift to all three levels.

Around Sedbergh

Dent

4 miles SE of Sedbergh off the A684

This charming village, the only one in Dentdale - one of Cumbria's finest dales - has a delightful cobbled main street with tall cottages lining the road. Visitors to this tranquil place will find it hard to believe that, in the 18th century, Dent was of greater importance than nearby Sedbergh. The impressive **St Andrew's Church** is Norman in origin though it underwent an almost complete rebuilding in the early 15th century. Inside can not only be seen the Jacobean three-decker pulpit that is still in use but also the local marble which paves the chancel.

Farming has, for many years, dominated the local economy but

Sedgwick Memorial Fountain

knitting, particularly in the village, has too played an important part. During the 17th and 18th centuries, the women and children, on whom this work fell, became known as the '**Terrible Knitters of Dent**' which, today, sounds uncomplimentary but the local use of the word terrible meant quite the opposite (like 'wicked' today!). Large amounts of dressed wool were turned by the knitters into stockings and gloves which were then exported out of the dale to local towns.

Viaduct carrying Settle to Carlisle Railway

Dent's most famous son is undoubtedly the 'Father of Geology', **Adam Sedgwick**. Born the son of the local vicar in 1785, Sedgwick went on to become the Woodwardian Professor of Geology at Cambridge University and also a friend of Queen Victoria and Prince Albert. The fountain of pinkish Shap granite in the village centre is Dent's memorial to this great geologist. Dent stone, with no iron pyrites likely to cause sparks, was popular for millstones used in gunpowder works. The little valley of Dentdale winds from the village up past old farms and hamlets to **Lea Yeat** where a steep lane hairpins up to Dent Station, almost five miles from the village. This is a marvellous place to begin a ramble into Dentdale or over the

Whernside. In the shadow of Whernside itself, **Whernside Manor** is a famous house with associations with the slave trade. Dent is the highest railway station in Britain, over 1,100 feet above sea level, and it lies on the famous Settle-Carlisle railway line.

Garsdale
5 miles E of Sedbergh on the A683

Lying just north of Dentdale, Garsdale is both a dale and a village and they are overlooked by the dramatic **Baugh Fell**. The River Clough follows down the dale from Garsdale Head, the watershed into Wensleydale, where a row of Midland Railway cottages lies alongside the former junction station on the Settle-Carlisle line. This is now a surprisingly busy little place during the summer months when, from time to time, preserved steam locomotives pause to take water from a moorland spring.

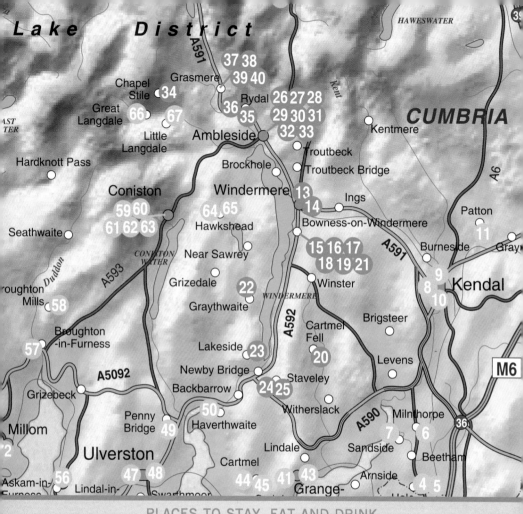

Lake District

CUMBRIA

HAWESWATER

Hardknott Pass

Chapel Stile **34**

Great Langdale **66** **67**

Little Langdale

Grasmere **37 38 39 40**

36 Rydal **35**

Ambleside

Brockhole

26 27 28 29 30 31 32 33

Kentmere

Troutbeck

Troutbeck Bridge

Seathwaite

Coniston

59 60 61 62 63

CONISTON WATER

Windermere **13 14**

Hawkshead **64 65**

Near Sawrey

Grizedale

Graythwaite

22

Ings

Bowness-on-Windermere

15 16 17 18 19 21

Winster

WINDERMERE

Cartmel Fell

Brigsteer

Patton

Burneside

Gray

9 8 10 Kendal

Levens

M6

Broughton Mills **58**

Duddon

Broughton -in-Furness **57**

A5092

Grizebeck

Millom

Penny Bridge **49**

Ulverston

Askam-in-Furness **56**

Lindal-in-

Swarthmoor

Lakeside **23**

Newby Bridge

Backbarrow

50 Haverthwaite

Cartmel

47 48

44 45 41 43 24 25

Staveley

Witherslack

Lindale

Grange-

20

A592

A590

Sandside

Arnside

Milnthorpe

Beetham

7 6

36

4 5

2 Around Windermere and Ambleside

This southeastern corner of the extensive Lake District National Park is Cumbria's best known and most popular area, with the main resort towns of Windermere, Bowness-on-Windermere and Ambleside, and, of course, Lake Windermere itself. They are certainly busy with tourists during the summer months but their charm and attraction remains for all to see. Also, with the unpredictability of Lakeland weather, they provide a whole host of indoor amusements to appeal to all ages.

The whole area opened up to tourism as a result of the Victorians' growing interest in the natural landscape and their engineering ability in providing a railway service. So these villages, once

Sunset over Windermere

little more than places where the fell
farmers congregated to buy and sell their
livestock and exchange gossip, grew into
inland resorts with fine Victorian and
Edwardian villas, houses, and municipal
buildings.

There are, also, many beautiful places
close to the bustling and crowded towns
that provide solitude. To the southeast
lies Cartmel Fell, while further north is
isolated Kentmere.

Windermere

Birthwaite village no longer features on
any map, thanks to the Kendal and
Windermere Railway Company which
built a branch line to it in 1847. With
an eye on tourist traffic, and considering
the name Birthwaite had little appeal,
they named the station Windermere
even though the lake is over a mile
distant. In the early days carriages and,
in later years, buses linked the station
with the landing stages in the village of
Bowness on the shores of the lake. As
the village burgeoned into a prosperous

Steam Boat on Lake Windermere

Victorian resort, it became popularly,
and then officially, known by the name
of its station, while Windermere water
was given the redundant prefix of Lake.

The Victorian heritage still
predominates in the many large houses

LAKES HOTEL & LAKES SUPERTOURS

1 High Street, Windermere,
Cumbria LA23 1PF
Tel: 015394 42751 Fax: 015394 46026
e-mail: admin@lakes-hotel.com
website: www.lakes-hotel.com

Lakes Hotel is a friendly Bed & Breakfast
establishment in the village centre. Built in
1860 as a bank, it has ten comfortable,
spacious bedrooms, all with private facilities,
central heating, tv, beverage tray, fridge and
hairdryer. Owner Andrew Dobson also runs
Lakes Supertours, offering full-day and half-

day Lakeland tours in comfortable mini-
coaches. Some tours include a lake cruise,
and one includes a trip on the Eskdale steam-
hauled narrow-gauge railway. All the tours
start from the forecourt of the hotel.

THE ABBEY COACH HOUSE

24 St Mary's Park, Windermere, Cumbria
Tel/Fax: 015394 44027
e-mail: abbeycoach@aol.com

The **Abbey Coach House** nestles in a quiet secluded cul-de-sac only 5 minutes walk from the village. The 19th century Lakeland stone former Coach House has been carefully and tastefully restored to provide two extremely comfortable self-catering holiday units. The bungalow has a twin bedroom, the other with two. Both have an additional bed settee in the lounge.

The grounds provide secure car parking and guests have the use of the garden and its facilities (including a barbecue).

here, originally built as country retreats for Manchester businessmen - the railway made it possible for them to reach this idyllic countryside in just over two hours. Hotels, boarding houses, comfortable villas and shops sprang up around the station and spread rapidly down the hill towards the lake until Birthwaite and Bowness were linked together.

Windermere's railway is still operating, albeit now as a single track branch line. The **Lakes Line** is now the only surviving Railtrack line to run into the heart of the Lake District. Diesel railcars provide a busy shuttle service to and from the main line at Oxenholme. The route, through Kendal, Burneside and Staveley, is a delight and provides a very pleasant alternative to the often crowded A591.

Within a few yards of Windermere Station, just across the busy main road, is a footpath that leads through the woods to one of the finest viewpoints in Lakeland, **Orrest Head**. This spectacular vantage point provides a 360 degree panoramic view that takes in the ten-mile length of Windermere, the Cumbrian hills and even the fells of the Yorkshire Pennines. In a region where glorious views open up at every turn, the vista from Orrest Head remains exceptional. In Victorian times, visitors wandered through such ravishing scenery carrying, not cameras, but small, tinted mirrors mounted in elaborate frames. Arriving at a picturesque spot, they placed themselves with their back to the view, held the mirrors above them and so observed the view framed as in a painting. The image they saw recalled the romantic landscapes of Claude Lorraine: the mirrors accordingly were known as **Claude Glasses**.

Around Windermere

Bowness-on-Windermere
2 miles S of Windermere on the A592

It is from this attractive, but seasonally very busy town right on the edge of Windermere that most of the lake cruises operate. Lasting between 45 and 90 minutes, the cruises operate daily and provide connections to the **Lakeside & Haverthwaite Steam Railway**, the **Fell Foot Country Park** and the **Visitor**

THE MARINERS INN

Lake Road, Bowness-on-Windermere,
Cumbria LA23 3AP
Tel: 015394 45678 Fax: 015394 44078
e-mail: steve@mariners-inn.co.uk
website: www.mariners-inn.co.uk

Handily situated on the main road linking Bowness and Windermere, **The Mariners** started life in the late-18th century as the home of a wealthy local merchant. Over its long lifetime it has played many roles, including ironmongers and fish & chip shop. Since becoming licensed premises, it has been the Coxswain's Cabin (noted for live jazz performances), the Robbie Burns and the Westmorland Arms. As The Mariner's, with leaseholders Steve and Helen at the helm, it welcomes visitors all day, every day for drinks, which include three real ales (and a fourth in summer), all from the local Jennings Brewery. The bar, with its

traditional trappings and nautical memorabilia, also stocks a full range of other beers, draught and bottled, lagers, stout and cider. The Mariners is also an excellent choice for a meal, and from Thursday to Monday, between 12 and 6, a variety of food to suit all tastes and appetites is served, making up a regular printed menu and a daily specials board. Soup, potato wedges, burgers, sandwiches and jacket potatoes make tasty lighter snacks, while among the main courses are chicken curry or Kiev, gammon and beef steaks, Cumberland sausage, battered cod, salmon hollandaise, scampi, steak & Jennings ale pie, a super steak & kidney suet pudding and the chef's special Mexican chilli. A selection of wines is available to enjoy with the fine food.

Live music, (check the website for a list of up coming bands), is performed in the downstairs bar from 9.30pm on Friday and Saturday evenings, when the inn has a late licence allowing drinks to be served until 1 am. The area around The Mariners offers an almost endless choice of things to see and do, and the inn has eight quality guest bedrooms, six doubles and two family rooms, all with en suite facilities. The tariff includes a generously served full English breakfast, and discounts apply for off-season and longer stays. Windermere, the largest lake in the whole country, is just moments way, with great views, the freshest of fresh air, sailing, fishing and many other activities available, and among other local attractions are the Windermere Steamboat Museum and the World of Beatrix Potter.

Centre at Brockhole - this centre (also easily reached by road) is idyllically situated in 30 acres of gardens and grounds and has two floors of interactive exhibitions. There are evening wine/champagne cruises during the summer months, and rowing boats and self drive motor boats are also available for hire all year round.

Aerial View, Bowness on Windermere

Not only is **Windermere** the largest lake in Cumbria but it is, at 11 miles long, the largest in England. Formed in the Ice Age by the action of moving glaciers, the lake is fed by the Rivers Brathay and Rothay, at the northern end, while the outlet is into the River Leven, at Newby Bridge. Windermere is actually a public highway or, more correctly, waterway, and this stretch of water, with its thickly wooded banks and scattered islands, has been used since Roman times as a means of transport. Roman Legionnaires used it for carrying stone to their fort at Galava, near present day Ambleside, at the head of the lake. Later, the monks of Furness Abbey fished here for pike and char. The name Windermere, however, comes from Viking times and is derived from Vinand's Mere, Vinand being the name of a Nordic chief.

Across from Bowness, the lake is almost divided in two by **Belle Island,** which is believed to have been

THE WHITE HOUSE HOTEL

Robinson Place, Bowness-on-Windermere, Cumbria LA23 3DQ
Tel: 015394 44803

A pair of connected cottages dating from the late 18th century were converted into what is now the **White House Hotel**. Very homely and comfortable, it has ten attractive, well-decorated bedrooms (non-smoking), two on the ground floor, all with en suite facilities. The bar is open to all for the service of drinks, and non-residents are also welcome for morning coffee, light lunches, afternoon tea and evening meals, which are served until 9pm. The owners since April 2003 are Dee and Gary Theobald, who are making an immediate success of this, their first venture into the hospitality business.

Lake Windermere

Curwen, who planted the surrounding trees.

Fishermen, too, find great enjoyment practising their skills on this well-stocked lake. Once considered a great delicacy in the 17th and 18th centuries, the char, a deep-water trout, is still found here - though catching it is a special art.

Away from the marinas and car parks is the old village where **St Martin's Church** is

inhabited by the Romans. During the Civil War, it was owned by Colonel Phillipson (the Royalist supporter who disgraced himself by riding into Kendal Parish Church) and his family had to withstand an 80-day siege, successfully, while the Colonel was away on another campaign. In 1774, the island was bought by a Mr English who constructed the round house which, at the time, caused such consternation that he sold the property and the island to Isabella

of particular interest. It has a magnificent east window filled with 14th and 15th century glass, and an unusual 300-year-old carved wooden figure of St Martin depicted sharing his cloak with a beggar.

On the lake shore just to the north of the village is the **Windermere Steamboat Centre** (see panel). Housed here is a unique collection of Lake Windermere's nautical heritage. The exhibits, mainly Victorian and

WINDERMERE STEAMBOAT MUSEUM

Rayrigg Road, Windermere,
Cumbria LA23 1BN Tel: 01539 445565

On the lake shore just to the north of the village is the **Windermere Steamboat Museum**, a unique collection of Victorian and Edwardian steam launches which includes the SL Dolly, the oldest mechanically powered boat in the world. Dolly celebrated her 150th birthday in 2000 and still has her original engine in working order despite its having lain on the bed of Ullswater for more than 60 years before being recovered. Guided tours of the museum are available and also around the Esperance, the inspiration for Captain Flint's boat in Arthur Ransome's Swallows and Amazons. Some of the launches are still in

working order and occasional cruises in one of these wonderful vintage craft are possible. Private charters of an Edwardian steam launch for up to 12 passengers can also be arranged, with catering provided if required. The Museum grounds also includes a model boat pond, shop, tea room, picnic area, a self-catering flat for 2 persons, and free parking.

Edwardian craft, include Dolly, the oldest mechanically powered boat in the world, and Beatrix Potter's rowing boat. The Swallows and Amazons exhibition features guided tours of Esperance, Arthur Ransome's inspiration for Captain Flint's Houseboat. The Museum grounds also includes a model boat pond, shop, tea room and picnic area.

Just down the road from the Steamboat Museum is the Old Laundry Visitor Centre, the home of **The World** of **Beatrix Potter**, one of the most popular visitor attractions in the country. Here visitors can enjoy fascinating re-creations of the Lakeland author's books, complete with the sounds, sights and even smells of the countryside. 2002 saw the centenary of the publication of the first Tale of Peter Rabbit, and to mark the occasion the Peter Rabbit Centenary springs to life every 15 minutes and features some previously unpublished illustrations from

NISSI RESTAURANT

Westmorland House, Lake Road, Bowness-on-Windermere, Cumbria LA23 3BJ
Tel: 015394 45055
e-mail: paulharris69@btopenworld.com

Paul Harris, an accomplished chef who trained with the stars, offers visitors to **Nissi Restaurant** the flavours of Greece and the Mediterranean in a friendly, stylish ambience. The classic meze, a selection of hot and cold dishes, makes a tasty and convivial start to a meal, followed perhaps by salmon antiboise, chicken with a creamy walnut, onion and nutmeg sauce, moussaka or a kebab. Mouth-

watering desserts round off a superb meal. Booking ahead is always strongly recommended (closed Monday), and for guests tarrying in Bowness the excellent Belsfield House hotel is close by.

the stories. Open all year, the complex also includes the Tailor of Gloucester Tea Room (children's menu and colouring sheets available) and the Beatrix Potter shop.

About a mile and a half south of Bowness, **Blackwell** (see panel opoposite) is a treasure trove of the Arts and Crafts Movement. Completed in 1900, it is the largest and most important surviving masterpiece of the architect MH Baillie Scott (1865-1945). Inspired by Lakeland flora and fauna, he designed every last detail of this outstanding house, creating a symphony of art nouveau stained glass, oak panelling, intricate plasterwork and fanciful metalwork. From the gardens there are wonderful views of Windermere and the Coniston fells.

Winster
4 miles S of Windermere on the A5074

This charming hamlet has an old post office, originally built in the early 17th century as a cottage, that is much photographed. South from the village runs the Winster Valley, which provided Wordsworth with one of his favourite walks. It was at **Low Ludderburn**, a couple of miles to the south, that Arthur Ransome settled in 1925 and here that he wrote his classic children's novel *Swallows and Amazons*. The house is still there but is not open to the public.

While living here, Ransome discovered the peaceful churchyard at **Rusland** and decided that was where he wanted to be buried. And when he died in 1967 that is indeed where he was buried, joined later by his second wife Eugenia.

Witherslack
9 miles S of Windermere off the A590

On the edge of the village is the **Latterbarrow Reserve** of the Cumbrian Wildlife Trust, a relatively small reserve that is home to some 200 species of flowering plants and ferns. Butterflies

---

THE MASONS ARMS

Strawberry Bank, Cartmel Fell,
Cumbria LA11 6NW
Tel: 015395 68486 Fax: 015395 68780
website: www.masonsarms.info

The two Helens, General Manager Helen Parker and chef Helen Barnes, make a first-rate team at the **Masons Arms**, which lies high up in a spectacular location on Cartmel Fell. Dating back to the late 16th century, this is really super, traditional old pub with flagstone floors, beamed ceilings, a magnificent vintage iron range and roaring log fires in winter. Recent re-furbishment has put

the interior into apple pie order without detracting in any way from the immense old-world appeal.

BLACKWELL

Bowness-on-Windermere, Cumbria LA23 3JR
Tel: 01539 722464 Fax: 01539 722494
e-mail: info@blackwell.org.uk
website: www.blackwell.org.uk

Located about a mile and a half south of Bowness, and occupying a superb position overlooking Lake Windermere and the Coniston fells, **Blackwell** is a treasure trove of the Arts and Crafts movement. Completed in 1900, the house was the work of the architect M.H. Baillie Scott who designed every last detail of this outstanding house, creating a symphony of art nouveau stained glass, oak panelling, intricate plasterwork and fanciful metalwork.

As well as being a perfect work of art in itself, Blackwell provides the perfect setting for changing exhibitions of the highest quality applied arts and crafts. Other attractions here include a licensed restaurant with an outdoor terrace and a book & gift shop.

and birds, including the spotted flycatcher, are a common sight among the plants that grow in the thin soil between the rocky outcrops. Further from the village is **Witherslack Hall**, once the summer residence of the Earls of Derby and now a school.

Newby Bridge

8 miles S of Windermere on the A592

The bridge here crosses the River Leven which runs from the southern tip of Windermere to Morecambe Bay. According to geologists, the mass of end moraines seen here show clearly that the village lay at the southernmost point of Windermere since they were deposited by the glacier while it paused having carved out the lake. Today, however, the village is some distance from the water's edge which can be reached on foot, by car, or by taking the steam train on the Lakeside & Haverthwaite Railway. As the village lies at the junction of two major south Cumbrian roads, it is also a popular tourist destination.

One mile north of the village, Fell Foot Park (National Trust) is a delightful 18-acre site of landscaped gardens and woodland laid out in late-Victorian times. Admission is free (although there's a car parking charge), and the grounds include picnic areas, a children's adventure playground, a splendid rhododendron garden, a gift shop and a tea room with outside tables where you can watch the lake traffic and also the steam trains chugging into Lakeside on the western bank. Rowing boats can be hired at the piers from which there are regular ferries across to Lakeside, and pleasure cruises operate during the summer school holidays.

Backbarrow

9 miles S of Windermere on the A592

This small village in the valley of the River Leven, which drains Windermere, was a hive of industry at one time. In 1711, the most ambitious iron furnace in

GRAYTHWAITE HOME FARM HOLIDAYS

Graythwaite, Ulverston, CumbriaLA12 8BA
Tel: 015395 31351 Fax: 015395 31764
e-mail: pewhitehead@lineone.net
website: www.graythwaiteholidays.com

On a private country estate on the western shores of Lake Windermere, **Graythwaite Home Farm Holidays** offer self-catering accommodation of the highest standard. Thirteen cottages and barn conversions are located within the secluded courtyard of the original Victorian farmstead, and the charm, character and serenity of Graythwaite can be enjoyed as it has been since the first days of the estate in the 1600s. With beautiful woodland and countryside all around,

many offer the alternative of an open fire – chopped logs are provided for those cottages. The cottages are available all year round and are equipped with everything needed to ensure a comfortable, peaceful self-catering stay. In operation since the early 1990s, they offer a superb base for relaxing and unwinding and for exploring the Lakes and the less known parts of the Lake District peninsulas.

children and adults alike can revel in the surroundings well away from the risk and intrusion of traffic.

Away from Home Farm are a further five cottages, each one totally private, with glorious views over Lake Windermere; guests of the Graythwaite Estate can enjoy the exclusive use of a private beach frontage to the Lake. Fishing can be arranged, and the private tarn is only a ten-minute walk away. An indoor heated swimming pool that is open all year and a small fitness suite are also available to guests. The 20 properties are individual in character and offer the very best accommodation for two to ten guests; all are centrally heated and

Short breaks are available outside the busiest season. Among the properties included: Coachman's Cottage (for two), the original coachman's cottage to Silverholme House, enjoys a romantic setting just 100 yards from Lake Windermere; Hullet Hall, which can sleep up to six in three bedrooms, has gardens running down to the Lake and has the bonus of its own private jetty; Hammerhole, which has five bedrooms accommodating up to ten guests in great comfort, is located in a secluded bay on the shores of the lake and has its own jetty and a private launch facility.

Cumbria was built here and the remains can still be seen along with the relics of the heyday of water power in the village.

Lakeside
10 miles S of Windermere off the A590

Located at the southwestern tip of Windermere, Lakeside sits beneath gentle wooded hills. It's the northern terminus of the Lakeside & Haverthwaite Railway, a 4-mile route through the beautiful Leven valley which was once part of a line stretching to Ulverston and Barrow-in-Furness. Throughout the season, hard-working steam locomotives chug along the track, their departure times set to coincide with boat arrivals from Bowness - a joint boat and train return ticket is available. The locomotives in use include 42073 and 42085, ex-LMR Fairburn 0-6-4 tank engines, and 5643, an ex-GWR 0-6-0 tank. Also present on display or under steam (when not occasionally required elsewhere) is FR20, built for the Furness Railway and Britain's oldest working standard gauge steam locomotive. Nearby lies Britain's only freshwater aquarium, the **Aquarium of the Lakes** (see panel) with the largest collection of freshwater fish in the UK and also a number of playful otters and diving ducks. A unique attraction for visitors is to walk along a re-creation of Windermere's lake bed along an underwater tunnel. There's also a shop and a café.

A mile or so north of Lakeside, **Stott**

Nearby, the **Aquarium of the Lakes** boasts the largest collection of freshwater fish in the UK. A walk-through tunnel along a re-created lake bed provides great views of char, perch and diving ducks, whilst in the Morecambe Bay displays, visitors come face to face with sharks and rays from around the local coast.

The mischievous otters are a special favourite with children and for the more earnest visitor there are educational displays on anything from leeches to lobsters. "The Quay" shop stocks a good range of quality gifts and souvenirs, and the "Café at the Quay" offers light refreshments and a good view of the lake.

Park Bobbin Mill (English Heritage) is a must for anyone interested in the area's industrial heritage. One of the best preserved in the country, it's a genuine working 19th century mill and stands in a lovely woodland setting at the southern end of the Lake. Visitors can join the inclusive 45-minute tour, watch wooden bobbins being made as they were 200 years ago and browse over the informative exhibition.

Ings

3 miles E of Windermere off the A591

A pleasant little village set alongside the River Gowan, Ings owes its fine Georgian church and charming almshouses to a certain Robert Bateman who was born here in the late 1600s. Wordsworth commemorated Bateman in a rather pedestrian poem which recounts how the villagers made a collection so that the young boy could travel to London. He prospered greatly, became a major ship owner and devoted a sizeable portion of his wealth to the benefit of his native village. Sadly, he never saw the completed church: less than a year after building began, he was murdered by Italian pirates.

Troutbeck Bridge

1 mile NE of Windermere on the A591

This small village in the valley of Trout Beck takes its name from the bridge here over the beck, just before the water runs into Windermere. During the 17th century, **Calgarth Hall** was owned by

THE RAILWAY HOTEL

1 The Banks, Staveley, Cumbria LA8 9NE
Tel: 01539 821385

Angela at the stoves and Stephen behind the bar make a very popular and successful team at the **Railway Hotel**, an end-of-terrace period building just a short walk from the village centre. The partners dispense genuine Cumbrian hospitality in generous measure, along with a good range of beers and wines and good-value home-cooked dishes · the sizzling steak platter is a great favourite. The

pub has a car park and beer garden, and for guests staying overnight there are two bedrooms equipped with tv and tea-makers.

WILF'S CAFÉ

Mill Yard, Back Lane, Staveley, Cumbria LA8 9LR
Tel: 01539 822329 Fax: 01539 822969
e-mail: food@wilfs-cafe.co.uk
website: www.wilfs-cafe.co.uk

Iain ('Wilf') Williamson and Charlotte Webb run a super local café on two floors of what was once a wood mill. **Wilf's Café** is popular with all ages, from youngsters with their parents to senior citizens, and Wilf and co-chef Martin Lovett prepare an excellent variety of well-priced dishes, from hearty breakfasts to salads, Wilf's famous veggie chilli and super cakes and pastries. When the sun shines, the wooden deck overlooking a weir on the River Kent is the place to be. Open 10-5, with regular speciality evenings.

Myles Phillipson, a local Justice of the Peace who wished to gain possession of nearby farmland. So he invited the landowner and his wife to a banquet at the Hall and then, having hidden a silver cup in their luggage, accused them of stealing.

At the resulting trial, Phillipson, who was the presiding judge, sentenced the couple to death as well as appropriating their land. As she was led away, the wife placed a curse on the judge saying that not only would his victims never leave him but that his family would also perish in poverty. The couple were executed but their skulls reappeared at Calgarth Hall and, no matter what Phillipson did (including burning them and throwing them into Lake Windermere) the skulls kept returning to the Hall. Moreover, the Phillipson family grew poorer and poorer until, in 1705, the family died out altogether.

Just north of the village lies the Royal Horticultural Society's four-acre garden at **Holehird**. In 1945, Edward Leigh Groves bequeathed the mansion and the estate 'for the better development of the health, education and social welfare services of the County of Westmoreland'. Some time later, the Lakeland Horticultural Society took over responsibility for the garden, which is still run by volunteers of that

society, whose primary aim is to promote 'knowledge on the cultivation of plants, shrubs and trees, especially those suited to Lakeland conditions'. Highlights include the borders in the walled garden, the many specimen trees, the summer-autumn heathers and the National Collections of astilbes and hydrangeas.

Troutbeck

3 miles NE of Windermere off the A592

Designated a conservation area, Troutbeck has no recognisable centre as the houses and cottages are grouped around a number of wells and springs which, until recently, were the only form of water supply. Dating from the 16th, 17th, and 18th centuries, the houses retain many of their original features, including mullioned windows, heavy cylindrical chimneys, and, in some cases, exposed spinning galleries, and are of great interest to lovers of vernacular architecture. **Troutbeck Church**, too, is worthy of a visit as there

Troutbeck Village

is a fine east window, dating from 1873, that is the combined work of Edward Burne-Jones, Ford Maddox Brown, and William Morris.

However, perhaps the best known building at Troutbeck is **Townend** (National Trust), another enchanting example of Lake District vernacular architecture. Built in 1626, the stone and slate house contains some fine carved woodwork, books, furniture and domestic implements collected by the Browne family, wealthy farmers who lived here for more than 300 years until 1944. Open from April to October, the house runs a regular 'living history' programme, so if you visit on a Thursday you can meet Mr George Browne - circa 1900. Another notable resident of Troutbeck was the '**Troutbeck Giant**' - Thomas Hogarth, uncle of the painter William Hogarth.

Kentmere

8 miles NE of Windermere off the A591

This hamlet, as its name implies, lies in part of the valley that was once a lake; drained to provide precious bottom pasture land. A large mill pond remains to provide a head of water on the River Kent for use at a paper mill. Inside **St Cuthbert's Church** is a bronze memorial to Bernard Gilpin, who was born at Kentmere Hall in 1517 and went on to become Archdeacon of Durham Cathedral. Known as The Apostle of the North, Gilpin was also a leader of the Reformation and, in 1558, he travelled

to London to face charges of heresy against the Roman Catholic Church. During the journey, Gilpin fell and broke his leg but, fortunately, while he was recovering Catholic Queen Mary died and was succeeded by Protestant Queen Elizabeth. The new queen restored Gilpin to favour and saved him from being burnt at the stake.

The beautiful valley of the River Kent is best explored on foot. A public footpath runs up its western side, past **Kentmere Hall**, a fortified pele tower that is now a private farmhouse. Following the river southwards, the **Dales Way** runs down into Kendal and on into the Yorkshire Dales.

Brockhole

3 miles NW of Windermere off the A591

The **Lake District Visitor Centre** at Brockhole provides enough activities for a full family day out. Lake cruises depart from the jetty here for 45-minute circular trips and groups of more than 20 can even organise their own private boat. The gardens and grounds were the work of Thomas H Mawson, a Lancastrian who trained in London and set up in business in Windermere in 1885. He soon became fashionable and landscaped the gardens of many wealthy industrialists. Within the beautifully landscaped grounds at Brockhole, visitors can join an organised walk accompanied by one of the gardening team, leave their children in the well-equipped adventure playground, enjoy a lakeside picnic or visit the rare breeds of sheep. A wide variety of events takes place during the season - among them a Medieval Living Weekend, a Taste of Cumbria Food Fair, a Christmas Craft Fair and much more. Brockhole itself is a fine Victorian mansion, originally built for a Manchester silk merchant. Here visitors can watch an audio visual presentation about the area, browse in the gift shop which stocks an excellent range of books, guides and maps, or take a break in the comfortable café which has an outdoor terrace overlooking the lake. Home baking to traditional Cumbrian recipes is the speciality, and many dishes feature local produce. There is good wheelchair access to all parts of the Visitor Centre and most of the grounds.

Ambleside is one of the busiest of the Lakeland towns, a popular centre for walkers and tourers, with glorious walks and drives radiating from the town in all directions. Ambleside offers a huge choice of pubs, restaurants, cafés, hotels and guest houses, as well as art galleries, a 2-screen cinema and a mix of traditional family-run shops supplemented by a modern range of retailers in the new **Market Cross Centre**. Because of its many shops specialising in outdoor clothing, the town was recently described as 'the anorak capital of the world' and it would certainly be hard to find a wider

Ambleside

5 miles NW of Windermere on the A591

Standing less than a mile from the head of Lake Windermere,

Ambleside Pier

selection anywhere of climbing, camping and walking gear.

Many of Ambleside's buildings are constructed in the distinctive grey green stone of the area which merges attractively with the green of the fields and fells all around. The centre of the town is now a conservation area and perhaps the most picturesque building here is **The Bridge House**, a tiny cottage perched on a packhorse bridge across Stock Ghyll. Today it's a National Trust shop and information centre, but during the 1850s it was the home of Mr and Mrs Rigg and their six children. The main room of this one-up, one-down residence measures just 13 feet by 6 feet, so living chez Rigg was decidedly cosy.

The Bridge House

In the cosy, atmospheric cellar of Ambleside's former Stamp House, **Stampers** is one of the town's favourite dining places. It has been owned since 1984 by Heather Tennant, who is also the chef, and her menu features local specialities as

STAMPERS RESTAURANT

The Old Stamp House, Church Street, Ambleside, Cumbria LA22 0BU
Tel: 015394 32775

well as dishes of worldwide inspiration.

Stampers is open most evenings from 6 till late, and booking is recommended at all times. Bookings can also be taken for lunch for parties of 10 or more. The fine food is complemented by an interesting selection of wines.

SMALLWOOD HOUSE HOTEL

Compston Road, Ambleside,
Cumbria LA22 9DJ
Tel: 015394 32330
website: www.smallwoodhotel.co.uk

A relaxed stay in a friendly, peaceful ambience is guaranteed at **Smallwood House**, which is run by resident proprietors Anthony and Christine Harrison. The house, in the centre of Ambleside, was built around 1880 using slate quarried from local mines, and the interior has been carefully updated for the comfort of

guests. The 12 bedrooms all have en suite facilities, tv, radio, tea-makers and hairdryers, and guests can unwind and plan their day in a pleasant lounge. Evening meals can be booked in advance (not on Sunday) and the hotel has a residential licence.

Close by, at **Adrian Sankey's Glass Works**, visitors can watch craftsmen transform molten material into glass in the age-old way and also purchase the elegant results - wine glasses, perfume bottles, lampshades, huge bowls and much more. The studio stands next to an 18th century water mill which Adrian Sankey, together with other local craftsmen, restored in 1995. Now, water flow permitting, you can watch the wheel in full working order and enjoy a coffee in the café-restaurant housed in a restored 15th century building.

A short walk from the mill brings the visitor to the **Armitt Museum** (see panel on page 40) and Library dedicated to the area's history since Roman times

and to its most famous literary luminaries, John Ruskin and Beatrix Potter. Among the highlights are Beatrix Potter's early watercolours - exquisite studies of fungi and mosses - and a fascinating collection of photographs by Herbert Bell, an Ambleside chemist who became an accomplished photographer.

The popular panoramic view of Ambleside, looking north from the path up **Loughrigg Fell**, reveals the town cradled within the apron of the massive Fairfield Horseshoe which rises to nearly 3,000ft. Within the townscape itself, the most impressive feature is the rocket-like spire, 180ft high, of **St Mary's Church**. The church was completed in 1854 to a design by Sir George Gilbert

Alison Harwood and Alan Hewartson are partners at **Lyndale**, a stone-built end-of-terrace house on the outskirts of Ambleside. Since the beginning of 2003 they have been offering Bed & Breakfast accommodation in six smart,

LYNDALE

Lake Road, Ambleside, Cumbria LA22 0DN
Tel: 015394 34244
e-mail: alison@lyndale-guesthouse.co.uk
web: www.lyndale-guesthouse.co.uk

comfortable bedrooms, two of them with en suite facilities and all with tv and tea/coffee making facilities.

The day starts with an excellent breakfast, and guests can set out on a day's walking or touring with a packed lunch.

SHEILA'S COTTAGE RESTAURANT

The Slack, Ambleside, Cumbria LA22 9DD
Tel: 015394 33079 Open daily: 11am-9pm
Reservations recommended

Sharyn and Mark Rush run **Sheila's Cottage**, a splendid licensed restaurant and tea room tucked away down a narrow lane. Behind the rough stone façade, there's old-world charm aplenty, and in this delightful setting friendly, efficient staff serve a day-long selection of home-cooked food. Traditional favourites such as Cumberland sausage with Bramley apple

mash sit comfortably alongside the more innovative dishes on the evening specials menu which includes fresh fish and local meat and game. Super desserts round off a meal to remember.

THE ARMITT MUSEUM

Rydal Road, Ambleside, Cumbria LA22 9PL
Tel: 01539 431212

A short walk from the mill brings you to **The Armitt**, an attractive new building which contains a museum and library dedicated to the area's history since Roman times and to its most famous literary luminaries, John Ruskin and Beatrix Potter. Visitors can "talk" to John Ruskin, watch a 19th century lantern slide show, and marvel at Beatrix Potter's pre-Mrs Tiggywinkle watercolours · exquisite scientific studies of fungi and mosses. Other exhibits include a lock of Ruskin's hair, a life mask of Harriet Martineau, the political writer and author of an early *Guide to the Lakes*, and a fascinating collection of photographs by Herbert Bell (1856-1946), an Ambleside

chemist who became an accomplished photographer, concentrating on lakeland scenes. The Armitt hosts regular exhibitions, lectures and concerts, and also has its own shop selling items produced exclusively for sale only at the museum.

Scott, the architect of London's St Pancras Station and the Albert Memorial. Inside the church is a chapel devoted to the memory of William Wordsworth and an interesting 1940s mural depicting the ancient ceremony of rush-bearing. The mural was painted by Gordon Ransome of the Royal College of Art during World War II when the college was evacuated to the town. The ceremony, dating back to the days when the floor of the church was covered by rushes, is still held on the first Saturday in July. Some 400 children process through the town bearing colourful decorated rushes and singing the specially commissioned Ambleside Rushbearer's Hymn.

A few weeks later the famous **Ambleside Sports** take place, an event distinguished by the variety of local traditional sports it features. In addition to carriage-driving, ferret or pigeon racing, and tugs of war, the Sports

FAR NOOK

Rydal Road, Ambleside, Cumbria LA22 9BA
Tel: 015394 31605
e-mail: farnook@tiscali.co.uk
website: www.farnook.co.uk

Far Nook is a detached 1930s' Lakeland stone house offering top-quality Bed & Breakfast accommodation in a lovely garden setting. Everything in the house reflects the high standards of owner Lesley Anne Higgins who looks after her guests in exemplary style. The three beautifully furnished bedrooms combine a high degree of comfort with modern amenities, and in the lounge guests can relax by the fire, enjoy the view or play a

board game. The day starts with an excellent breakfast featuring local bacon and sausages and home-made bread. No smoking or pets.

Loughrigg Fell

cruises. Rowing boats and self drive motor boats can also be hired. Just to the west of the pier is **Borrans Park**, a pleasant lakeside park with plenty of picnic spots, and to the west of the park, the site of Galava Roman Fort. There is little to be seen of the fort but the setting is enchanting. Also well worth a visit is nearby **Stagshaw Garden** (NT), a spring woodland garden which contains a fine collection of shrubs, including some impressive rhododendrons, azaleas and camellias. Parking is very limited and vehicular access is hazardous, so it's best to park at Waterhead car park and walk.

Perhaps the most unusual visitor attraction in Ambleside is the **Homes of Football**, described by the Sunday Times as a national treasure. It began as a travelling exhibition of football photographs and memorabilia but now

include Cumberland and Westmorland wrestling (a little like Sumo wrestling but without the rolls of fat), muscle-wrenching fell racing, and hound trailing.

Another experience not to be missed while staying at Ambleside is a boat cruise on Lake Windermere to Bowness. There are daily departures from the pier at **Waterhead**, about a mile south of the town. At Bowness, there are connections to other lakeland attractions and, during the summer months, evening wine

ROTHAY MANOR

Rothay Bridge, Ambleside, Cumbria LA22 0EH
Tel: 015394 33605 Fax: 015394 33607
e-mail: hotel@rothaymanor.co.uk
website: www.rothaymanor.co.uk

Built in 1830 as a private residence, **Rothay Manor** stands in its own grounds close to the head of Lake Windermere. The Nixon family have established it as one of the country's leading country house hotels, outstanding in terms of service, comfort and food. The lounges retain an elegant Regency air, and the 17 beautifully appointed bedrooms, including family rooms, have en suite bathrooms, tv and telephone. The cooking is top-class, and the hotel is open to non-residents for morning

coffee, lunch, afternoon tea and dinner. Special interest holidays, from painting and bridge to walking and gardening, are a feature of this very special hotel.

BRAMBLES CAFÉ

Chapel Stile, Nr Ambleside,
Cumbria LA22 9JE Tel: 015394 37500

Delicious home-cooked food is served
throughout the day at **Brambles Café**, which
is located above the Langdale Co-Op at
Chapel Stile, on the B5343 west of Ambleside.
Wooden slatted floors and rustic wooden
furniture make a simple, stylish setting for
enjoying everything on owner Samantha
Rodway's cooking, which runs from soup,
salads and sandwiches to breakfasts, light
lunches, quiches, cakes and scrumptious
sweets. Take away food is available, and

picnic lunches can be supplied to order. The
café is open from 9 to 5.30 in summer, 10 to
4.30 in winter.

has a permanent home in Lake Road.
Photographer Stuart Clarke recorded
games and grounds at every kind of
venue from the Premier League down to
amateur village teams. There are now
60,000 photographs on file and a
massive selection on show, framed and
for sale. Some of the memorabilia retail
for £200 or more but a free picture
postcard of your favourite soccer ground
is included in the modest entrance fee.

From Ambleside town centre, a steep
road climbs sharply up to the dramatic
Kirkstone Pass and
over to Ullswater. The
pass is so called
because of the rock at
the top which looks
like a church steeple.
Rising to some 1,489
feet above sea level,
the road is the highest
in the Lake District
and, though today's
vehicles make light
work of the climb, for
centuries the Pass

presented a formidable obstacle. The
severest incline, known as **The Struggle**,
necessitated passengers to step out of
their coach and to make their way on
foot, leaving the horses to make the
steep haul with just the empty coach.

Rydal
*7 miles NW of Windermere on the
A591*

In 1813, following the deaths of their
young children Catherine and Thomas,
William and Mary Wordsworth were too
grief-stricken to stay on at the Old

Rydal Water

Rectory in Grasmere. They moved a couple of miles down the road to **Rydal Mount**, a handsome house overlooking tiny **Rydal Water**. By now, the poet was well-established and comparatively prosperous. A salaried position as Westmorland's

Rydal Mount

Distributor of Stamps (a tax official), supplemented his earnings from poetry. Although Wordsworth only ever rented the house, it is now owned by his descendants and has been open to the public since 1970. The interior has seen

GLEN ROTHAY HOTEL & BADGER BAR

Keswick Road, Rydal, Nr Ambleside, Cumbria LA22 9LR Tel: 015394 34500
e-mail: jhpckrng9@aol.com
website: www.theglenrothay.com

A fine country house hotel and a comfortable, friendly pub - at the **Glen Rothay Hotel** and **Badger Bar** owner John Pickering offers both in great walking country north of Ambleside. The eight guest bedrooms are styled to enhance the character of the 17th century building; some have four-poster or canopied

beds, and all have en suite bathrooms, telephone, tv and fine views. Badger Bar is a great favourite with hotel guests and passing visitors, and Cumbrian produce is to the fore in the pub lunches and in the evening à la carte.

WHITE MOSS HOUSE

Rydal Water, Nr Grasmere, Cumbria LA22 9SE
Tel: 015394 35295 Fax: 015394 35516
e-mail: sue@whitemoss.com
website: www.whitemoss.com

In a glorious setting by beautiful Rydal Water, **White Moss House** has been owned and run by Peter and Sue Dixon for well over 20 years. In that time they have earned innumerable accolades for care, comfort and the consistently outstanding food and wine. Five prettily decorated bedrooms are in the 18th century main house, while on the hillside above is the hideaway Brockstone Cottage.

Peter puts the finest local ingredients to marvellous use in his evening meals, and the fine food is complemented by a fabulous wine list.

little change, retaining a lived-in atmosphere. It contains first editions of the poet's work and many personal possessions, among them the only surviving portrait of his beloved sister, Dorothy. William was a keen gardener and the four-acre garden remains very much as he designed it.

Grasmere

9 miles NW of Windermere on the A591

In 1769 Thomas Gray described Grasmere as "a little unsuspected paradise". Thirty years later, Wordsworth himself called it "the loveliest spot that man hath ever found". Certainly,

Grasmere enjoys one of the finest settings in all Lakeland, its small lake nestling in a natural scenic amphitheatre beside the compact, rough-stone village.

For lovers of Wordsworth's poetry, Grasmere is the pre-eminent place of pilgrimage. They come to visit **Dove Cottage** where Wordsworth lived in dire poverty from 1799 to 1808, obliged to line the walls with newspaper for warmth. The great poet shared this very basic accommodation with his wife Mary, his sister Dorothy, his sister-in-law Alice and, as almost permanent guests, Coleridge and De Quincey. (Sir Walter Scott also stayed, although he often

THE ROWAN TREE

Church Bridge, Grasmere, Cumbria LA22 9SU
Tel: 015394 35528

By the bridge facing the churchyard where Wordsworth is buried, the **Rowan Tree** is a vegetarian licensed restaurant and café serving anything from a cup of coffee to a five-course dinner. Behind the handsome stone façade the feel is intimate and the look stylishly contemporary, and the 76 covers include 30 outside overlooking the river. All the dishes on the menu · some with a Mediterranean slant · are freshly cooked on

the premises, and the Rowan Tree, which is owned and run by Barry and Gillian Calveley, is open from 10 to 5 and 6 to 9 daily.

Fresh local produce is the basis of the super snacks and meals served at **The Wild Daffodil**, a family-run licensed café and restaurant well placed for the attractions of Grasmere. Carl McAllister is the chef, helped by

THE WILD DAFFODIL

Stock Lane, Grasmere, Cumbria LA22 9SL
Tel: 015394 35770 Fax: 015394 47788

his father, while Sarah greets and serves.

The choice of home-cooked dishes extends from an all-day breakfast to hot and cold snacks and daily roasts, with teas, coffees, draught beer and wines to accompany. Service in the café is from 9.30 to 6, at which time the different but similarly wide-ranging restaurant menu takes over until last orders at 9pm.

sneaked off to the Swan Hotel for a dram since the Wordsworths were virtually teetotallers.) Located on the outskirts of the village, Dove Cottage has been preserved intact: next door is an award-winning museum dedicated

Dove Cottage

to Wordsworth's life and works. Dove Cottage, Rydal Mount, another of the poet's homes near Grasmere, and his birthplace, Wordsworth House at Cockermouth, are all owned by the **Wordsworth Trust** which offers a discount ticket covering entrance to all three properties.

In 1808, the poet moved to **The Rectory** (private) opposite St Oswald's Church. In his long poem, *The Excursion*, he describes the house and its lovely garden beside the River Rothay.

The church, too, is remembered in the same poem:

Not raised in nice proportions was the pile,
But large and massy, for duration built,
With pillars crowded and the roof upheld
By naked rafters intricately crossed,
Like leafless underboughs in some thick
wood.

In 1850, the Poet Laureate was buried beneath yew trees he himself had planted in **St Oswald's** churchyard. He was joined here by his sister Dorothy, in 1885, and his wife Mary, in 1889. In

Interior of Dove Cottage

Kinquering Kongs their titles take.

You have hissed all my mystery lessons.

You have deliberately tasted two worms and you can leave Oxford by the town drain.

Yes indeed: the Lord is a shoving leopard.

Grasmere town cemetery is the grave of **William Archibald Spooner**, sometime Warden of New College, Oxford. He gave his name to Spoonerisms, in which the initial letters of two words are transposed, with amusing results. Here are a few of his gems, some genuine, others perhaps apocryphal:

Grasmere Village Church

FOREST SIDE HOTEL & RESTAURANT AND GRASMERE LODGE

Forest Side, Grasmere, Cumbria LA22 9RN
Tel: 015394 35250 Fax: 015394 35947
e-mail: hotel@netcomuk.co.uk

Built by the Earl of Lonsdale as a very grand hunting lodge, **Forest Side** offers guests superior non-smoking accommodation in 34 well-equipped bedrooms, personal attention, traditional English cuisine and wonderful views from the lower slopes of Butter Crag. Within the 40 acres of landscaped grounds of the hotel, **Grasmere Lodge** provides a self-

catering alternative in five apartments sleeping two to four, with seven supplementary rooms for additional guests. The tariff includes temporary membership of a nearby health and fitness club. Grasmere village is close by.

He spent many holidays in Grasmere with his wife at her house, How Foot.

Like Ambleside, Grasmere is famous for its **Sports**, first recorded in 1852, which still take place in late August. The most celebrated event in the Lake District, they attract some 10,000 visitors and feature many pursuits unique to Cumbria such as Cumberland and Westmorland wrestling as well as the more

Grasmere Lake

understandable, though arduous, fell running.

Collectors of curiosities who happen to be travelling north on the A591 from Grasmere should look out for the vintage black and yellow AA telephone box on the right hand side of the road. Still functioning, **Box 487** has been accorded Grade II listed building status by the Department of the Environment.

Denotes entries in other chapters

3 The Cartmel and Furness Peninsulas

The southernmost coast of Cumbria is a region that is sometimes overlooked by visitors to the county. This is a great pity as it has much to offer the tourist including a rich history as well as splendid scenery. Lying between the lakes and mountains of the Lake District and the sandy estuaries of Morecambe Bay, this is an area of gentle moorland, craggy headlands, scattered woodlands, and vast expanses of sand.

It was once a stronghold of the Cistercian monks, whose influence can still be seen in the buildings and fabric of the landscape. This is Cumbria's ecclesiastical centre and there were several monasteries here; two in particular are well worth visiting today. There is little left of Cartmel Priory except the church and gatehouse which lie in the heart of this charming old market town. However, the remains of Furness Abbey, once the second richest in England, are extensive and occupy a particularly pleasant site.

Before the great boom of the local iron ore mining industry, the peninsular villages and market towns relied on farming and fishing and, before some of the river estuaries silted up, there was also some import and export trade. The rapid growth of Barrow-in-Furness, which will be forever linked with the shipbuilding industry, changed the face of much of the area, but as the iron industry declined so did the town.

The arrival of the railways in the mid-

Holker Hall

The Cumbria Grand Hotel

Lindale Road, Grange-over-Sands,
Cumbria LA11 6EN
Tel: 015395 32331 Fax: 015395 34534
e-mail:
salescumbria@strathmorehotels.com
website: www.strathmorehotels.com

Originally built in 1880 as the Hazlewood Hydro, the **Cumbria Grand Hotel** certainly lives up to its name. It stands in 20 acres of beautifully maintained grounds that include a woodland nature walk, a tennis court, putting green and children's play area. The Cumbria Grand is part of the Strathmore family of quality hotels, which enjoy a well-deserved reputation for providing excellent hospitality combined with outstanding comfort and courteous, efficient service.

Accommodation at the Cumbria Grand is top of the range: all 122 rooms, from singles to family rooms, have en suite bathroom, tv with radio, telephone and central heating, and most enjoy views over the bay or woodland. Mini-suites and executive bedrooms have extra amenities including hairdryer, trouser press and additional telephone/modem point, and for really special occasions there are three four-poster rooms. Rooms can be booked on a Bed & Breakfast or Dinner, Bed & Breakfast basis. The hotel is a great place for wining and dining, and the experienced executive chef and his team produce a good variety of dishes complemented by a well-chosen wine list.

Bar meals are served from 11am right through to 9 o'clock in the evening, and in the non-smoking restaurant a multi-choice carvery operates every evening. Non-residents are welcome for meals, and booking is advisable. Live entertainment is laid on during some evenings, and permanent diversions include table tennis and a full-size snooker table. (The hotel has from the start always been alive to the leisure needs of its guests and there was a billiards room as early as 1891; at that time, too, there were regular dances and concerts, a dark room for the new hobby of photography and a special cycle house to cater for the popular pastime of cycling.)

Located only 12 miles from the M6 (leave at Junction 36), the hotel is well situated for a variety of occasions, from residential and day conferences to wedding receptions and dinner dances. Parking is available for up to 150 cars, the five function rooms can accommodate from 20 to 300, and the peaceful rural setting and spacious grounds offer admirable flexibility for outdoor activities. Facilities for golf (there's a course next door), fishing, water sports, climbing and pony trekking are all within easy reach, and the surrounding area also has much to offer the tourist, including the attractive town of Grange-over-Sands itself.

19th century saw the development of genteel resorts such as Grange-over-Sands overlooking the treacherous sands of Morecambe Bay. Grange is still an elegant little town and has been spared the indignity of vast amusement parks and rows of slot machines, retaining its character as a quiet and pleasant holiday centre.

Morecambe Bay from Grange-over-Sands

Grange-over-Sands

Grange, as it's known locally, is an attractive little town set in a natural sun-trap on the north shore of Morecambe Bay. 'Grange', or 'Graunge', is a French word meaning granary: the monks of nearby Cartmel Priory stored their grain here until Henry VIII dissolved England's monasteries in 1536. Much of its Victorian charm can be credited to the **Furness Railway Company** which developed the town after building the Lancaster to Whitehaven line in 1857. At that time, the whole of the Cartmel and Furness Peninsulas were part of Lancashire, a detached area whose main link with the rest of the county was the dubious route across Morecambe Sands. The railway provided a safe alternative to this hazardous journey. At Grange the company built an elegant mile-long promenade (now traffic free) and set out the colourful ornamental gardens. Prosperous merchants built grand

country homes here and it wasn't long before local residents began referring to their town as the 'Torquay of the North'.

Though Grange doesn't have a beach to rival that of its brash neighbour across Morecambe Bay, it does enjoy an exceptionally mild climate, the mildest in the northwest, thanks to the Gulf Stream. It is still a popular place, particularly with people who are looking for a pleasant and quiet place to retire. It was a favourite with Beatrix Potter, who recorded that on one visit to the town she met a "friendly porker", a meeting that inspired *The Tale of Pigling Bland*. There's no connection of course, but today the town boasts a butcher's shop, Higginsons, which has been voted the Best Butcher's Shop in England.

The route to Grange, across the sands of **Morecambe Bay**, is a treacherous one, though it was used not only by the Romans but also by the monks of Furness Abbey and, later, even by stage coaches looking to shorten their journey time. Avoiding the quicksands of the

THE KENTS BANK HOTEL

96 Kentsford Road, Kents Bank, Nr
Grange-over-Sands, Cumbria LA11 7BB
Tel/Fax: 015395 32054
e-mail:
tcapper@kentsbankhotel.freeserve.co.uk
website: www.kentsbankhotel.co.uk

Tim and Rachael Capper owned and ran a restaurant in Kendal before taking over the reins at the **Kents Bank Hotel**. It was the first hotel in the area when it opened in 1872, built to look after passengers in the coaches that once crossed the treacherous Morecambe at low tide at this point. The hotel has recently been refurbished to give

today's traveller a commendably high standard of comfort and amenity, and the eight guest rooms offer all the options, from singles to family rooms; all have tv, radio and hospitality tray. Bedrooms at the front enjoy splendid views out across Morecambe Bay, as do the residents' lounge and the dining room.

The hotel is open all day for both residents and non-residents, and in the 'locals' bar snacks, well-kept cask ales and an amazing selection of over 100 whiskies are on offer. The restaurant seats 30, and there's room for another 50 diners in the bar areas. Diners can choose between the regular printed menu and the specials board; typical options on the former include both British classics and more exotic dishes: mussels cooked with garlic and cream;

pan-fried red snapper with a lime and fresh coriander dressing; battered cod & chips; ribeye steak with the usual garnishes; ratatouille of Tuscan vegetables wrapped in filo pastry, served with a sweet and sour sauce. Lunch is served daily from 12 to 2.30, afternoon tea from 3 to 5 and evening meals from 6 to 9; booking is recommended for Saturday evening and also for the very popular Sunday lunch, when the main courses offer a choice of meats and a vegetarian alternative.

The Kents Bank Hotel, which is open all year round and centrally heated, provides an ideal base for exploring the delights of the Cartmel Peninsula, and the main Lakeland attractions and the Yorkshire Dales National Park are within an easy drive. In the immediate vicinity there are many pleasant walks, including guided walks across the Bay in summer. The hotel is efficiently geared up to catering for private functions and small meetings and conferences. Private guests arriving by rail can be met by arrangement at the nearby railway station.

bay, which have taken many lives over the centuries, is a difficult task. Back in the 16th century, the Duchy of Lancaster appointed an official guide to escort travellers over the shifting sands and also provided him with a house at Grange. The town still has an official guide who takes groups on a 3-hour walk across the bay. The sands are extremely dangerous since "the tide comes in with the merciless speed of a galloping horse" - a crossing should never be attempted without the help of a qualified guide.

Away from the hotels, shops, and cafés of the town there are some lovely walks and none is more pleasant than the path behind Grange which climbs through magnificent limestone woodlands rich in wild flowers. The path finally leads to the 727-foot **Hampsfell Summit** and **The Hospice**, a little stone tower from which there are unforgettable views over the bay and, in the opposite direction, the craggy peaks of the Lake District. The Hospice was provided by Grange's Vicar, the Rev Thomas Remington, in

1834 to provide a refuge for travellers who found themselves stranded on the fell overnight. An external flight of stairs leads to a flat roof and, as the Vicar observed in a poem attached to the wall:

"The flight of steps requireth care,
The roof will show a prospect rare".

Grange is also the starting point of the **Cistercian Way**, an exceptionally interesting 33 mile long footpath through Furness to Barrow which takes in, naturally, many Cistercian sites.

Around Grange-over-Sands

Lindale
2 miles NE of Grange-over-Sands off the A590

This small village was the birthplace of a man who defied the scepticism of his contemporaries and built the first successful iron ship. 'Iron Mad' John Wilkinson also built the first cast iron

---

LYMEHURST HOTEL

Kents Bank Road, Grange-over-Sands, Cumbria LA11 7EY
Tel: 015395 33076
e-mail: enquiries@lymehurst.co.uk
website: www.lymehurst.co.uk

Lymehurst Hotel is a handsome limestone Victorian building with a spacious, airy feel in ten well-appointed en suite bedrooms; several with sitting areas are ideal for longer stays. Days start with an excellent leisurely breakfast, and three-course evening meals are available by arrangement. This lovely place · owned and run since September 2002 by Jan and Steve Gentle - is further enhanced by a

beautiful sitting room and a suntrap terrace. Numerous local walks start near the hotel, and Grange-over-Sands has plenty to interest visitors.

Wilkinson Obelisk

crossroads is also cast in iron. The admirers who erected it however omitted to provide the iron column with a lightning conductor. A few years later it was struck to the ground by a lightning bolt. The obelisk lay neglected in shrubbery for some years but has now been restored and towers above the village once again. Just outside Lindale, at **Castle Head**, is the imposing house that Wilkinson built by the River Winster.

Cartmel
2 miles W of Grange-over-Sands off the B5278

One of the prettiest villages in the Peninsula, Cartmel is a delightful cluster of houses and cottages set around a square from which lead winding streets and arches into back yards. The village is dominated by the famous **Cartmel Priory**, founded in 1188 by Augustinian canons. According to legend, it was originally intended to be sited on nearby Mount Bernard but St Cuthbert

barges and later created the castings for the famous Iron Bridge at Coalbrookdale. After his death in 1808 he was buried in an iron coffin (naturally) in an unmarked grave, and the lofty **Wilkinson Obelisk** to his memory that stands near the village

Uplands Hotel

Haggs Lane, Cartmel, Cumbria LA11 6HD
Tel: 015395 36248 Fax: 015395 36848
e-mail: uplands@kencomp.net
website: www.uplands.uk.com

Since it opened in March 1985, **Uplands Hotel** has established itself as one of the leading hotels in the region, with superior accommodation, terrific food and a warm, friendly ambience generated by resident owners Tom and Diana Peter. The five en suite bedrooms are comfortably furnished and prettily decorated, with bath or shower en suite, tv, radio, telephone, books and magazines. Tom's cooking is truly

memorable, and guests and non-residents can enjoy lunch Friday to Sunday and dinner every evening except Monday. The hotel stands in two acres of lovely gardens.

Cartmel Gatehouse

appeared in a vision to the monastic architect and ordered him to build the Priory between two springs of water, one flowing north and the other south. The next morning, water was found to be trickling in two different directions from the foundation stones and this is where the church stands today.

Like all monastic institutions, the priory was disbanded in 1537 and several of its members were executed for participating in the Pilgrimage of Grace. Today, substantial remains of the 12th century Gatehouse (National Trust) survive, but the rest of the Priory was cannibalised to build many of the village's cottages and houses. After the

MARKET CROSS COTTAGE

The Square, Cartmel, Cumbria LA11 6QB
Tel: 015395 36143
e-mail:
dburgess@marketcross.freeserve.co.uk

Market Cross Cottage is a charming Grade II listed building dating from the 1660s; it stands next to the noted 12th century Gatehouse in the heart of Cartmel overlooking the main square. Since the early 1990s it has been the home of Eileen and Duncan Burgess, and in this warm, friendly ambience they offer characterful Bed & Breakfast accommodation in four delightful bedrooms - three en suite, the other with its own private bathroom. The interior of this lovely old house is very much in keeping with its age, but guests will find that nothing is lacking in modern comforts.

The day gets off to an excellent start with a full English breakfast, and a three-course evening meal is available by arrangement. On the ground floor of the cottage, Eileen and Duncan run a traditional tea room with oak beams and a huge stone fireplace. Home baking takes centre stage here among a range of delicious things to eat, and booking

is advisable for the ever popular Sunday lunch. The accommodation is available all year round, while the tea room is open from 10 to about 4.30 every day except Monday (but open Bank Holidays). Market Cross Cottage is a non-smoking establishment.

Dissolution, only the south aisle of the **Church of St Mary and St Michael** was still standing but, in 1620, George Preston of Holker began restoring the entire building and the richly carved black oak screens and stall canopies date from this restoration. St Mary & St Michael's has recently been described as "the most beautiful church in the northwest".

Inside, in the southwest corner of the church, is a door known as **Cromwell's Door**. The holes in it are said to have been made by indignant parishioners firing at Parliamentarian soldiers who had stabled their horses in the nave. Cromwell's troops were certainly in the area in 1643 and, to further establish the story, fragments of lead were found in the wood during restoration work in 1955.

Other features of interest include the glorious 45ft high east window (inspired by York Minster), the 14th century tomb of Lord and Lady Harrington, a fine Jacobean screen and some floor tablets referring to people who had drowned trying to cross the sands of Morecambe Bay. By the chancel screen are two sculptures by Josephina de Vasconcellos - one of St Michael, the other depicting the rest on the flight to Egypt. Cartmel is also famous for its attractive **Racecourse**, set beside the River Eea, on which meetings are held in May, July and August. Located close to the village, the course must be one of the most picturesque in the country and it is certainly one of the smallest. A holiday atmosphere descends on the village for race days and, though the competition is fierce, it is a wonderful and relaxing day out. The fixtures for 2003 are May 24th, 26th and 28th; July 17th; and August 23rd and 25th.

Flookburgh
3 miles SW of Grange-over-Sands on the B5277

An ancient Charter Borough, Flookburgh is still the principal fishing village on Morecambe Bay. Roads from the square lead down to the shore where fishermen still land their catches of cockle, shrimps and (less often nowadays) flukes, the tasty small flat fish from which the village takes its name. In **Coach House**, Winder Lane, is an unusual attraction in the form of a miniature village. 120 buildings made of local Coniston slate are accurate down to the last detail.

Cark-in-Cartmel
3 miles SW of Grange-over-Sands on the B5278

Cumbria's premier stately house, **Holker Hall** is one of the homes of the Cavendish family, the Dukes of Devonshire. An intriguing blend of 16th century, Georgian and Victorian architecture, is a visitor-friendly place with no restraining ropes keeping visitors at a distance, a fire burning in the hearth and a lived-in, family atmosphere. There's an impressive cantilevered staircase, a library with some 3,500 leather bound books (plus a few dummy covers designed to hide

Holker Hall and Gardens

gardens, water features, a 125-acre deer park, picnic and children's play areas, a gift shop and café. Also within the grounds is the **Lakeland Motor Museum** (see panel on page 58) which, as well as boasting a completely restored 1920s garage, has more than 100 vehicles on show among well over 20,000 well-presented exhibits. The cars may hold centre stage, but there's a great deal more, including 'magnificent motorbikes, superb scooters, bygone bicycles and triumphant tractors'. Housed in a quaint former Shire horse stable and its courtyard, the museum also honours leading figures from the world of motoring, among them Walter Owen Bentley, Frederick Henry Royce, Henry Ford, Colin Chapman and Alec Issigonis. A special exhibit is devoted to the attempts of Sir Malcolm and Donald Campbell to beat the world water speed record on Coniston Water. In August 2003 the museum celebrates its 25th anniversary all month, with a very special weekend of activities on the 16th and 17th.

electricity sockets), and an embroidered panel said to be the work of Mary, Queen of Scots.

Holker's 25 acres of award-winning gardens have featured in BBC-TV's *An English Country Garden*, and each year host the **Holker Garden Festival** which has been hailed as the 'Chelsea of the North'. The gardens are the pride of Lord and Lady Cavendish, who developed the present layout from the original 'contrived natural landscape' of Lord George Cavendish 200 years ago. The Great Holker Lime and the stunning spring display of rhododendrons are among the delights not to be missed. Here, too, are a wonderful rose garden, an azalea walk and a restored Victorian rockery. Lord and Lady Cavendish put their pride into words: "If you gain from your visit a small fraction of the pleasure that we ourselves get from them, then the work of generations of gardeners will not have been in vain."

The Holker Hall estate contains a wide variety of other attractions - formal

Ulverston

It was way back in 1280 that Edward I granted Ulverston its market charter; more than seven centuries later, colourful stalls still crowd the narrow streets and cobbled market square every

LAKELAND MOTOR MUSEUM

Holker Hall and Gardens, Cark-in-Cartmel,
Grange-over-Sands, Cumbria LA11 7PL
Tel/Fax: 015395 58509

A nostalgic reminder of transport bygones, the **Lakeland Motor Museum** has more than 100 vehicles on show ranging from pioneer vehicles of the early 1900s through to the exuberant models of the swinging 40s and fabulous 50s. As well as these classic cars, the Museum also houses a fascinating collection of "magnificent motorbikes, superb scooters, bygone bicycles and triumphant tractors!" Also amongst the 10,000 exhibits, probably the most extensive presentation of automobilia on display in the UK, are

"Authentic automobilia, reminiscent rarities, micro cars and mechanical marvels". This unique and carefully maintained collection is housed in a quaint former Shire horse stable and its courtyard. Prominent contributors to 20th century motoring are all honoured - amongst them Walter Owen Bentley, Colin Chapman, Henry Ford, Cecil Kimber, William Lyons, Alec Issigonis and Frederick Henry Royce. The world of agriculture is not neglected either, with Henry Ferguson and the horticultural reformer Charles H. Pugh both featured. Interpretive displays and strategically positioned push-button narrative centres, together with a well-researched exhibit listing, provide added interest and enjoyment.

The recent recovery of Donald Campbell's *Bluebird* from the depths of Coniston Water gives an added interest to the Campbell

Legend Bluebird Exhibition which pays tribute to Sir Malcolm Campbell and his son Donald who between them captured 21 world land and water speed records for Britain. Highlights of the exhibition include full size detailed replicas of the 1935 *Bluebird* car and the famous jet hydroplane, *Bluebird K7*. There's even a replica of Donald Campbell's lucky mascot, teddy bear Mr Whoppit, together with a continuous video detailing the lives, careers, failures and achievement of these two sporting celebrities.

Also on site is an exhibition celebrating Britain's horticultural heritage, a comprehensive display of vintage mechanical rotavators, trimmers, cutters and rollers, plus a fine collection of historical lawnmowers. The Potting Shed contains a display of gardening hand tools and other equipment of the past, as well as a re-creation of a pre-war glasshouse. Other attractions include the Coach House Café and a gift shop.

Market Street, Ulverston

Thursday. It's a picturesque scene but a walk up nearby **Hoad Hill** is rewarded with an even more striking view of the town. The great expanse of Morecambe Bay with a backdrop of the Pennines stretches to the south, the bulk of Ingleborough lies to the east, Coniston Old Man and the Langdale Pikes lie to the west and north. Crowning the hill is a 100ft-high **Replica of the Eddystone Lighthouse**, raised here in 1850 to commemorate one of Ulverston's most distinguished sons, Sir John Barrow. Explorer, diplomat and author, he served as a Lord of the Admiralty for more than forty years, his naval reforms contributing greatly to England's success in the Napoleonic Wars.

An even more famous son of Ulverston was Stanley Jefferson, born at number 3, Argyle Street on June 16th, 1890. Stanley is far better known to the world as Stan Laurel. His thirty-year career in more than 100 comedy films with Oliver Hardy is celebrated in the town's **Laurel and Hardy Museum** (see panel on page 60) in King Street. The museum was founded in 1976 by the late Bill Cubin, who devoted his life to the famous duo and collected an extraordinary variety of memorabilia, believed to be the largest in the world. Everything is here, including letters, photographs, personal items, and even furniture belonging to the couple. The museum is now looked after by Bill Cubin's daughter Marion

OLDE ULVERSTON TEA ROOMS

2 Lower Brook Street, Ulverston,
Cumbria LA12 7EE
Tel/Fax: 01229 580280
e-mail: supersue@aol.com

Super home-cooked food is served daily at the **Olde Ulverston Tea Rooms**, which Sue Hillman runs with her daughter Caroline and a trio of local ladies. Susan's menu runs from soup and sandwiches to jacket potatoes, toasted snacks and scrumptious pastries, and the daily specials board tempts with the likes of savoury pies, roasts and hearty casseroles. There are seats for 30 inside, with another 20

in the courtyard on good days. The tea rooms are open Monday to Saturday in summer, Tuesday to Saturday in winter.

The Cartmel and Furness Peninsulas

LAUREL AND HARDY MUSEUM

4c Upper Brook Street, Ulverston (town centre), Cumbria LA12 7BH

Tel: 01229 582292

The world famous museum devoted to **Laurel & Hardy** is based in Ulverston, the town where Stan was born on 16th June 1890. Everything you want to know about them is here. The late Bill Cubin, the founder of the museum, devoted his life to these famous comedians and collected an amazing variety of memorabilia, believed to be the largest in the world, including letters, photographs, personal items and furniture. A large

extension gives ample room to browse and a small cinema shows films and documentaries all day. Disabled persons have full access.

who continues to extend its amenities. A large extension has been added to the modest 17th century house and there is also a small cinema showing films and documentaries throughout the day. The museum is open seven days a week all year round except during January. Another son of Ulverston was Lord Norman Birkett, who represented Britain at the Nuremberg Trials and Mrs Wallis Simpson when she filed for divorce prior to marrying King Edward VIII.

Yet another great man associated with the town is George Fox, founder of the Quakers. Despite an extremely rough reception from the citizens of Ulverston when he preached here in the 1650s, Fox later married Margaret, widow of Judge Fell of nearby Swarthmoor Hall. This lovely late-16th century manor house, set in extensive gardens, was the birthplace of the Quaker movement and was for a time the home of its founder George Fox.

Ulverston itself, with its fascinating alleys and cobbled streets, is a delightful place to wander around. The oldest building in the town is the **Church of St Mary** which, in parts, dates from 1111. Though it was restored and rebuilt in the mid-19th century and the chancel was added in 1903, it has retained its splendid Norman door and some magnificent stained glass, including a window designed by the painter Sir Joshua Reynolds. The present tower dates from the reign of Elizabeth I as the original steeple was destroyed during a storm in 1540.

Ulverston also boasts England's shortest, widest and deepest **Canal**. Visitors can follow the towpath walk alongside which runs dead straight for just over a mile to Morecambe Bay. Built by the famous engineer John Rennie and opened in 1796, the canal ushered in a half-century of great prosperity for Ulverston as an inland port. At its peak, some 600 large ships a year berthed here but those good times came to an abrupt end in 1856 with the arrival of the railway. The railway company's directors bought the canal and promptly closed it. The town's other attractions include **The Lakes Glass Centre**, which features the high-quality Heron Glass and Cumbria Crystal. Also at the Centre is the **Gateway to Furness Exhibition**, providing a colourful snapshot of the history of the Furness Peninsula. There's more history at the **Ulverston Heritage Centre**, which also has a gift shop selling souvenirs and crafts made in Cumbria, while modern entertainment is provided at the Coronation Hall theatre complex and the traditional Roxy Cinema.

The open area to the north of the town, known as **The Gill**, is the starting point for the 70-mile Cumbria Way. The route of the Cumbria Way was originally devised by the Lake District area of the Ramblers Association in the mid-1970s and provides an exhilarating journey through a wonderful mix of natural splendour and fascinating heritage. The first section is the 15-mile walk to Coniston.

Around Ulverston

Haverthwaite

5 miles NE of Ulverston off the A590

Haverthwaite is the southern terminus of the **Lakeside & Haverthwaite Railway** (see panel on page 62), a branch of the Furness railway originally built to transport passengers and goods to the steamers on Lake Windermere. It was one of the first attempts at mass tourism in the Lake District. Passenger numbers peaked in the 1920s, but the general decline of rail travel in the 1960s led to the railway's closure in 1967.

However, a group of dedicated rail enthusiasts rescued this scenic stretch, restored its engines and rolling stock to working order and now provide a full service of steam trains throughout the season (see also under Lakeside in Chapter 2).

THE BRITANNIA INN

Penny Bridge, Nr Ulverston,
Cumbria LA12 7RJ
Tel: 01229 861480
e-mail: good-food@britpub.co.uk
website: www.britpub.co.uk

Just off the A5092 in the village of Penny Bridge, the 17th century **Britannia Inn** is a favourite choice with the local community for both food and drink, and tenet/chef Frank and barman Andy are winning new friends all the time. Frank is a superb chef, and everything on his menu is home-made – even the bread. Options run from sandwiches and snacks to Cumberland hotpot, wild mushroom risotto,

fish pie and steaks. Booking is recommended at the weekend. Wednesday is quiz night at this most convivial place.

THE LAKESIDE & HAVERTHWAITE RAILWAY

Haverthwaite Station, nr Ulverston,
Cumbria LA12 8AL
Tel: 015395 31594

From the Victorian station at Haverthwaite, beautifully restored steam locomotives of the **Lakeside & Haverthwaite Railway** haul comfortable coaches through the Leven Valley. With connections at Lakeside by way of Windermere Lake Cruises, the train offers a unique perspective from which to enjoy the ever-changing lake and river scenery of this picturesque part of the Lake District. This former Furness Railway branch line runs for 3.5 miles, with a journey time of around 20 minutes, giving passengers a leisurely and relaxing trip. Whilst at Haverthwaite, visitors can sample a delicious home baked scone in the licensed Station Restaurant - an ideal way to start or end the journey.

Swarthmoor

1 mile S of Ulverston off the A590

This small village of whitewashed cottages, now almost entirely incorporated into Ulverston, also has a curious 16th century hall. **Swarthmoor Hall** stands in well-kept gardens and, although a cement rendering disguises its antiquity, the mullion windows and leaded panes give a clue to its true age. It was built in around 1586 by George Fell, a wealthy landowner. It was his son, Judge Thomas Fell, who married

Margaret Askew, who, in turn, became a follower of George Fox after hearing him preach in 1652. At that time, many people were suspicious of Fox's beliefs but Margaret was able to persuade her husband to use his position to give Fox protection and shelter, and the hall became the first settled centre of the Quaker Movement. Missionaries were organised from here and the library was stocked with both Quaker and anti-Quaker literature. Judge Fell died in 1658 and, 11 years later, Margaret married George Fox. The hall is open during the summer and it gives a fascinating insight into the history of the early Quakers.

Lindal-in-Furness

3 miles SW of Ulverston on the A590

The **Colony Country Store** combines the aromatic character of an old-fashioned country general stores with the cost-cutting advantages of a Factory Shop. There's a huge range of textiles, glassware, ceramics and decorative accessories for the home, but the Colony is also Europe's leading manufacturer of scented candles, supplying millions of scented and dinner candles every year to prestigious stores around the world. The 30 fragrances include classic Rose, fruity Fresh Peach and French Vanilla. From a viewing gallery visitors can watch the traditional skills of hand pouring and dipping being used to create a variety of candle styles. And for a small additional fee, you can try your hand at dipping your own candle. Open daily all year round, The Colony has a restaurant serving hot meals and snacks, and free parking.

Great Urswick
3 miles S of Ulverston off the A590

The ancient village **Church of St Mary and St Michael** is noted for its unusual and lively woodcarvings that were created by the Chipping Campden Guild of Carvers. As well as the figure of a pilgrim to the left of the chancel arch, there are some smaller carvings in the choir stall of winged children playing musical instruments. Also worthy of a second look is the 9th century wooden cross which bears a runic inscription.

Lying between Great Urswick and Bardsea and overlooking Morecambe Bay is **Birkrigg Common**, a lovely area of open land. Here, on the east side of the common, is the **Druid's Circle**, with two concentric circles made up of 31 stones up to three feet high. The cremated human remains found around the site in 1921 indicate that is was used for burials. There are also several other prehistoric sites in the area.

Bardsea
2 miles S of Ulverston off the A5087

The village stands on a lovely green knoll overlooking the sea and, as well as having a charming, unhurried air about it, there are some excellent walks from here along the coast either from its Country Park or through the woodland.

Just up the coast, to the north, lies **Conishead Priory**, once the site of a leper colony that was established by Augustinian canons in the 12th century. The monks from the priory used to act as guides across the dangerous Cartmel Sands to Lancashire. After the Dissolution, a superb private house was built on the site and the guide service was continued by the Duchy of Lancaster. In 1821, Colonel Braddyll demolished the house and built in its place the ornate Gothic mansion that stands here today. He was also responsible for the atmospheric ruined folly on **Chapel Island** that is clearly visible in the estuary.

Latterly, **Conishead Priory** has been a private house, a hydropathic hotel, a military hospital and a rest home for Durham miners; it is now owned by the Tibet Buddhist Manjushri Mahayana Buddhist Centre, who came here in 1977. During the summer months, visitors are welcome to the house, which is open for tours, and there is a delightful woodland trail to follow through the grounds. A new Buddhist temple was opened in 1998, based on a traditional design which symbolises the pure world (Mandala) of a Buddha.

Barrow-in-Furness

Undoubtedly the best introduction to Barrow is to pay a visit to the **Dock Museum** (free admission), an impressive glass and steel structure which hangs suspended above a Victorian Graving Dock. Audio-visual displays and a series

THE HARBOUR HOTEL

The Strand, Barrow-in-Furness,
Cumbria LA14 2HG
Tel: 01229 820066

Tenants Margaret and Philip Savage have a warm welcome for visitors to the **Harbour Hotel**, a friendly pub close to the town centre. It's open all day, every day, and behind the smart blue and cream frontage the open-plan bar area is bright and spotless. Besides the usual range of drinks, the Harbour serves a good choice of hearty home-cooked dishes lunchtime and evening Wednesday to Saturday and from 12 to 5 on Sunday. On the social side, pool and darts are played in the bar, Friday is karaoke night and there's live music on Saturday.

THE DOCK MUSEUM

The Dock, North Road, Barrow-in-Furness,
Cumbria LA14 2PW
Tel: 01229 894444

The Dock Museum is a spectacular modern museum built over an orginal Victorian dock. Its displays trace the fascinating history of Barrow showing how it grew from a tiny nineteenth century hamlet to the biggest iron and steel centre in the world and a major

the museum's nationally important collection of glass negatives.

The Dock Museum has a fully landscaped waterfront site, with paths linking to the Cumbria Coastal Way, an adventure playground and picnic area. A wide range of tempting snacks and hot meals are available in our Strollers Coffee Shop. The museum has no admission charge and car parking is also free.

shipbuilding force in just 40 years.

New for 2001 is a permanent exhibition entitled "Shipbuilders to the World" which opens in May to coincide with Barrow's submarine centenary. This impressive exhibition looks at the development of shipbuilding in the town and will include an exciting interactive display using images from of exhibits describe how Barrow grew from a tiny hamlet in the early 1800s to become the largest iron and steel centre in the world and also a major shipbuilding force in just 40 years. The original population of just 200 had, by 1874, increased to over 35,000.

The museum has some spectacular models of ships of every kind, an Art Gallery hosting both permanent and travelling exhibitions, and a high tech interactive film show where characters from Barrow's history come to life to tell the town's story. Other attractions at the museum include a themed adventure playground, a Museum Shop and a coffee shop.

It was James (later Sir James) Ramsden who established the first Barrow Iron Ship Company in 1870, taking advantage of local steel production skills. In 1896, the firm was acquired by **Vickers**, a name forever linked with Barrow, and for a number of years was the largest armaments works in the world. Sir James was also the General Manager of the Furness Railway and the town's first mayor. At the Ramsden Square roundabout is a statue to Sir James, and at the next roundabout is a statue of HW Schneider, one of the men who developed the Furness iron mines and was involved in the Barrow Haematite

GLEN GARTH HOTEL & RESTAURANT

359 Abbey Road, Barrow-in-Furness, Cumbria LA13 9JY
Tel: 01229 825374 Fax: 01229 811744
e-mail: glengarth@btconnect.com
website: www.glengarthhotel.com

Glen Garth Hotel & Restaurant is a distinguished late 19th century property just off the town centre. The hotel offers 15 high-quality guest bedrooms, all decorated and furnished in traditional style and all with en suite facilities. Some are family rooms, and children are very welcome (but not pets). The food at Glen Garth is excellent, and in the elegantly appointed non-smoking restaurant, owner Yvonne Patterson and head chef Cathy Goude offer a choice of à la carte and bistro menus between 7 and 9 Monday to Saturday evenings. On Sunday evenings supper is served from the bar supper menu. Morning coffee is available, and the hotel is licensed for residents and diners.It is also a

popular venue for Weddings and Functions.

Glen Garth stands back from the road that leads to Furness Abbey, one of the region's leading visitor attractions. The Abbey was once the second richest in England, and the extensive red sandstone remains occupy a very pleasant and peaceful site in the Vale of Deadly Nightshade. Guests at Glen Garth can enjoy the fresh air and build up an appetite for supper with a walk on the Cistercian Way, which starts in Barrow and passes the Abbey en route to Grange-over-Sands.

THE RAMS HEAD HOTEL

110 Rawlinson Street, Barrow-in-Furness,
Cumbria LA14 2DY
Tel: 01229 821728

The Rams Head Hotel is a large, imposing late-Victorian building on a corner site an easy walk from the town centre. It operates both as a hotel and as a pub and has been run since the early 1990s by Thomas and Paula Halfpenny. A good standard of budget overnight accommodation is provided in seven bedrooms with shared bathroom facilities, making it a practical base for visitors to this busy town, whose Dock Museum is

one of the region's most important attractions. The Rams Head's pub hours are 4pm to 11pm Monday to Wednesday, noon to 11pm Thursday to Sunday.

Steel Company.

Today, Barrow is the Peninsula's prime shopping centre, with all the familiar High Street stores mingling with local specialist shops, and the largest indoor market in the area which is open on Mondays, Wednesdays, Fridays and Saturdays. The town also boasts a wide range of entertainment facilities - multiplex cinema, 10-pin bowling, fitness centre and leisure club, and three first class golf courses all within easy reach.

Barrow is also the western starting point of the **Cistercian Way**, a 33-mile walk to Grange-over-Sands through wonderfully unspoilt countryside. En route it passes Furness Abbey in the Vale of Deadly Nightshade, prehistoric sites on the hills surrounding Urswick Tarn and many other historical places of interest. The Way is marked on public roads and footpaths, and a fully

GLEASTON WATER MILL

Gleaston, Ulverston, Cumbria LA12 0QH
Tel: 01229 869244 Fax: 01229 869764
website: www.watermill.co.uk

Where is **Gleaston Water Mill**? Take up the challenge and follow the signs from the

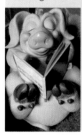

A5087, down the country lanes of rural Cumbria and past the ruins of Gleaston Castle, to find it - it will be worth your efforts. The historic water driven corn mill is in working order and abounds with atmosphere, artefacts, archaeologists and an apiary. Guided talks, walks and tours can be

arranged. The Dusty Miller's café is fully licensed.

Pig's Whisper is a rare treat for pig lovers of all ages. This gallery offers gift items from the sublime to the pigiculous. And don't forget the Boggard!

descriptive leaflet is available from Tourist Information Centres.

Around Barrow-in-Furness

Gleaston

3 miles E of Barrow-in-Furness off the A5087

This village is typical of the small, peaceful villages and hamlets that can be found in this part of the peninsula. Here, standing close by the ruins of **Gleaston Castle**, can be found **Gleaston Water Mill** (see panel opposite). The present buildings date from 1774, with the massive original wooden gearing still in place. The machinery is operational most days - an 18ft water-wheel and an 11ft wooden pit wheel serviced by an intriguing water course. Evening tours with supper are available by prior arrangement.

Foulney Island

5 miles E of Barrow-in-Furness off the A5087

The island, like its smaller neighbour Roa Island, is joined to the mainland by a causeway. The site of the local

lifeboat station, the island is small and sheltered from the Irish Sea by Walney Island.

Piel Island

5 miles SE of Barrow-in-Furness via foot ferry from Roa island

Though this tiny island was probably visited by both the Celts and the Romans, its first recorded name is Scandinavian - Fotheray - from the Old Norse meaning 'fodder island'. In 1127 the islands were given to the Savignac Monks by King Stephen and, after the order merged with the Cistercian monks in the middle of the 12th century, the monks of Furness Abbey began to use Piel Island as a warehouse and storage area.

Piel Castle, on the island, was a house fortified in the early part of the 14th century and at the time it was the largest of its kind in the northwest. Intended to be used as one of the abbey's

Piel Castle, Piel Island

warehouses and to offer protection from raiders, in later years the castle also proved to be a useful defence against the King's Customs men and a prosperous trade in smuggling began. The castle has, over many years, been allowed to fall into ruin and now presents a stark outline on the horizon.

One of the most exciting events in Piel's history occurred on 4th June 1487 when a man claiming to be the Earl of Warwick, one of the Princes in the Tower allegedly murdered by Richard III, landed on the island. If true, the Earl was indisputably the true King of England. In reality, this 'Earl of Warwick' was Lambert Simnel, the son of a joiner. Supported by an army of German and Irish mercenaries, Simnel set out across Furness to march on London. However, when he arrived in the capital it was as the prisoner of Henry VII who had defeated Simnel's troops at Stoke. Somewhat contemptuously, Henry gave Simnel employment in the royal kitchens.

Walney Island
2 miles W of Barrow-in-Furness on the A590

This 10-mile-long island is joined to the Furness Peninsula by a bridge from Barrow docks and is home to two important nature reserves that are situated at either end of the island. **North Walney National Nature Reserve** covers some 350 acres within which are a great variety of habitats including sand dunes, heath, salt marsh,

shingle, and scrub. As well as having several species of orchid and over 130 species of bird either living or visiting the reserve, there is also an area for the preservation of the Natterjack toad, Britain's rarest amphibian. Unique to the Reserve is the Walney Geranium, a plant that grows nowhere else in the world. North Walney also boasts a rich prehistoric past, with important archaeological sites from mesolithic, neolithic, Bronze, and Iron Age times.

Situated on the island's long foot, **South Walney Nature Reserve** is home to the largest nesting ground of herring gulls and lesser black-backed gulls in Europe. It is also the most southerly breeding ground of such species as the oystercatcher, tern, and ringed plover, and in all, over 250 bird species have been recorded. A stopover for many migratory birds, the reserve has considerable ecological interest with mudflats, sandy beaches, rough pasture, and fresh water. There are waymarked trails around the reserve, with a number of hides.

The island's southernmost tip, **Walney Point**, is dominated by a 70ft lighthouse which was built in 1790 and whose light was, originally, an oil lamp.

Dalton-in-Furness
5 miles N of Barrow-in-Furness off the A590

Lying in a narrow valley on the part of Furness which extends deep into Morecambe Bay, it is difficult to imagine that this ancient place was once the leading town of Furness and an important centre for administration and justice. The 14th century pele tower, **Dalton Castle**, was built with walls six feet thick to provide a place of refuge for the monks of Furness Abbey against Scottish raiders and it still looks very formidable. Over the centuries, in its twin role as both prison and court, it has been substantially altered internally although it still retains most of its original external features. It is now owned by the National Trust and houses a small museum with an interesting display of 16th and 17th century armour, along with exhibits about iron mining, the Civil War in Furness, and the life and work of George Romney, the 18th century portrait painter (see below).

Dalton Castle

Dalton became established as a market town in the 13th century when the Cistercians began to hold fairs and markets in the town. Indeed, the influence of the monks was great here as, before the Dissolution, it was the Abbot who held court and administered justice. Not surprisingly, Dalton's decline coincided with the departure of the monks and also with the growing importance of Ulverston and Greenodd as ports.

The red sandstone **Church of St Mary** was designed by the celebrated Victorian architects Paley and Austin

and, in the graveyard, lies George Romney, who was best known in his day for his many portraits of Nelson's mistress, Lady Hamilton, with whom he formed a romantic attachment, in spite of having a wife in Kendal. His grave is marked with the inscription 'pictor celeberrimus'. Also worth seeking out in the graveyard is the plaque which outlines the devastating effect of the bubonic plague which swept through the town in 1662. Of the total population at the time of 612, no fewer than 320 fell victim to the plague.

Visitors to Dalton will find that it is

time well spent looking around the many fascinating facades in and close to the market place, such as the unique, cast-iron shop front at No 51, **Market Street**. In the market place itself is an elegant, **Victorian Drinking Fountain** with fluted columns supporting a dome of open iron work above the pedestal fountain. Nearby stands the market cross and the slabs of stone that were used for fish-drying in the 19th century.

From the mostly pedestrianised Tudor Square, visitors can board a bus to the award-winning **South Lakes Wild Animal Park** which has been designated the Region's Official Top Attraction by the Cumbria Tourist Board. It's the only place in Britain where you can see rare Amur and Sumatran tigers (the world's biggest and smallest tigers). At feeding time (14.30 each day) they climb a 20ft vertical tree to 'catch' their food. Ring-tailed lemurs wander freely through the park, visitors can walk with emus and hand feed the largest collection of kangaroos in Europe. The 17 acres of natural parkland are also home to some of the rarest animals on earth, among them the red panda, maned wolves and tamarin monkeys as well as some 150 other species from around the world, including rhinos, giraffes, tapirs, coatis and the ever-popular meerkats. Other attractions include a Safari Railway, adventure play area, many picnic spots, a gift shop and café.

To the south of the town lies **Furness Abbey** (English Heritage), a magnificent ruin of eroded red sandstone set in fine parkland, the focal point of south Cumbria's monastic heritage. Among the atmospheric remains can still be seen the canopied seats in the presbytery and the graceful arches overlooking the cloister, testaments to the abbey's former wealth and influence. Furness Abbey stands in the **Vale of Deadly Nightshade**, a shallow valley of sandstone cliffs and rich pastureland. The abbey itself was established in 1123 at Tulketh, near Preston, by King Stephen. Four years later it was moved

ASKAM HOTEL

1-3 Victoria Street, Askam-in-Furness, Cumbria LA16 7BX
Tel: 01229 466161

In the village of Askam-in-Furness, half a mile off the main A595, the **Askam Hotel** has a dual role of Bed & Breakfast hotel and public house. On the accommodation side are three non-smoking upstairs bedrooms, all with tv and tea & coffee making facilities. Downstairs, the bar is a popular local meeting place, and a fine selection of ales includes Jennings Bitter and Cumberland Ale. Accommodation is available all year round, and the bar is open every evening and Saturday and Sunday lunchtimes (all day, every day during the summer school holidays). Cash and cheques only.

to its present site and, after 20 years, became absorbed into the Cistercian Order. Despite its remoteness, the abbey flourished, with the monks establishing themselves as guides across the treacherous sands of Morecambe Bay. Rich endowments

Furness Abbey

of land, including holdings in Yorkshire and Ireland, led to the development of trade in products such as wool, iron, and charcoal. Furness Abbey became the second wealthiest monastery in Britain after Fountains Abbey in Yorkshire. After Dissolution, in 1537, the abbey became part of Thomas Cromwell's estate and it was allowed to decay into a picturesque and romantic ruin. It is now owned by English Heritage who have a small Interpretative Centre nearby detailing its history. Off the A595 Dalton to Askam road, **Sandscale Haws** is one of the most important sand dune systems in Britain, supporting an outstanding variety of fauna.

Grizebeck
15 miles N of Barrow-in-Furness on the A595/A5092

This small village on the edge of the Lake District National Park nestles against the flanks of the **Furness Fells**. Although it stands at the junction of

roads leading to the Furness Peninsula and the South Cumbria coast, the village and the area around is peaceful and unhurried, offering the visitor an inviting alternative to some of the busier and more crowded Lakeland towns.

Broughton-in-Furness
19 miles N of Barrow-in-Furness on the A595/A593

At the heart of this attractive, unspoilt little town is the **Market Square** with its tall Georgian houses, commemorative obelisk of 1810, village stocks, fish slabs and some venerable chestnut trees. The old Town Hall, occupying the whole of one side, dates back to 1766 and now houses the town's Tourist Information Centre and the Clocktower Gallery, which exhibits paintings, ceramics, mirrors and glassware. On August 1st each year, Broughton's Lord of the Manor comes to the Square to read out the market charter granted by Elizabeth I, while Councillors dispense pennies to

THE BLACK COCK INN

Princes Street, Broughton-in-Furness,
Cumbria LA20 6HQ
Tel/Fax: 01229 716529
e-mail: blackcockinn@yahoo.co.uk
web: www.theblackcockinncumbria.co.uk

The **Black Cock Inn** is a really delightful old-world village hostelry full of charm, atmosphere and history. Alexandra Jarvis, a local lady, has been associated with public houses for over 25 years, but this is her first venture with her husband Dale. They've been here since 2000, and have made it one of the most popular places for miles around, particularly for food. In summer the black-and-white front of the inn is adorned with colourful window boxes and flower tubs, and the inside is just as warm and welcoming whatever the season. The bar is a great place for lovers of real ale, with no fewer than five brews always on tap · Bombardier, Theakstons Best, Cool Cask and Black Bull, and a regularly changing guest. Food is served every session,

and even though there are seats for 90 (including 20 in a non-smoking section) it's always best to book to be sure of a table.

Daily specials supplement the printed menu, which makes fine use of fresh local ingredients and offers an excellent choice of dishes both traditional and less familiar. Starters include mussels cooked with white wine, garlic and parsley, deep-fried camembert with a redcurrant dip, sticky chicken wings and nachos topped with cheese, salsa, guacamole and soured cream. Among the mouthwatering main courses are

haddock cooked in stout batter served with chips and mushy peas, minty lamb Henry, chicken breast griddled with Cajun spices, and terrific steamed puddings · chicken & ham or beef & mushroom. A special steak board lists the day's prime cuts, which can be served plain or with one of the tasty home-made sauces. The fine food is complemented by well-chosen, well-priced wines from a helpfully annotated list.

The inn also offers four superior en suite guest bedrooms · two doubles, a family room and a suite. The tariff includes a hearty English breakfast, and there are discounts for stays of more than three nights. Children under 11 sharing their parents' room stay free. To the rear of the inn, accessible through the bar, is a courtyard beer garden. The 17th century Black Cock, which is open every lunchtime and evening and all day on Saturday and Sunday, is situated at the heart of the attractive little town of Broughton-in-Furness, with some of the Lake District's finest scenery within easy reach.

LICKLE VALLEY COTTAGES

Lane End Farm, Broughton Mills, Broughton-in-Furness, Cumbria LA20 6AX
Tel: 01229 716332
website: www.licklevalleycottages.co.uk

In an area noted for excellent walking and beautiful scenery, **Lickle Valley Cottages** provide the perfect base for a relaxed self-catering holiday. 17th century Rose Cottage sleeps six in comfort, and careful refurbishment has retained its period character while offering all the modern amenities. Across from a working farm, Honeysuckle Cottage makes a cosy hideaway for two, and both cottages have pleasant little gardens. Owned and run by Margaret and

Allan Harrison, the cottages, which have a 4-star ETB rating, are available all year round. No smoking or pets.

any children in the crowd.

One of the town's famous short-term residents was Branwell Brontë who was employed here as a tutor at **Broughton House**, a splendid double-fronted, three-storey town house just off the Square. Branwell apparently found time to both enjoy the elegance of the town and to share in whatever revelries were in train. Wordsworth often visited Broughton as a child. Throughout his life he loved this peaceful corner of Lakeland and celebrated its charms in some 150 poems; his 20th century poetical successor, Norman Nicholson, was similarly enchanted.

Some of the Lake District's finest scenery - the Duddon Valley, Furness Fells, Great Gable and Scafell are all within easy reach, and about 3 miles west of the town is **Swinside Circle**, a fine prehistoric stone circle, some 60 feet in diameter, containing 52 close-set stones and two outlying 'portal' or gateway stones.

About 3 miles north of the town, the peaceful hamlet of **Broughton Mills** will attract followers of the Coleridge Trail. During the course of his famous 'circumcursion' of Lakeland in August 1802, the poet stopped to refresh himself at the **Blacksmith's Arms** where he 'Dined on Oatcake and Cheese, with a pint of Ale, and 2 glasses of Rum and water sweetened with preserved Gooseberries'. The inn, built in 1748, is still there and barely changed since Coleridge's visit.

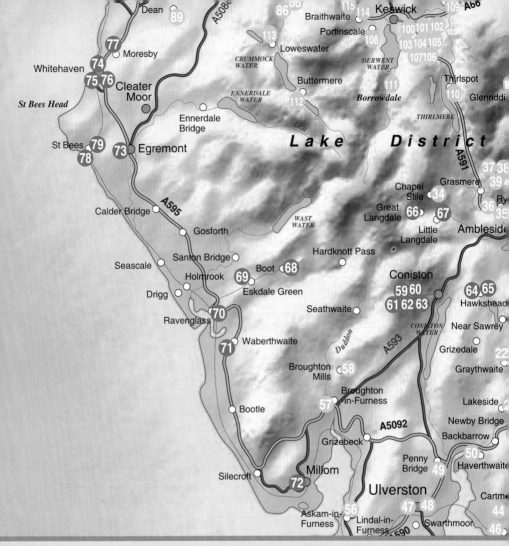

Dean
89
A508...
86
115
114 Keswick
109 A6...
77
Braithwaite
100 101 102
Moresby
113
Portinscale
108
103 104 105
Whitehaven
74
Loweswater
107 106
75 76
Cleater
CRUMMOCK
WATER
DERWENT
WATER
Moor
111
Thirlspot
St Bees Head
ENNERDALE
WATER
Buttermere
Borrowdale
110
Glenriddi
Ennerdale
Bridge
112
THIRLMERE
St Bees
79
73
Egremont
Lake   District
A591
37 38
78
Chapel
Stile
34
Grasmere
39
Calder Bridge
A595
Great
Langdale
66
67
36
Ry
35
Gosforth
Little
Langdale
Ambleside
Seascale
Santon Bridge
WAST
WATER
Hardknott Pass
Coniston
Holmrook
Boot
68
59 60
64 65
Drigg
69
61 62 63
Hawkshead
Eskdale Green
Seathwaite
Near Sawrey
Ravenglass
70
CONISTON
WATER
Grizedale
22
71
Waberthwaite
Duddon
A593
Graythwaite
Broughton
Mills
58
Lakeside
Bootle
Broughton
in-Furness
Newby Bridge
57
Backbarrow
A5092
Grizebeck
Penny
Bridge
50
Silecroft
Millom
49
Haverthwaite
72
Ulverston
Cartm...
47 48
44
Askam-in-
Furness
56
Lindal-in-
Furness
Swarthmoor
46
A590

PLACES TO STAY, EAT AND DRINK

● Denotes entries in other chapters

4 Coniston and Southwest Cumbria

hree distinct areas lie within the southwest quarter of Cumbria. The enchanting scenery around Coniston Water and its environs is very much on the tourist trail, and also has strong literary connections. John Ruskin, the 19th century author, artist, and critic made his home at Brantwood on the shore of Coniston and the lake is also the setting for many of the adventures recounted in *Swallows and Amazons* as told by Arthur Ransome. Wordsworth went to school in Hawkshead where the desk he defaced with his name can still be seen. But probably the most popular of Coniston's literary denizens is Beatrix Potter, who, after holidaying at Near Sawrey as a child, later bought a house at Hill Top

Wast Water

PLACES TO STAY, EAT AND DRINK

Denotes entries in other chapters

as well as many acres of farms which she bequeathed to the National Trust. Further west is Cumbria's 'Empty Quarter', a vast terrain of magnificent mountains and desolate fells beloved of climbers and walkers. England's highest mountain, Scafell Pike, rises here; the country's deepest lake, Wast Water, sinks to a depth of some 200ft and is surrounded by sheer cliffs soaring up to 2,000ft, and the village of Wasdale Head claims to have the smallest church in England.

Bordering this untamed landscape is the narrow coastal strip, stretching from Whitehaven down to Millom, which has its own identity as well as a quiet charm. The coastline is dominated by small 18th and 19th century iron mining communities set between the romantic outline of the Lakeland fells and the grey-blue waters of the Irish Sea. The famous Ravenglass and Eskdale Railway carries many visitors from the coast up one of Cumbria's most picturesque valleys. There are also several genteel Victorian resorts along the coast, including the popular village of Seascale. One of the area's most controversial sites, the nuclear power station at Sellafield, closed in the spring of 2003.

Coniston

Beatrix Potter, John Ruskin, Arthur Ransome, Sir Donald Campbell - all of them have strong connections with **Coniston Water**, the third largest and one of the most beautiful of the central Cumbrian lakes. Beatrix Potter lived at Sawrey near Lake Windermere but she owned the vast **Monk Coniston** estate at the head of Coniston Water. On her death, she bequeathed it to the National Trust, a body she had helped to establish and to which she devoted much of her time and fortune.

Ruskin came to Coniston in 1872, moving into a house he had never seen. Brantwood, on the eastern side of the lake, is open to the public and enjoys superb views across the water to the

WATERHEAD HOTEL

Coniston, Cumbria LA21 8AJ
Tel: 015394 41244 Fax: 015394 41193
e-mail: wh@pofr.co.uk
website: www.pofr.com

The **Waterhead Hotel** enjoys a stunning location in five acres of grounds and lawns running down to the shores of Coniston Water. A hotel for more than 100 years, it has 21 beautifully appointed en suite bedrooms, all with remote control tv and tea/coffee making facilities; there are two family rooms, and one room on the ground floor has been adapted for wheelchair users. Table d'hote dinners featuring local produce are served in

the non-smoking restaurant, and anyone is welcome to drop in for a drink, morning coffee or afternoon tea.

great crumpled hill of the **Old Man of Coniston**, 800 metres high. From its summit there are even more extensive vistas over Scotland, the Isle of Man, and on a clear day as far as Snowdonia.

Arthur Ransome's *Swallows and Amazons* has delighted generations with its tales of children's adventures set in and around the Lake District. As a child he spent his summer holidays near Nibthwaite at the southern

Gondola Steam Launch, Coniston

end of the lake and recalled that he was always "half-drowned in tears" when he had to leave. Later he bought a house overlooking Coniston Water and many locations in his books can be recognised today: **Peel Island**, for example, at the southern end of the lake, is the Wildcat Island of his books.

Sir Donald Campbell's associations with the lake were both glorious and tragic. In 1955 he broke the world water speed record here; twelve years later, when he was attempting to beat his own record, his boat, **Bluebird**, struck a log while travelling at 320mph. In March 2001 his widow was present as the tailfin of the boat was at last hauled up to the surface. For 34 years the 15ft rear section had lain on a bed of silt, 140ft down and right in the middle of the lake. Plans are still under way for the boat to be restored and placed on display at the Ruskin Museum, but it could take some time. Sir Donald's body was later

recovered and was buried on September 12th 2001 in the village cemetery - an event that was comparatively little covered by the media, who were obviously concerned with the tragic events in New York and Washington the day before.

Nowadays, boats on Coniston Water are restricted to a 10 mph limit which is an ideal speed if you're travelling in the wonderful old steamship, the **Gondola**. So called because of its high prow which enabled it to come in close to shore to pick up passengers, *Gondola* was commissioned by Sir James Ramsden, General Manager of the Furness Railway Company and first Mayor of Barrow, and was launched on Coniston Water in 1859. She retired in 1936, but found a new career as a houseboat in 1945. Abandoned after a storm in the 1960s, she was saved by a group of National Trust enthusiasts and restored and rebuilt by Vickers Shipbuilding. She was

View of Coniston Lake

Man of Coniston overlooks the village and it was from this mountain, and some of the surrounding hills, that copper was extracted. Mined from the days of the Romans, the industry's heyday in Coniston was in the 18th and 19th centuries but, with the discovery of more accessible deposits, the industry went into decline and the village returned to pre-boom peacefulness. At 2,631 feet, the Old Man of Coniston is a considerable climb but many make the effort and the summit can be bustling with fell walkers enjoying the glorious views.

relaunched in 1980. Up to 86 passengers can now travel in opulent comfort on her regular trips around the lake. Coniston Launch also offers lake cruises in its two timber launches, and at the boating centre craft of every kind are available to rent.

Coniston village was once an important copper mining centre and was also widely known for the beautiful decorative green slate, quarried locally, which is used on so many of the public buildings. The great bulk of the Old

Just south of the village and beside the lake is **Coniston Hall**, the village's oldest building. Dating from the 16th century, it was the home of the Le Fleming family, the largest landowners in the area. Coniston's most famous inhabitant was, however, John Ruskin, the 19th century author, artist, critic,

BANK GROUND

East of Lake Road, Coniston,
Cumbria LA21 8AA
Tel: 015394 41264 Fax: 015394 41900
e-mail: info@bankground.com
website: www.bankground.com

Set in 60 acres of fell and woodland with its own jetty on Coniston Water, **Bank Ground** offers a magical combination of peace, comfort, a traditional Lakeland welcome and glorious surroundings. Long-time owners the Batty family offer a choice of Bed & Breakfast or Self Catering accommodation. The former

comprises seven superb rooms in the farmhouse, while the latter consists of four adjoining cottages and The Barn, which can sleep up to 14 guests in six bedrooms. Bank Ground was the setting for Arthur Ransome's children's story *Swallows and Amazons*.

RUSKIN · THE MUSEUM

The Institute, Yewdale Road, Coniston,
Cumbria LA21 8DU
Tel: 015394 41164 Fax: 015394 41132
e-mail: vmj@ruskinmuseum.com
website: www.ruskinmuseum.com

The Ruskin Museum tells the Story of
Coniston. From the dynamic geological history
(volcanic rocks can be seen through the
museum window and explored in the geology
section inside) to 300 years of colourful but
raw excavation in the old Coppermines (an

accessible CD Rom gives you a wonderful
virtual trip).

From the inspirational art work (including
originals plus sketches on computer) and
heart warming philosophies of John Ruskin, to
the dramatic, suspense-filled saga of Donald
Campbell's record breaking attempts on
Coniston Water (poignant Powerpoint display
of photos, including KTs recovery in 2001,
plus video of the fatal crash and memorabilia)
the heritage of this unique area offers
something for everyone. "Coniston's superb
museum... is the most thought provoking in
the Lakes." *The Rough Guide to the Lake
District, 2000.*

social commentator and one of the first
conservationists. He lies buried in
Coniston churchyard and the **Ruskin
Museum** (see panel above) nearby
contains many of his studies, pictures,
letters, and photographs as well as his
collection of geological specimens.
Visitors can also see a pair of his socks,
his certificate of
matriculation from Oxford,
and his funeral pall made of
Ruskin lace embroidered with
wild flowers. The lace was so
called because Ruskin had
encouraged the revival of flax
hand-spinning in the area.
Lace pieces made to his own
designs and based on the
sumptuous ruffs worn by

sitters in portraits by Titian, Tintoretto
and Veronese were attached to plain
linen to make decorative cushions, table
covers and bedspreads - many of these
are on display.

From the jetty at Coniston, a short
ferry trip takes you to John Ruskin's
home, **Brantwood** (see panel on page

Brantwood, Coniston

JUMPING JENNY AT BRANTWOOD

Brantwood House, Coniston,
Cumbria LA21 8AD
Tel: 015394 41715 Fax: 015394 41819

Since taking over in 1991, Chris and Gillie Addison have never stopped winning new friends at **Jumping Jenny**, their delightful coffee house and restaurant overlooking Coniston Water. Splendid home cooking, with Chris in charge of savouries and Gillie looking after sweets, brings in the crowds, and as a very special prelude to a meal the owners can arrange a trip on the lake. The restaurant occupies the former stables of John Ruskin's home, Brantwood House, and takes its name from Ruskin's rowing boat. Jumping Jenny is open every day except Monday and Tuesday during December to February.

80), which occupies a beautiful setting on the eastern shores of Coniston Water. It was his home from 1872 until his death in 1900. When he arrived for the first time he described the house, which he had bought for £1,500 without ever seeing it, as "a mere shed". He spent the next 20 years extending the house, by adding another 12 rooms, and laying out the gardens. The view from the Turret Room he had built was, Ruskin declared, "the best in all England". Sadly, Ruskin's later years were blighted by mental illness, "He was", said a biographer, "at times quite mad".

Visitors today can wander around rooms filled with Ruskin's watercolours, paintings by Turner (who was one of his heroes), see his study which is lined with wallpaper he designed himself, and

BRANTWOOD

Coniston, Cumbria LA21 8AD
Tel: 015394 41396 Fax: 015394 41263

Brantwood is the most beautifully situated house in the Lake District. It enjoys the finest lake and mountain views in England and there is no other house in the district with such a diversity of cultural associations. The home of John Ruskin from 1872 until his death in 1900, Brantwood became an intellectual powerhouse and one of the greatest literary and artistic centres in Europe. Tolstoy, Mahatma Gandhi, Marcel Proust and Frank Lloyd Wright can all be numbered amongst Ruskin's disciples.

Today, Brantwood still retains that special feeling which has given inspiration to so many, and Ruskin's thinking still has the keenest relevance. The house is filled with Ruskin's drawings and watercolours, together with much of his original furniture, books and personal items. The video presentation and special displays provide a fascinating insight into the work of this great man and his life in a Victorian country house.

Every Thursday during the season there'll be lace making demonstrations and readings from Ruskin's writing are performed regularly in the study. An excellent bookshop specialises in Ruskin and related art and literature.

watch a 20-minute video which provides a useful introduction to his life and works. Every Thursday during the season there are lace-making demonstrations and readings from Ruskin's works are performed regularly in the study. There's also a well-stocked bookshop, a craft gallery and 250 acres of grounds where there are well-marked nature trails and where a theatre season is held during the summer.

Around Coniston

Grizedale
3 miles SE of Coniston off the B5285

The village lies at the heart of the 9,000-acre **Grizedale Forest** which was acquired by the Forestry Commission in 1934 and is famous for its Theatre and Sculpture. The Commission's original intention of chiefly cultivating the forest for its timber met with much resistance and, over the years, many pathways have been opened and a variety of recreational activities have been encouraged. The Visitor Centre vividly illustrates the story of the forest as well as showing how the combination of wildlife, recreation, and commercial timbering can work together hand in hand. The forest, too, is famously the home of some 80 tree sculptures commissioned since 1977. All are created from natural materials found in the forest and they have been made by some of Britain's best known contemporary artists, including Andy

Sculpture Trail Grizedale Forest

Goldsworthy, as well as by artists from all over the world. The great beauty of these sculptures is their understated presence: there are no signposts pointing to the exhibits and visitors are left entirely on their own to discover these wonders though there is a printed map obtainable from the Visitor Centre.

Near Sawrey
4 miles E of Coniston on the B5285

Though this little village will not be familiar to many visitors to the Lake District, its famous inhabitant, Beatrix Potter, almost certainly will be. After holidaying here in 1896, the authoress fell in love with the place and, with the royalties from her first book, *The Tale of*

Peter Rabbit, she purchased **Hill Top** in 1905. After her marriage in 1913 to a local solicitor, she actually lived in another house in the village, Castle Cottage (private), and used the charming 17th century cottage as her study. Oddly, she wrote very little after the marriage, spending most of her time dealing with the management of the farms she had bought in the area.

Tarn Hows

Following Beatrix Potter's death in 1943, the house and the land she had bought on the surrounding fells became the property of the National Trust and, in accordance with her will, Hill Top has remained exactly as she would have known it. One of the most popular Lakeland attractions, Hill Top is full of Beatrix Potter memorabilia, including some of her original drawings. The house is very small, so it is best avoided at peak holiday times. **Tarn Hows**, part

of the 4,000-acre Monk Coniston estate bought and sold on to the National Trust, was created to resemble a Swiss lake and is very rich in flora and fauna - it has been designated a Site of Special Scientific Interest.

Hawkshead
3 miles E of Coniston on the B5285

There are more Beatrix Potter connections in the enchanting little village of Hawkshead. Her solicitor husband, William Heelis, worked from

THE OLD SCHOOL HOUSE

Main Street, Hawkshead, Cumbria LA22 0NT
Tel: 015394 36403

A 300-year-old former schoolmaster's house is now a very peaceful, civilised and comfortable Bed & Breakfast establishment. Resident owners of **The Old School House**, Eileen and Peter Johnston, have six letting bedrooms and guests have the use of a lounge with tv. The house is a short stroll from the centre of a village that has been described as the prettiest in the Lake District; its many attractions include the Beatrix Potter Gallery and the school which William Wordsworth

attended. The house is set back behind trim hedges, with a pretty garden and open countryside at the back. There is ample off road private parking.

an office in the Main Street here and this has now been transformed into **The Beatrix Potter Gallery**. The gallery features an exhibition of her original drawings and illustrations alongside details of the author's life.

Hawkshead has specific Wordsworth connections too. **Hawkshead Grammar School** was founded in 1585 by Edwin Sandys, Archbishop of York, and between 1779 and 1787 the young William Wordsworth was a star pupil. The earliest of his surviving

The Beatrix Potter Gallery

poems was written to celebrate the school's 200th year. The school is open from Easter to September and visitors can inspect the classrooms during the summer holidays, see the desk where William carved his name and have a look around the headmaster's study. Ann Tyson's Cottage, where Wordsworth lodged while he attended the school, has also survived. It stands in Wordsworth Street and is now a guest house.

Situated at the head of **Esthwaite Water**, enjoying glorious views of Coniston Old Man and Helvellyn, Hawkshead has a history that goes back to Viking times. Its name is Norse in origin, derived from Haukr who built the original settlement. It's a delightful village of narrow cobbled lanes with a pedestrianised main square dominated by the Market House, or Shambles, and another square linked to it by little

snickets and arched alleyways which invite exploration. The poet Norman Nicholson observed that "The whole village could be fitted into the boundaries of a large agricultural show; yet it contains enough corners, angles, alleys and entries to keep the eye happy for hours".

Hawkshead was once an important market town serving the surrounding area and at that time most of the land here was owned by the monks of Furness Abbey. The only building to remain from those monastic times is the **Courthouse**, to the north of the village, part of a medieval manor house built by the monks.

The **Church of St Michael & All Angels**, with its massive 15th century tower, seems rather grand for the village but it too was built at a time when Hawkshead was a wealthy town. Inside,

THE MINSTRELS' GALLERY

The Square, Hawkshead,
Cumbria LA22 0NZ
Tel: 015394 42435 Fax: 015394 36178
e-mail:
    bookings@lakeland-hideaways.co.uk
website: www.lakeland-hideaways.co.uk

Minstrels' Gallery Tearooms are located in a building that dates from the early 15th century and was one of the village's many inns and alehouses. It later saw service as a grocer's and sweet shop, private house, apothecary, guest house and potter's studio and it is now run as a traditional tea room. The original gallery, where musicians would once have entertained the public, can still be seen upstairs, and during recent refurbishment the original main entrance at the rear of the building was unearthed. Much of the old interior remains, with lots of beams

and panelling, and in this delightfully old-world setting Steph the chef heads a team preparing a tempting selection of light meals and teatime treats. On the savoury side are filled jacket potatoes served with salad and coleslaw, sandwiches, toasties and warmed baguettes with mouthwatering fillings such as Cumberland sausage and fried onions or brie and bacon served with homemade chutney.

The Vegetarian specials each day along with the daily specials board adds to the choice with flavour-packed pies and hot pots and summer salads. Cabinets display the excellent home-made cakes and biscuits, among which teabread, carrot cake and lemon drizzle cake are just a few of the favourites. Meals are a sheer delight from the

first mouthful to the last, which could be sticky toffee pudding served with custard, whipped cream or ice cream. Drinks include speciality coffees and leaf teas, hot chocolate (made with melted Belgian chocolate), milk shakes and organic lemonade. Children of all ages are very welcome, and for the very young bottle warming and high chairs can be provided. The Gallery is open every day from 9 to 5, sometimes later in the summer months; evening bookings can be taken for parties of ten or more.

The Gallery's owner Ruth Thomason and her partners Anne and Gary have another string to their bow in the shape of **Hideaways Cottages**. They offer a wide range of self-catering holiday cottages in and around Hawkshead to suit all needs, from romantic one-bedroom cottages set among rolling hills to larger houses in the centre of the village. Most of them have central heating and wood-burning fires, making them ideal year-round bases for exploring Hawkshead, often called 'the prettiest village in the Lake District', and the surrounding area, which includes Esthwaite Water, Coniston Water, Windermere and the 9,000-acre Grizedale Forest with its nature trails, scenic picnic sites and a fascinating collection of sculptures.

Church of St Michael & All Angels

there are some remarkable wall paintings from the late 1600s and also look out for the "Buried in Woolen" affidavit near the vestry door. In 1666 the Government had decreed that corpses must not be buried in shrouds made from "flaxe, hempe, silke or hair, or other than what is made of sheeps wool onely". The idea was to help maintain the local woollen industry and this was one way of ensuring that even the dead got to help out. The church is the focal point of the annual Lake District Summer Music Festival and a popular venue for concerts and recitals. In the churchyard is a war memorial erected in 1919 and modelled on the ancient runic cross at Gosforth.

Some lovely walks lead from Hawkshead to **Roger Ground** and Esthwaite Water, possibly the least frequented of the Lakes, and also to the nearby hamlet of **Colthouse** where there's an early Quaker Meeting House built around 1690. Esthwaite Water was much loved by Wordsworth, as he shows in *The Prelude*:

My morning walks were early; oft before
the hours of school
I travelled round our little lake, five miles
Of pleasant wandering. Happy time!

Great Langdale
9 miles N of Coniston on the B5343

One of the most dramatic of the Lake District waterfalls is **Dungeon Ghyll**,

MILLBECK FARM AND SIDE HOUSE FARM & COTTAGE

Great Langdale, Nr Ambleside,
Cumbria LA22 9JU
Tel: 015394 37364 Fax: 015394 37570
e-mail: millbeck@lineone.net

In great walking country near the head of the lovely Langdale Valley, **Millbeck Farm** is a working farm with a 400-year-old farmhouse. Full of character, with oak beams, original panelling and log fires, the farmhouse offers Bed & Breakfast accommodation in three warm, spotless bedrooms. Sue and Eric Taylforth also run **Side House**, where charming self-catering accommodation is

offered in two very well equipped cottages in the farmhouse (three bedrooms) and the adjacent former dairy (two bedrooms). Millbeck Farm is a noted supplier of Herdwick lamb and Angus beef.

Langdale Pikes, Great Langdale

famous peaks of Crinkle Crags, Bowfell and the Langdale Pikes provide some serious challenges for hikers and ramblers.

Seathwaite

5 miles W of Coniston via minor road off the A593

A mere 5 miles or so from Coniston as the crow flies, by road Seathwaite is nearly three times as far. It stands in one of the Lake District's most tranquil and least known valleys, **Dunnerdale**. Little has changed here since the days when William Wordsworth, who knew the area as Duddon Valley, captured its

which tumbles 60 feet down the fellside. The 'dungeon' is actually a natural cave. Nearby is the well known Old Dungeon Ghyll Hotel, which makes an excellent starting point for walks in this spectacularly scenic area where the

THE THREE SHIRES INN

Little Langdale, Nr Ambleside,
Cumbria LA22 9NZ
Tel: 015394 37215 Fax: 015394 37127
e-mail: enquiry@threeshiresinn.co.uk
website: www.threeshiresinn.co.uk

The Stephenson family and their staff extend a warm welcome at the **Three Shires Inn**, where guests can appreciate friendly hospitality in a peaceful, scenic setting. The traditional slate and stone inn was built in 1872 near the meeting point of the old counties of Westmorland, Lancashire and

Cumberland. The valley of Little Langdale is the most peaceful and unspoilt in the central Lake District. The Inn has been sympathetically extended and upgraded to provide 10 comfortable en-suite

bedrooms as well as a walkers bar and residents' lounge, which have log fires on cooler days, and a restaurant. There are delightful views over the Tilberthwaite fells from the bedrooms as well as from the garden terrace and hotel verandahs. Traditional ales, a large selection of malt whiskies and well chosen wines are on offer in the bar, where meals are served every lunch time and evening. A four course dinner is served between 7pm and 8pm in the restaurant. Smoking is restricted to the bar and residents' lounge only.

natural beauty in a sequence of sonnets. In his poem *The Excursion*, he wrote about the Rev Robert Walker, the curate of Seathwaite. Nicholas, or 'Wonderful Walker' as Wordsworth referred to him, served the church

Hardknott Fort, Hardknott Pass

here for some 67 years though he also filled various other jobs such as farm labourer and nurse as well as spinning wool and making his own clothes. Fell walkers and hikers who prefer to escape the masses will delight not only in the solitude of this glorious valley but also in the wide variety of plant, animal, and birdlife that have made this haven their home.

Hardknott Pass

5 miles W of Coniston off the A593

Surrounded by the fell of the same name, this pass is one of the most treacherous in the Lake District yet it was used by the Romans for the road between their forts at Ambleside (Galava) and Ravenglass (Glannaventa). Of the remains of Roman occupation, **Hardknott Fort** on a shoulder of the fell, overlooking the Esk Valley, is the most substantial and

also provides some of the grandest views in the whole of the Lake District. The walls of the fort, known as Mediobogdum, still stand up to 2 metres high, and within them the foundations of the commander's house, headquarters building and granary can be seen.

Boot

8 miles W of Coniston off the A595

Lying at the eastern end of the **Ravenglass and Eskdale Railway**, this is a wonderful place to visit whether arriving by train or car. A gentle walk from the station at Eskdale brings you to this delightful village with its pub, post office, museum, waterfall and nearby St Catherine's Church in its lovely secluded riverside setting. Perhaps because of the rugged walking country to the east, the village is well supplied with both a campsite and bunkhouse available.

Brook House Inn & Restaurant

Boot, Eskdale, Cumbria CA19 1TG
Tel: 019467 23288 Fax: 019467 232160
e-mail: stay@brookhouseinn.co.uk
website: www.brookhouseinn.co.uk

Built around 1870, **Brook House Inn** enjoys glorious views of the spectacular Eskdale countryside and is the ideal base for exploring the many contrasts of the Lake District. The rugged mountains, gentle riverbanks and lake shores are enjoyed by experienced and novice walkers alike. Owned and run by the Thornley family, **Brook House Inn** has eight beautifully appointed bedrooms with en suite facilities, central heating, tv, radio and superb views of the local fells. Gareth Thornley is an excellent chef and his home-cooked dishes from around the world are served from noon

through to 8.30pm. Vegetarian options, daily specials and a childrens menu are also available. Along with a good selection of real ales and a range of guest beers from Cumbrian breweries such as Yates, Hesket Newmarket and Great Gable, there is a varied wine list and a choice of over 100 malt whiskies. Dalegarth Station, on the Ravenglass & Eskdale Light Railway, is just a short walk from Brook House.

Eskdale Green

10 miles W of Coniston off the A595

One of the few settlements in this beautiful and unspoiled valley, the village lies on the route of the Ravenglass and Eskdale Railway. Further up the valley lies a group of buildings that make up Eskdale Mill where cereals have been ground since 1578, when it is recorded that the brothers Henry and Robert Vicars were the tenants, paying an annual rent of eight shillings (40p). The original machinery for grinding oatmeal is in full working order and operated daily. Power for the two waterwheels is provided by

Whillan Beck which surges down from England's highest mountains, the Scafell range. Visitors can enjoy a picnic in the picturesque mill grounds, browse in the gift shop or explore the Mill's history in the informative exhibition. The mill may be reached by crossing a 17th century packhorse bridge over the beck.

Eskdale Green

FORESTHOW GUEST HOUSE

Eskdale Green, Cumbria CA19 1TR
Tel: 019467 23201 Fax: 019467 23190
e-mail: facrter@easynet.co.uk
web: www.forest-how-eskdale-cumbria.co.uk

Foresthow is a handsome Victorian house standing in unspoilt countryside in the beautiful Eskdale Valley. For the past ten years Chris and Neil Carter have been offering a friendly welcome and very pleasant Bed & Breakfast accommodation in eight individually appointed bedrooms, four of them with en suite facilities. They are renowned for their excellent multi-choice breakfasts, and they are also happy to provide packed lunches. Guests can enjoy the lovely gardens and orchard, walk among the nearby fells and take a trip on the Ravenglass and Eskdale steam railway.

Ravenglass

Lying as it does at the estuary of three rivers - the Esk, the Mite, and the Irt - as well as enjoying a sheltered position, it is not surprising that Ravenglass was an important port from prehistoric times. The Romans built a naval base here around AD78 which served as a supply point for the military zone around Hadrian's Wall. They also constructed a fort, **Glannaventra**, on the cliffs above the town, which was home to around 1,000 soldiers. Little remains of Glannaventra except for the impressively preserved walls of the Bath House. Almost 12 feet high, these walls are believed to be the highest Roman remains in the country.

In the 18th century Ravenglass was a base for smugglers bringing contraband in from coastal ships - tobacco and French brandy. Today, the estuary has silted up but there are still scores of small boats and the village is a charming resort, full of atmosphere. The layout has changed little since the 16th century; the main street is paved with sea pebbles and leads up from a shingle beach. Once, iron-ore was brought to the estuary by narrow gauge railway from the mines near Boot, in Eskdale, about eight miles away.

One of the town's major attractions is the 15" narrow gauge **Ravenglass and Eskdale Railway** which runs for seven miles up the lovely Mite and Esk River valleys. Better known as "La'al Ratty", it was built in 1875 to transport ore and quarried

Ravenglass Estuary

MUNCASTER CASTLE

Ravenglass, Cumbria CA18 1RQ
Tel: 01229 717614 Fax: 01229 717010

Muncaster Castle is an impressive castellated mansion which has been owned by the Pennington family since 1208. Back in 1464 the Penningtons gave shelter to King Henry VI after his defeat at the Battle of Hexham. On his departure Henry presented them with his enamelled glass drinking bowl saying that as long as it remained unbroken the Penningtons would live and thrive at Muncaster. It remains intact and the Penningtons are indeed still here · your audio tour guide is narrated by Patrick Gordon-Duff-Pennington, the present owner, who enlivens the tale with old legends and family anecdotes. The tour also introduces visitors to the many Muncaster treasures (including tapestry, silver, and porcelain collections), the stunning Great Hall, Salvin's octagonal library and the barrel ceiling in the drawing room.

Muncaster is also famous for its gardens and, in particular, the rhododendrons, azaleas, and camellias which are best viewed between March and June. The woodland gardens themselves cover some 77 acres and, as well as the beauty of the vegetation,

there are some splendid views over the Lakeland fells. These extensive grounds also contain a fascinating Owl Centre which is home to more than 180 birds of 50 different species. Here, visitors can meet the birds daily at 14.30 (late March to early November) when a talk is given on the work of the centre and, weather permitting, the owls display their flying skills.

Other attractions include a very well-equipped children's play area with an aerial runway, scramble net and fireman's pole; a nature trail and orienteering course, plant centre, gift shop and licensed café. The gardens and owl centre are open daily throughout the year; the castle is open each afternoon from the end of March to the end of October (closed Saturday).

stone from the Eskdale Valley and opened the following year for passenger traffic. Since then the railway has survived several threats of extinction. The most serious occurred at the end of the 1950s when the closure of the Eskdale granite quarries wiped out the railway's freight traffic at a stroke. However, at the auction for the railway in 1960 a band of enthusiasts outbid the scrap dealers and formed a company to keep the little railway running.

Today, the company operates 12 locomotives, both steam and diesel, and 300,000 people a year come from all over the world to ride on what has been described as 'the most beautiful train journey in England'. The La'al Ratty is still the best way to explore Miterdale and Eskdale and enchants both young and old alike. There are several stops along the journey and at both termini there is a café and a souvenir shop. At the Ravenglass station there is also a museum which brings to life the history of this remarkable line and the important part it has played in the life of Eskdale.

A mile or so east of Ravenglass stands **Muncaster Castle** (see panel opposite), which has been in the ownership of the Pennington family since 1208. In 1464 the Penningtons gave shelter to King Henry VI after his defeat at the Battle of Hexham. On his departure Henry presented them with his enamelled glass drinking bowl, saying that as long as it remained unbroken the Penningtons would survive and thrive at Muncaster. Apart from the many treasures, the stunning Great Hall, Salvin's octagonal library and the barrel ceiling in the drawing room, Muncaster is also famous for its gardens. The collection of species rhododendrons is one of the finest in Europe, gathered primarily from plant-hunting expeditions to Nepal in the 1920s, and there are also fine azaleas, hydrangeas and camellias as well as many unusual trees. For many visitors the chief attraction is the **World Owl Centre**, where many endangered owl species are bred. Snowy owls have become great favourites on the back of the Harry Potter craze, and many visitors have enquired about keeping them as pets. The staff at the Centre have to point out that the snowy owl is a mighty predator with a 5ft wingspan. Mighty as he is, he is not the mightiest of the owls at the Centre: that honour goes to the Eurasian eagle owl, whose full splendour can be seen at the daily

demonstrations. Muncaster's latest attraction is the Meadow Vole Maze (these little creatures are the staple diet of barn owls, and visitors can find out what it's like to be a vole on the run from a hungry owl).

Originally part of the Muncaster Castle Estate, **Muncaster Water Mill** can be traced back to 1455, though it is thought that this site may be Roman. The situation is certainly idyllic, with the mill race still turning the huge wooden water wheel and the Ravenglass and Eskdale Railway running alongside. In November 1996, Pam and Ernie Priestley came to the mill and Ernie put his years of engineering experience to use as the miller. The mill is open every day from Easter to the end of October, working just as it has done for hundreds of years. Visitors can see the machinery in action, and also enjoy some delicious refreshments in the 17th century byre tea rooms. Naturally, the organic flour ground here is used in all the cakes, breads, and scones, and the flour is also on sale.

Around Ravenglass

Waberthwaite
4 miles S of Ravenglass on the A595

No visit to west Cumbria is complete without the inclusion of a trip to RG Woodall's shop. Found in the heart of this village, Richard Woodall is world famous for his sausages, in particular for the Waberthwaite Cumberland Sausage,

BROWN COW INN

Waberthwaite, Cumbria LA19 5YJ
Tel: 01229 717243 Fax: 01229 717295
e-mail: keith-freda@browncowinn.com
website: www.browncowinn.com

In a convenient location on the A595 about three miles south of Ravenglass, the **Brown Cow Inn** is a delightful hostelry with a well-deserved reputation for its excellent food. Not only is the food good, it is available throughout the day, from 10am (last orders 9.30pm). You can start the day with a full English or Continental breakfast, have a break for morning tea or coffee, return for Afternoon or High Tea, and of course enjoy lunch and dinner here as well.

The resident owners are Keith and Freda Hitchen, and Keith keeps the customers happy with his splendid cooking. His menu includes local delicacies such as Waberthwaite Ham and Cumberland Gammon or Sausage, as well as fish dishes, Indian dishes, a vegetarian special and a good choice of meals for children. Keith is

generous with his servings but smaller portions are available at a reduced rate. A choice of two roasts are avaiable from noon on Sundays and there is a take away service. Meals are served in the non-smoking dining room, in the bar with its blazing open fire or in the snug.

The drinks on offer here include three real ales - Theakstons Best and two rotating guest ales and if you're looking for somewhere to stay, The Brown Cow has a self catering flat which can sleep up to four people. Credit cards (except Amex and Diners) are accepted and children are welcome.

and is the proud possessor of a Royal Warrant from the Queen.

Bootle

7 miles S of Ravenglass on the A595

This ancient village is particularly picturesque and quaint. The river Annas flows beside the main road and then dives under the village on its way to the sea. High up on **Bootle Fell**, to the southeast of the village, lies one of the best stone circles in Cumbria. Over the years, many of the 51 stones that make up the **Swinside Stone Circle** have fallen over. When it was originally constructed and all the stones were upright, it is likely, as they were also close together, that the circle was used as an enclosure.

Silecroft

10 miles S of Ravenglass off the A595

Perhaps of all the villages in this coastal region of the National Park, Silecroft is the perfect example. Just a short walk from the heart of the village is the beach, which extends as far as the eye can see. On the horizon lies the distant outline of the Isle of Man. There is also a **Site of Special Scientific Interest** close by, a tract of coastal scrubland which provides the perfect habitat for the rare Natterjack toad.

Millom

13 miles S of Ravenglass on the A5093

This small and peaceful town stands at

the mouth of the River Duddon with the imposing **Black Combe Fell** providing a dramatic backdrop. Originally called Holborn Hill, the present day name was taken from nearby **Millom Castle** which is now a private, working farm. Like many neighbouring towns and villages in Furness, Millom was a small fishing village before it too grew with the development of the local iron industry. **Millom Folk Museum**, recently relocated, tells the story of the town's growth and there is also a permanent memorial here to Norman Nicholson (1914-1987) who is generally regarded as the best writer on Lakeland life and customs since Wordsworth himself. Nicholson's book *Provincial Pleasures* records his affectionate memories of Millom, the town where he spent all his life. Other displays include a full-scale reproduction of a drift and cage from nearby Hodbarow mine. South of Millom, at Haverigg, is the **RAF Millom Museum** situated in the former Officers Mess. Visitors to the site will find a fascinating collection of over 2,000

photographs of the wartime activities of the RAF in the area, various artefacts connected with the period and a number of items recovered from local crash sites. The museum also has a fine collection of aero engines including a Rolls Royce Merlin, a Westland Whirlwind helicopter, the cockpit section of a De Havilland Vampire jet trainer and an example of the HM14 or Flying Flea. The Duddon Estuary is an important site for wildlife, and the RSPB site at **Hodbarrow** is home not only to birds but to many kinds of flora and fauna. **Hodbarrow Beacon**, which still stands, was built in 1879 as a lighthouse to assist vessels taking iron ore from the mines to destinations in Europe.

Holmrook

2 miles N of Ravenglass on the A595

Situated on the banks of the River Irt, where it is possible to fish for both salmon and sea trout, this small village also lies on the Ravenglass and Eskdale Railway line. Though the village Church

CHAT N AVA CHEW CHEW

Station Buildings, Millom, Cumbria LA18 5AA
Tel: 01229 771590

Local residents and visitors to Millom make tracks for the railway station not just to catch a train but to enjoy the good food and hospitality dispensed at **Chat N Ava Chew Chew**. Owner Sue Day and her son-in-law Gav are the cooks, while daughter Mandy greets and serves in the fine old station building. Customers have plenty of choice, from pastries, sandwiches and jacket potatoes to hot snacks and traditional Sunday lunches. Children are very welcome, and there are

books and toys to keep them amused. No smoking. Closed Wednesday in winter.

of St Paul is not of particular note, inside there is not only a 9th century cross of Irish style but also memorials to the Lutwidges, the family of Lewis Carroll.

Drigg

2 miles N of Ravenglass on the B5343

The main attractions here are the sand dunes and the fine views across to the Lakeland mountains and fells. There is an important nature reserve, **Drigg Dunes**, on the salt marshes that border the River Irt but - take note, adders are common here. The reserve is home to Europe's largest colony of black-headed gulls.

Santon Bridge

3 miles NE of Ravenglass off the A595

The churchyard of **Irton Church**, reached from Santon Bridge via an unclassified road, offers the visitor not only superb views of the Lakeland fells to the west but also the opportunity to see a beautiful Anglican Cross, in excellent condition, that is certainly 1,000 years old. Though the original runic inscription has been eroded away over time, the fine, intricate carving can still be seen. The Bridge Inn here plays host each November to the 'World's Biggest Liar' competition (see Gosforth below).

Seascale

4 miles N of Ravenglass on the B5343

One of the most popular seaside villages in Cumbria, Seascale enhanced its resort status in 2000 by restoring the **Victorian Wooden Jetty** to mark Millennium Year. Stretching out into the Irish Sea, it is the focal point for fishing, beach casting, wind surfing and water-skiing, and also provides the starting point for many walks, including the Cumbrian Coastal Way which passes along the foreshore. This fine sandy beach enjoys views over to the Isle of Man and the Galloway Mountains of Scotland while, behind the village, the entire length of the western Lakeland hills presents an impressive panorama.

Two Victorian buildings stand out: the **Water Tower**, medieval in style and with a conical roof, and the old **Engine Shed** which is now a multi-purpose Sports Hall.

A couple of miles north of the village is the site of the world's first commercial nuclear power station. The Magnox power station at Calder Hall shut down in the spring of 2003 after 46 years in operation; the closure was brought forward from 2006 because of the competition from low-priced wholesale electricity.

Gosforth

5 miles N of Ravenglass on the A595

On the edge of this picturesque village, in the graveyard of **St Mary's Church**, stands the tallest ancient cross in England. Fifteen feet high, the **Viking Cross** towers above the huddled gravestones in the peaceful churchyard. Carved from red sandstone and clearly influenced by both Christian and pagan traditions, the cross depicts the crucifixion, the deeds of Norse gods and Yggdrasil, the World Ash Tree that Norsemen believed supported the universe. The interior of the church also contains some interesting features. There's a **Chinese Bell**, finely decorated with Oriental imagery, which was captured in 1841 at Anunkry, a fort on the River Canton, some delightful carved faces on the chancel arch and a collection of ancient stones the most notable of which dates from Saxon times and depicts the Lamb of God trampling on the serpents of pagan faith.

A major attraction in this appealing village is **Gosforth Pottery**, where Dick and Barbara Wright produce beautifully crafted work and also give pottery lessons.

To the east of Gosforth runs Wasdale, the wildest of the Lake District valleys but easily accessible by road. The road leads to **Wast Water**, which is just 3 miles long but is the deepest lake in England. The southern shores are dominated by huge screes some 2,000 feet high that plunge abruptly into the lake and they provide an awesome backdrop to this tranquil stretch of water. A

lake less like Windermere would be hard to find as there are no motorboats ploughing their way up and down the lake; this is very much the country of walkers and climbers and from here there are many footpaths up to some of the best fells in Cumbria.

Wasdale Head, just to the north of the lake, is a small, close-knit community with a far-famed Inn that has provided a welcome refuge for walkers and climbers since the mid-1800s. who have been out discovering Wasdale and the lake. **Wasdale Church** is claimed to be the smallest in England - although this title is hotly disputed by Culbone in Somerset and Dale Abbey in Derbyshire. The church was built in the 14th century and it is hidden away amidst a tiny copse of evergreen trees. Local legend suggests that the roof beams came from a Viking ship and it is certainly true that until late Victorian times, the church had only an earth floor and few seats.

Hiking, Scafell Pike

THE RED LION HOTEL

2 Market Place, Egremont,
Cumbria CA22 1AE
Tel: 01946 824050 Fax: 01946 825758
e-mail: redlionhotel@btopenworld.com

One of the biggest plaster red lions you'll ever see adorns the front of the **Red Lion Hotel**, which is easy to spot on the main street of Egremont. The hotel started life in the early 18th century as a coaching inn, and

it became an important stopping place on what was then the main Whitehaven to Barrow road.

Its early prominence was a distant memory when John and Debbie came here in 1998, but they have invested a great deal of time and effort in a major refurbishment programme that has seen its gradual restoration, and when that programme is completed the good old days will definitely have returned. Work has already been finished on the 11 letting bedrooms, which offer a choice of accommodation to suit all types of guests. The rooms run from plain and simple with shared facilities to top of the range rooms with en suite facilities, and the tariff,

which includes a full English breakfast, varies accordingly. In the bar areas, where refurbishment has just been completed, a full range of beers, including real ales, is served, and a happy hour operates from Thursday to Sunday.

John and Debbie have widened the scope of their pub by serving good pub food every lunchtime and evening, and they have also made it one of the town's most popular meeting places and social spots. Entertainment includes regular karaoke and disco sessions, and at weekends they run a night club in a function room next to the hotel. At other times, this room is available for private parties. Egremont, which lies among the low hills of the Ehen Valley, is a little town with a lot of history, and is well worth taking time to explore. It's famous for its castle, for its annual medieval festival and most of all for Crab Fayre Day in September, when the entertainment includes the World Gurning Championships with contestants vying to pull the ugliest face with their heads stuck through a horse's collar.

Thanks to the efforts of John and Debbie, the Red Lion Hotel has become an excellent base from which to enjoy all the fun of the fair and everything else the town has to offer.

As well as the deepest lake and the smallest church, Wasdale also boasts the highest mountain, **Sca Fell Pike** (3,205ft) - and the world's biggest liars. This latter claim goes back to the mid-1800s when Will Ritson, "a reet good fibber", was the publican at the inn. Will enthralled his patrons with tall stories of how he had crossed foxes with eagles to produce flying foxes and had grown turnips so large he could hollow them out to make a comfortable residence. In the same spirit, the 'World's Biggest Liar' Competition takes place every November, usually at the Bridge Inn at Santon Bridge, when contestants from all over the country vie in telling the most enormous porkies.

Calder Bridge
7 miles N of Ravenglass on the A595

From this small, grey, 19th century settlement there is an attractive footpath to **Calder Abbey**. It was founded by monks of Savigny in 1134 but amalgamated with the Cistercians of Furness Abbey when it was ransacked by the Scots a few years later. After the Dissolution the monastery buildings lapsed slowly into the present-day romantic ruin. Part of the tower and west doorway remain, with some of the chancel and transept, but sadly these are unsafe and have to be viewed from the road. To the northeast of the village, the River Calder rises on Caw Fell. **Monk's Bridge**, the oldest packhorse bridge in Cumbria, was built across it for the monks of Calder Abbey.

Egremont
12 miles N of Ravenglass on the A595

This pretty town is dominated by **Egremont Castle** with walls 20ft high and an 80ft tower. It stands high above the town, overlooking the lovely River Ehen to the south and the market place to the north. The castle was built between 1130 and 1140 by William de Meschines on the site of a former Danish fortification. The most complete part still standing is a Norman arch that once guarded the drawbridge entrance. Nearby is an unusual four-sided sundial and the stump of the old market cross dating from the early 13th century.

A legend concerning the castle is related in Wordsworth's poem, *The Horn of Egremont*. Apparently, a great horn hanging in the castle could only be blown by the rightful lord. In the early 1200s, the rightful lord, Eustace de Lucy was on a Crusade to the Holy Land, together with his brother Hubert. The dastardly Hubert arranged with local hit men to have Eustace drowned in the Jordan. Hubert returned to Egremont but during the celebration feast to mark his inheritance a mighty blast on the horn was heard. The hit men had reneged on the deal: Eustace was still alive. Hubert prudently retired to a monastery.

Egremont's prosperity was based on the good quality of its local red iron ore and jewellery made from it can be bought at the nearby **Florence Mine Heritage Centre**. Visitors to the mine, the last deep working iron ore mine in Europe, can join an underground tour (by prior arrangement) and discover why the miners became known as the Red Men of Cumbria. The

Egremont Crab Fair

museum here also tells story of the mine, which was worked by the ancient Britons, and there is a re-creation of the conditions that the miners endured at the turn of the 20th century.

In September every year the town celebrates its **Crab Fair**. Held each year on the third Saturday in September, the Fair dates back more than seven centuries - to 1267 in fact, when Henry III granted a Royal Charter for a three-day fair to be held on "the even, the day and the morrow after the Nativity of St. Mary the Virgin". The celebrations include the "Parade of the Apple Cart" when a wagon loaded with apples is driven along Main Street with men on the back throwing fruit into the crowds. Originally, the throng was pelted with crab apples - hence the name Crab Fair - but these are considered too tart for modern taste so nowadays more palatable varieties are used. The festivities also feature a greasy pole competition (with a pole 30 feet high), a pipe-smoking contest, wrestling and hound-trailing. The highlight, however,

is the **World Gurning Championship** in which contestants place their heads through a braffin, or horse collar, and vie to produce the most grotesque expression. If you're toothless, you start with a great advantage!

Lowes Court Gallery, in a listed 18th century building, holds fine art exhibitions throughout the year. The premises also house the Tourist Information Centre.

Whitehaven

The first impression is of a handsome Georgian town but Whitehaven was already well established in the 12th century as a harbour for use by the monks of nearby St Bees Priory. After the reformation, the land was acquired and developed by the Lowther family in order to expand the coal industry. Whitehaven's growth in those years was astonishing by the standards of the time - it mushroomed from a hamlet of just 6 thatched cottages in 1633 to a sizeable, planned, town with a population of more than 2,000 by 1693. Its 'gridiron' pattern of streets, unusual in Cumbria, will be familiar to American visitors and the town boasts some 250 listed buildings. By the mid-1700s, Whitehaven had become the third largest port in Britain, its trade based on coal and other cargo business, including importing tobacco from Virginia, exporting coal to Ireland, and transporting emigrants to the New World. When the large iron-steamships arrived however, the harbour's shallow draught halted expansion and the port declined in favour of Liverpool and Southampton. For that reason much of the attractive harbour area - now full of pleasure craft and fishing smacks - and older parts of the town remain largely unchanged.

The harbour and its environs have been declared a Conservation Area and located here is **The Beacon** (see panel below), where, through a series of innovative displays, the history of the town and its harbour are brought to life. Looking a bit like a small lighthouse, the museum deals with the history of the whole of Copeland (the district of Cumbria in which Whitehaven lies) with special emphasis on its mining and maritime past. The displays reflect the many aspects of this harbour borough with a collection that includes paintings, locally made pottery, ship models, navigational instruments, miners' lamps, and surveying equipment. The Beilby 'Slavery' Goblet, part of the museum's collection, is one of the masterpieces of English glass-making and is probably the finest example of its kind in existence. Also here are the **Harbour Gallery**, with an ongoing arts programme, and the **Met Office Gallery**, where visitors can monitor, forecast and broadcast the weather. They can also learn about the "American Connection" and John Paul Jones' attack on the town in 1778, or settle down in the cinema to

THE BEACON

West Strand, Whitehaven, Cumbria, CA28 6LY
Tel: 01946 592302 Fax: 01946 598150
e-mail:
   thebeacon@copelandbc.gov.uk
website: www.copelandbc.gov.uk

Situated on Whitehaven's attractive harbourside, **The Beacon** is home to the town's museum collection. It traces the social, industrial and maritime heritage of the area, using local characters, audio-visual displays and fascinating museum pieces. The Met Office Weather Gallery, where you can monitor, forecast and broadcast the weather, offers panoramic views of the town and coast.

Also, don't miss the Harbour Gallery, which offers free entry to the changing exhibitions; our gift shop and café. Guided heritage walks are available through town and over the headland to Haig Colliery Mining Museum.

HAIG COLLIERY MINING MUSEUM

Solway Road, Kells, Whitehaven,
Cumbria CA28 9BG
Tel: 01946 599949 Fax: 01946 61896
e-mail: museum@haigpit.com
website: www.haigpit.com

Situated within the former site of Haig Pit, on the cliffs high above Whitehaven with magnificent views of the Scottish Hills and the Isle of Man, **Haig Colliery Mining Museum** offers a wealth of information on the coal mining history of Whitehaven and West Cumbria. The Museum houses the world's only two Bever Dorling & Co Ltd, steam Winding engines, one of which is restored to full working order and operated daily.

Learn about the numerous disasters in the area, which took the lives of over 1200 men, women and children, some as young as six years of age. See living conditions of local people, and the social history of Whitehaven told using lively displays and tales from the guides of their ancestor's life from the 1700's onwards. Explore the site and uncover centuries of history brought back to life using

locomotives, a roadroller, mining machinery, the shaft tops, and cages unfolding the many aspects of colliery equipment through the ages and the men that operated them, often in terrible conditions below and above ground.

An optional guided walking tour available from the historic harbourside to the ruins of Saltorn Pit, the world's first undersea pit, first sunk in 1729. On route the guide will recount tales of centuries of mining history, stories of disasters, bravery and lucky escapes while crossing the Wellington Pit site, with only the candlestick chimney remaining, up the incline to view 'Jonathan Swift's House', the author of Gullivers Travels. See the 'cairn' at King Pit site, the worlds deepest coal mine shaft in it's day, before walking across the coastal path to Saltorn Pit engine house, in its dramatic setting at the bottom of the cliffs below Haig.

watch vintage footage of Whitehaven in times past. John Paul Jones had been an apprentice seaman at Whitehaven before going to the New World, where he became well known in the War of Independence. In 1777 he became Captain of the privateer The Ranger and led a raid on Whitehaven with the intention of firing the ships in the harbour. Thwarted by light winds, the party raided the fort and spiked the guns, then managed to damage only three ships before retreating under fire.

There's more history at **The Rum Story**, which tells the story of the town's connections with the Caribbean. The display is housed in the original 1785 shop, courtyards, cellars and bonded warehouses of the Jefferson family, the

oldest surviving UK family of rum traders. Visitors can learn about the various processes involved in the making of rum, travel through realistic re-creations of far-off villages and experience the sights, sounds and smells of life on board the slave ships.

In Solway Road, Kells, the **Haig Colliery Mining Museum** (see panel above) features the world's only Bever Dorling Winding Engines, various displays about the mining industry and exhibits on mining disasters. Haig Colliery was the last deep coal mine worked in the West Cumberland coalfield. Sunk between 1914 and 1918, it closed in 1986 and was later sold for restoration. As well as the elegant Georgian buildings that give the town its air of distinction, there are two fine parish churches that are worth a visit. Dating from 1753, **St James' Church** has Italian ceiling designs and a beautiful Memorial Chapel (dedicated to those who lost their lives in the two World Wars and also the local people who were killed in mining accidents) while the younger **St Begh's Church**, which was built in the 1860s by E.W. Pugin, is striking with its sandstone walls. In the graveyard of the parish church of **St Nicholas** is buried Mildred Gale, the grandmother of George Washington. In 1699, this widow and mother of three married George Gale, a merchant who traded from Whitehaven to Maryland and Virginia. Her sons were born in Virginia but went to school in Appleby. When their mother died they returned to Virginia; one of them, Augustin, became the father of George Washington, first President of the United States of America.

Whitehaven is interesting in other ways. The grid pattern of streets dating back to the 17th century gives substance to its claim to be the first planned town in Britain. Many of the fine Georgian buildings in the centre have been restored and **Lowther Street** is a particularly impressive thoroughfare.

GLENFIELD

Corkickle, Whitehaven, Cumbria CA28 7TS
Tel: 01946 691911
e-mail: GlenfieldHotel@aol.com
web: www.whitehaven.org.uk/glenfield.html

Glenfield is an elegant late-Victorian town house hotel just a five-minute walk from the Georgian town of Whitehaven. Ten minutes from the historic harbour and marina it is convenient for the start of the Coast-to-Coast walk and cycle routes. Owners Margaret and Andrew Davies are the most welcoming of hosts, their guests can look forward to home-from-home comfort and the guarantee of a relaxing break. Accommodation comprises of lovingly restored, spacious bedrooms that range from single to family rooms. All have superb en-suite facilities. Margaret is a fine traditional cook, incorporating local produce whenever possible, Her breakfast is really something to look forward to.

Evening meals are served in the tranquil dining room, and snacks can be ordered from the licensed Resident's Bar to be enjoyed by the open fire or, when the weather is fine, on the patio. Glenfield can cater for a range of small private functions. It is situated only a few minutes walk from Corkickle rail station and provides the perfect base to combine the varied attractions of Whitehaven with some of Englands most spectacular mountain scenery only a short drive away. So whether you are an active walker seeking the sanctuary of the less-visited western fells or wish to visit some of the delights of West Cumbria including the Cumbrian coast, the Western lakes, local golf, Sellafields world class visitor centre or Roman Ravenglass, Glenfield is for you. For those without their own transport access to the Lake District is available from Corkickle station along the Cumbrian coastline and then into the heart of Eskdale by The Ravenglass and Eskdale steam line running along one of the most picturesque valleys in England.

Also of note is the **Harbour Pier** built by the canal engineer John Rennie, and considered to be one of the finest in Britain. There is a fascinating walk and a Nature Trail around **Tom Hurd Rock**, above the town.

The town has a curious literary association with Jonathan Swift, the poet, satirist, journalist and author of *Gulliver's Travels*. As a sickly infant in a poverty-stricken Dublin home, Swift was wet-nursed by a young girl from Whitehaven named Sarah. She was suddenly called to the deathbed of a relative in Cumbria from whom she expected a legacy. By now Sarah was so attached to the child she could not bear a separation and carried him off with her to Whitehaven. Later, guilt-stricken, she wrote to Mrs Swift admitting what she had done and received an answer asking her to continue looking after Jonathan, Mrs Swift being concerned about the effect on the boy's delicate health of another sea crossing. Swift stayed with the girl for 3 years and was clearly well looked after in every way - by the time he returned to Dublin he was in robust health and "could read any chapter in the Bible".

Around Whitehaven

St Bees

3 miles S of Whitehaven on the B5343

St Bees Head, a red sandstone bluff, forms one of the most dramatic natural features along the entire coast of northwest England. Some four miles long and 300 feet high, these towering, precipitous cliffs are formed of St Bees sandstone, the red rock which is so characteristic of Cumbria. Far out to sea, on the horizon, can be seen the grey shadow of the Isle of Man and, on a clear day, the shimmering outline of the Irish coast. From here the 190-mile **Coast to Coast Walk** starts on its long journey across the Pennines to Robin Hood's Bay in North Yorkshire.

Long before the first lighthouse was built in 1822, there was a beacon on the headland to warn and guide passing ships away from the rocks. The present 99ft high lighthouse

St Bees

MORESBY HALL

Moresby, Nr Whitehaven, Cumbria CA28 6PJ
Tel: 01946 696317
e-mail: hiddenplaces@moresbyhall.co.uk
website: www.moresbyhall.co.uk

Moresby Hall is a Grade I listed 16th century building described by English Heritage as 'one of the most important buildings in Cumbria'. With its semi-rural location it is a perfect base from which to explore the Western Lake District, and Whitehaven, just a few minutes away, is a town full of historic interest. The owners Jane and David Saxon welcome guests from near and far, whether travelling for business or leisure, and are already winning repeat bookings since opening in May 2001.

The four beautiful en suite guest bedrooms are superbly equipped, with tv, trouser press, tea & coffee trays, hairdryer, iron and even a foot spa. Top of the range is the De Asby suite with a sumptuous

carved four-poster bed, a hydro massage power shower and steam enclosure en suite. Moresby Hall is renowned for its hearty English breakfasts, and dinner can be pre-booked, with everything on an imaginative daily changing menu prepared by Jane from top-quality local produce. In the oldest part of the property, 'Rosmerta' and 'Brighida' cottages accommodate from 2 to 6 guests; both are superbly equipped and are offered on either B&B or self-catering terms. Open all year, Moresby Hall is a non-smoking establishment.

dates from 1866-7, built after an earlier one was destroyed by fire. St Bees Head is now an important Nature Reserve and the cliffs are crowded with guillemots, razorbills, kittiwakes, gulls, gannets, and skuas. Bird watchers are well-provided for with observation and information points all along the headland. There is a superb walk of about eight miles along the coastal footpath around the headland from St Bees to Whitehaven. The route passes Saltam Bay and Saltam Pit, which dates from 1729 and was the world's first undersea mineshaft. The original lamp house for the pit has been restored and is now used by HM Coastguard.

St Bees itself, a short walk from the headland, is a small village which lies

huddled in a deep, slanting bowl in the cliffs, fringed by a shingle beach. The village is a delightful place to explore, with its main street winding up the hillside between old farms and cottages. It derives its name from St Bega, daughter of an Irish king who, on the day she was meant to marry a Norse prince, was miraculously transported by an angel to the Cumbrian coast.

According to legend, on Midsummer Night's Eve, St Bega asked the pagan Lord Egremont for some land on which to found a nunnery. Cunningly, he promised her only as much land as was covered by snow the following morning. But on Midsummer's Day, three square miles of land were blanketed white with snow and here she founded her priory.

HARTLEY'S BEACH SHOP

St Bees Foreshore, St Bees, Cumbria
CA22 0ES
Tel/Fax: 01946 820175

In a super location overlooking the foreshore at St Bees, **Hartley's Beach Shop & Tea Rooms** has become one of the most popular places in the region to pause for a drink and a snack. It's a particularly welcome amenity for anyone starting or finishing a spell of exercise on the Coast to Coast Walk, which starts more or less outside and runs across the Pennines to Robin Hood's Bay in North Yorkshire.

The long-established owners are the Richardson family, and the business is shared by Les and Eileen Richardson, their son Mark and their daughter-in-law Shirley. Hartley's is open every day between mid-March and New Year's Day, from 9am to 5pm (high season 8am to 7pm). There are non-smoking seats for 48 inside, and when the weather permits tables and chairs are set outside. Home-made cakes, toasted tea cakes and scones are the speciality, along with the famous ice creams, while on the savoury side the choice comprises soup, beans on toast and made-to-order sandwiches with a variety of generous, tasty fillings · tuna savoury, corned beef & onion, chicken mayonnaise and ham with cheese & pineapple are just a few of the options. Coffee is the favourite beverage, coming in several varieties and two sizes.

The Beach Shop, on the righthand side of the long, low modern building, is stocked with a wide range of foodstuffs, drinks, gifts and all that walkers and campers might need. In 1981 the family took over the ice cream business, which had been founded 50 years previously, and the range runs to more than 30 flavours, with a selection of sorbets as well. Their ice cream shop, in Church Street, Egremont, is open from March to early January, from 11am to 5pm and until 7 o'clock in the busy summer months. St Bees is a place of many attractions, including the priory church, the school (Rowan Atkinson is a former pupil), a nature reserve and wonderful walks along the coastal footpath. And for the past 20 years and more no visit to St Bees has been complete without sampling the goodies on offer at Hartley's.

(Incidentally, this 'miracle' snowfall is a not uncommon feature of a Cumbrian summer on the high fells.)

The Priory at St Bees grew in size and importance until it was destroyed by the Danes in the 10th century: the Benedictines later re-established the priory in 1129. **The Priory Church of St Mary and St Bega** is all that is now left and although it has been substantially altered there is still a magnificent Norman arch and a pre-Conquest, carved Beowulf Stone on a lintel between the church and the vicarage, showing St Michael killing a dragon. The most stunning feature of all is much more modern, a sumptuous Art Nouveau metal work screen. In the south aisle is a small museum.

Close by the church are the charming Abbey Cottages and **St Bees School** with its handsome clock-tower. The school was founded in 1583 by Edmund Grindal, Archbishop of Canterbury under Elizabeth I, and the son of a local farmer. The original red sandstone quadrangle bears his coat-of-arms and the bridge he gave to the village is still in use. Among the school's most famous alumni is the actor and comedian Rowan Atkinson, creator of the ineffable Mr Bean.

An anonymous resident of St Bees has also achieved fame of a kind. In 1981, archaeologists excavating a ruined chapel discovered a lead lined coffin containing one of the best preserved medieval bodies in England. It was the

FAIRLADIESBARN GUEST HOUSE

Main Street, St Bees, Cumbria CA27 0AD
Tel: 01946 822718 Fax: 01946 825838
e-mail: info@fairladiesbarn.co.uk
website: www.fairladiesbarn.co.uk

Fairladies is a 17th century sandstone barn situated on the main street of the coastal village of St Bees, the most westerly point in Cumbria. The barn was initially converted in the 1980s into a guest house and self-contained flats, and the current accommodation has recently been smartly refurbished by the owners John and Susan Carr. They now offer 11 top-quality bedrooms, ten of them en suite, the other with private facilities; six of the rooms are on the ground floor, and all rooms have tv and tea/coffee trays.

Rooms 7 and 8, a double and a twin with a shared shower room and a kitchenette, make an ideal choice for a family or a few

friends. The tariff includes an excellent breakfast that will set guests up for a day exploring the numerous local attractions. Packed lunches can be provided on request. Fairladies has a large private car park and attractive gardens. The amenities of St Bees, including the village stores, pubs, the railway station and the beach, are all within easy walking distance. Open all year round, Fairladies is a non-smoking establishment.

corpse of a local lord who had died during the Crusades. Some of the artefacts including a shroud and hair found with the body, can be seen in St Bees Church, together with pictures of the body and the setting in which it was found. Research is continuing into his identity and that of a female skeleton found nearby.

Cleator Moor
3 miles SE of Whitehaven on the B5295

The name of this once-industrial town derives from the Norse words for cliff and hill pasture. Cleator developed rapidly in the 19th century because of the insatiable demand during the Industrial Revolution for coal and iron ore. As the Cumbrian poet Norman Nicholson wrote:

From one shaft at Cleator Moor
They mined for coal and iron ore.
This harvest below ground could show
Black and red currants on one tree.

Cleator is surrounded by delightful countryside and little evidence of the town's industrial past is visible. But there is a thriving business nearby - the **Kangol Factory Shop** in Cleator village which stocks a huge range of hats, scarves, bags, caps and golf wear.

Ennerdale Bridge
7 miles E of Whitehaven off the A5086

Wordsworth described Ennerdale's church as "girt round with a bare ring of mossy wall" - and it still is. The bridge here crosses the River Ehen, which, a couple of miles upstream runs out from

Ennerdale Water

Ennerdale Water, one of the most secluded and inaccessible of all the Cumbrian lakes. The walks around this tranquil lake and through the quiet woodlands amply repay the slight effort of leaving the car at a distance. The Coast to Coast Walk runs the whole length of Ennerdale and this section is generally considered to be by far the most beautiful.

PLACES TO STAY, EAT AND DRINK

● Denotes entries in other chapters

5 The North Cumbrian Coast

The North Cumbrian coast, from Workington in the south to the Solway Firth in the north, is one of the least known parts of this beautiful county but it certainly has a lot to offer. It is an area rich in heritage, with a network of quiet country lanes, small villages, old ports, and seaside resorts. The coast's largest town, Workington, on the site of a Roman fort, was once a large port, prospering on coal, iron and shipping. It later became famous for fine-quality steel, and though its importance has declined, it is still the country's largest producer of railway lines. Further up the coast is Maryport, again a port originally built by the Romans.

However, Maryport has not gone down the industrial route to the extent of its neighbour and, as well as being a quaint and picturesque place, it is also home to a fascinating museum dedicated to the town's maritime past. A short distance inland lies Cockermouth on the edge of the Lake District National Park, a pretty market town with some elegant Georgian buildings. However, most visitors will be more interested to see and hear about the town's most famous son, the poet William Wordsworth, who was born here in 1770.

The northernmost stretch of coastline, around the Solway Firth, is an area of tiny villages with fortified towers standing as mute witness to the border

PLACES TO STAY, EAT AND DRINK

● Denotes entries in other chapters

struggles of long ago. These villages were the haunt of smugglers, wildfowlers, and half-net fishermen. What is particularly special about this coastline is its rich birdlife. The north Cumbrian coast was also the setting for Sir Walter Scott's novel *Redgauntlet*, and the fortified farmhouse by the roadside beyond Port Carlisle is said to be the White Ladies of the novel.

Wordsworth House

Cockermouth

Cockermouth fully earns its designation as a 'gem town' recommended for preservation by the Department of the Environment. A market town since 1226, Cockermouth has been fortunate in keeping unspoilt its broad main street, lined with trees and handsome Georgian houses, and dominated by a

statue to the Earl of Mayo. The Earl was Cockermouth's MP for ten years from 1858 before being appointed Viceroy of India. His brilliant career was brutally cut short when he was stabbed to death by a convict at a prison settlement he was inspecting on the Andaman Islands.

But Cockermouth boasts two far more famous sons. Did they ever meet, one wonders, those two young lads growing up in Cockermouth in the 1770s, both of them destined to become celebrated for very different reasons? The elder boy was Fletcher Christian, who would later

THE GLOBE HOTEL

Main Street, Cockermouth,
Cumbria CA13 9LE
Tel: 01900 822126 Fax: 01900 823705

The Globe Hotel has stood in the middle of Main Street since about 1750. Many distinguished visitors have enjoyed its hospitality, including the author Robert Louis Stevenson and the scientist John Dalton, and today's guests can look forward to a winning combination of period charm and modern comfort. The 28 bedrooms, most with en suite facilities, range from singles to family rooms, and the hotel, which is owned by Helen and Peter Brown, has two well-stocked bars, and

an excellent restaurant. In a separate function room a disco takes place on Friday night and live entertainment on Saturday.

lead the mutiny on the *Bounty*; the younger lad was William Wordsworth, born here in 1770 at Lowther House on Main Street, an imposing Georgian house now maintained by the National Trust. Now known as **Wordsworth House**, it was built in 1745 for the Sheriff of Cumberland and then purchased by the Earl of Lowther; he let it to his land agent, John Wordsworth, William's father. All five Wordsworth children were born here, William on 7th April 1770. Many of the building's original features survive, among them the staircase, fireplace, and fine plaster ceilings. A few of the poet's personal effects are still here and the delightful walled garden by the River Cocker has been returned to its Georgian splendour. The garden is referred to in *The Prelude*.

Interior of Wordsworth House

Wordsworth was only eight years old when his mother died and he was sent to school at Hawkshead, but later he fondly recalled walking at Cockermouth with his sister Dorothy, along the banks of the rivers Cocker and Derwent to the

ruined castle on the hill. Built in 1134 by the Earl of Dunbar, **Cockermouth Castle** saw plenty of action against Scottish raiders (Robert the Bruce himself gave it a mauling in 1315), and again during the Wars of the Roses; in

THE BUSH

Main Street, Cockermouth,
Cumbria CA13 9JS
Tel: 01900 822064

The Bush is a beautifully kept inn whose black-and-white frontage is a familiar landmark on Cockermouth's main street. Maureen Williamson worked here as manager before taking over the lease in 2002, since when she has reinforced the inn's reputation for excellent hospitality, well-kept ales and super food. The local Jennings Brewery provides Best Bitter, Cock a Hoop, Sneck Lifter and Cumberland Ale among a wide selection of liquid refreshment, and Maureen's

appetising home cooking is available every lunchtime; on Sunday afternoon, between 2.30 and 6, The Bush also serves her famous soups and a good choice of sandwiches.

Cockatoo Restaurant And Traditional Fish & Chips

16 Market Place, Cockermouth, Cumbria
CA13 9NQ
Tel: 01900 826205

Janet and Tony Blades brought many years' experience as fish fryers when they opened **Cockatoo Restaurant and Traditional Fish & Chips** at Eastertime 2003. The premises are spotlessly clean after top-to-toe refurbishment, a pristine setting for enjoying the most traditional of English dishes, which hold a unique place in the nation's affections. A menu of all the much-loved classics is served, along with daily specials like trout, salmon and plaice, and the occasional meaty treat such as steak & kidney pie or pudding.

There are two parts to the business: at the front is the takeaway section, with service from 11.30 to 9 (closed Sundays in winter); there are a few seats in this area, and another 30 in the restaurant to the rear, which features an attractive mural of an alfresco eating scene. Last orders in this part, which is licensed for diners, are at 8 o'clock in the evening.

A market town since 1226, Cockermouth is a place well worth taking plenty of time to explore, with places of interest that range from the Castle, the National Trust's Wordsworth House and museums

concerned with printing and mining to the renowned Jennings Brewery. For visitors staying in town Janet and Tony can provide not only their excellent fish and chips but very comfortable Bed & Breakfast accommodation in the town-centre Croft House at 6/8 Challoner Street, Tel: 01900 827533. This smartly turned-out period building has three en suite double rooms, three en suite twins (one on the ground floor has wheelchair access) and an en suite family room with a double bed and a bunk bed. All the rooms have tv, tea/coffee making facilities and electric shaver points. Croft House prides itself on being a fresh air establishment, so no smoking on the premises.

the course of the Civil War it was occupied by both sides in turn. Mary, Queen of Scots, took refuge at the castle in 1568 after her defeat at the Battle of Langside. Her fortunes were so low that she was grateful for the gift of 16 ells (about 20 yards) of rich crimson velvet from a wealthy merchant. Part of the castle is still lived in by the Egremont family; the remainder is usually only open to the public during the Cockermouth Festival in July.

Opposite the Castle entrance, **Castlegate House** is a fine Georgian house, built in 1739, which hosts a changing programme of monthly exhibitions of the work of Northern and Scottish artists - paintings, sculptures, ceramics and glass. To the rear of the house is a charming walled garden which is open from time to time during the summer.

Just around the corner from Castlegate House is the **Toy & Model Museum** (see panel) which exhibits mainly British toys from around 1900 to the present. There are many visitor operated

THE CUMBERLAND TOY & MODEL MUSEUM

Banks Court, Market Place, Cockennouth,
Cumbria CA13 9NG Tel: 01900 827606
e-mail: Rod@toymuseum.co.uk
website: www.toymuseum.co.uk

Winner of the 1995 National Heritage Shoestring Award for achieving the best results with limited resources, the museum exhibits a wide selection of mainly British toys from c1900 to the present. There are many visitor operated displays and buttons to press including 0 and 00 tinplate trains, Scalextric cars, Meccano, Lego models and even a helicopter to fly.

Among the displays are prams, dolls' houses and railways in both a "loft" and garden shed. Are you brave enough to look at the monster at the bottom of the water butt?  There is a family quiz and worksheets that are linked to National Curriculum topics while small children can find the little teddy bears, ride the rocking horse or play with the wooden bricks. The museum features the street windows and inside of an old toy shop. There are always new things to see ·including those you missed the first time! Whether you are 8 or 88 there should be something to remind you of your childhood.

STRATHEARN HOUSE

6 Castlegate, Cockermouth,
Cumbria CA13 9EU Tel: 01900 826749
e-mail@ waters.boyle@virgin.net
website:
www.smoothhound.co.uk/hotels/castlegate

In a handsome terrace close to the town centre, **Strathearn House** is a Grade II listed Georgian townhouse with an imposing pillared portico. The interior is equally gracious, with a fine staircase and attractive period furnishings. New owners Sarah Waters and Liam Boyle have carried out extensive refurbishment and offer Bed & Breakfast accommodation in seven pleasantly appointed bedrooms, four of them with en suite facilities. Strathearn is a very pleasant, civilised base for touring the region.

THE BELLE VUE INN

Papcastle, Cockermouth,
Cumbria CA13 0NT
Tel/Fax: 01900 823518
e-mail: helenglvr@aol.com

The Belle Vue Inn is the social hub of a small village located just five minutes' drive from the centre of Cockermouth, birthplace of William Wordsworth. It stands a little way off the main A595 where it meets the A594, and is well worth a visit to enjoy the cordial hospitality of leaseholders John and Helen Glover, who took over the reins when they arrived at the beginning of 2002 with their son Matthew, now aged 4. Behind the slate-

roofed greystone façade the inn has a particularly bright, welcoming feel that is enhanced by attractive use of wood and greenery.

The Belle Vue is open every session for the service of drinks, which always include at least three real ales · Jennings Bitter and Cumberland Ale, a seasonal ale from a smaller brewery and the occasional second guest. Old Smoothie is another option among a good selection of beers, lagers, cider and stout. Excellent pub meals are also served every lunchtime (12-2) and every evening (6-9), and there's plenty of room in the bar and in the non-smoking restaurant. Sandwiches, served on white or brown bread with a salad garnish, provide tasty quick snacks, and at the serious end they

take the form of hot baguettes filled with rump steak or Cumberland sausage and caramelised onions, or crispy bacon topped with melted cheese. Home-cooked beef, ham and turkey are the basis of appetising meat platters, and elsewhere on the menu are traditional pub favourites such as chilli con carne, meat or vegetarian lasagne, chicken (roast, sizzling strips or tikka masala), breaded mushrooms with a creamy garlic mayonnaise, scampi, deep-fried cod, steak pie and lamb Jennings · shoulder cooked slowly in a mint and garlic marinade. A specials list widens the choice still further, and vegetarians are very well catered for.

Children are always welcome, and they can choose from their own little section of the menu. Desserts like treacle sponge pudding or chocolate lumpy bumpy cake end a meal on a wicked but delicious note. The food is complemented by a well-annotated wine list that is strong on New World wines. Everything on the list is available by glass or bottle.

displays including 0 and 00 gauge vintage tinplate trains, Scalextric cars, Lego models and even a 1950s helicopter to fly. There are prams and dolls houses, and a working railway in a garden shed.

Almost next door, **Jennings Brewery** offers visitors a 90-minute tour which ends with the option of sampling some of their ales - Cumberland Ale, Cocker Hoop or the intriguingly named Sneck Lifter. The last independent brewing company in Cumbria, Jennings have been brewing traditional beers since the 1820s and today there are more than 100 Jennings pubs across the north of England. In addition to the tours, Jennings has a shop selling gifts and leisure wear, the latter boldly emblazoned with the names of its various brews.

A short walk from the Brewery brings you to the **Kirkgate Centre**, which is housed in a converted Victorian primary school. Run by volunteers, the Centre offers a wide range of events and activities including live music, amateur and professional drama, films, dance, workshops, exhibitions of art and local history.

Two more visitor attractions stand either side of Wordsworth House in the Main Street. The **Printing House Museum** occupies a building dating back to the 16th century and follows the progress of printing from its invention by Johann Gutenberg in 1430 to the end of the letterpress era in the 1960's, when computers took over. On display is a wide range of historical presses and printing equipment, the earliest being a Cogger Press dated 1820. Visitors are offered the opportunity to gain hands-on experience by using some of the presses to produce cards or keepsakes.

Located just south of the town, the **Lakeland Sheep & Wool Centre** provides an introduction to life in the Cumbrian countryside with the help of a spectacular visual show, 19 different breeds of live sheep and a wide variety of exhibits. The Centre also hosts indoor sheepdog trials and sheep-shearing displays for which there is a small charge. Open all year round, the Centre has ample free parking, a shop selling woollen goods and gifts, a large café-restaurant and even en suite accommodation.

Around Cockermouth

Brigham
2 miles W of Cockermouth off the A66

St Bridget's Church, which was probably founded as part of a nunnery, contains many interesting features, including pre-Norman carved stones, a rare 'fish window' and a window dedicated to the Rev John Wordsworth, son of William and vicar of Brigham for 40 years. One of the tombs in the graveyard is that of Charles Christian, the father of Fletcher Christian, the *Bounty* mutineer. Fletcher himself was baptised in the church on the day of his birth, as it was thought unlikely that he would survive.

NEW HOUSE FARM

Lorton, Nr Cockermouth,
Cumbria CA13 9UU
Tel: 01900 85404 Fax: 01900 85478
e-mail: hazel@newhouse-farm.co.uk
website: www.newhouse-farm.co.uk

Seventeen acres of beautiful gardens and pastureland provide a glorious setting for **New House Farm**. Owned and run since 1990 by Hazel Thompson, this outstanding Bed &

room. Children over 6 are welcome, and special arrangements can be made for younger children.

Awarded 5 Diamonds by the AA, this non-smoking establishment is indeed 'a very special country guest house', and its location makes it an ideal base for touring one of the loveliest parts of the country. Bookings can be made on a Bed & Breakfast or Dinner, Bed & Breakfast basis, and rates vary with the seasons and with the length of stay. The farm stands by the B5289 in Lorton Vale, south of Cockermouth. That gem of a town is full of interest, as is Keswick, a short drive in the other direction.

Bassenthwaite Lake, Derwent Water and other lesser known lakes are almost on the doorstep, along with the spectacular Whinlatter Pass and Forest Park. The Lortons, High and Low, are peaceful,

Breakfast establishment is a magnificent farmhouse dating back to the 17th century and surrounded by the superb Lortondale countryside.

Local mountains give their names to the five letting bedrooms, each individually decorated and furnished with comfort and style in mind. They all have en suite facilities and offer wonderful views, and one of the rooms is on the ground floor. Guests have the use of two elegant, relaxing lounges, and breakfast is served in the separate dining

enchanting places, and behind the former's village hall the yew tree of Wordsworth's poem still stands. Right next door to New House Farm, and in the same ownership, is The Barn, a handsome building dating from the 1880s.

It has been converted into a charming tea room, with seats for 40 and opening hours from 11 to 5 between March and the end of October. Besides serving excellent traditional teas, it also offers appetising home cooked hot and cold snacks throughout the day.

HUDDLESTONE COTTAGE & THE HAYLOFT

Pooley House, Redmain, Nr Cockermouth,
Cumbria CA13 0PZ
Tel: 01900 825695 Fax: 01900 829228
e-mail: hudcot@lakesnw.co.uk
website: www.lakesnw.co.uk/hudcot

In the pretty rural hamlet of Redmain, **Huddlestone Cottage and The Hayloft** provide a peaceful retreat within the Lake District National Park. Stone barns attached to 17th century Pooley House have been converted to offer quality self-catering accommodation for 2 to 4 guests, and both the cottage and the Hayloft feature original stone walls, polished pine floors, open-plan living areas and fully equipped kitchens. The grounds behind the properties include lawns, woodland wildlife area with pond and organic vegetable and herb garden.

Bridekirk

2 miles N of Cockermouth off the A595

The village **Church** contains one of the finest pieces of Norman sculpture in the country, a carved font with a runic inscription and a mass of detailed embellishments. It dates from the 12th century and the runic inscription states that:

Richard he me wrought
And to this beauty eagerly me brought.

Richard himself is shown on one side with a chisel and mallet. Not only is this a superb example of early English craftsmanship but it is exceedingly rare to find a signed work. Ancient tombstones stand round the walls of this cruciform church and inside it has unusual reredos of fleur-de-lys patterned tiles.

High & Low Lorton

5 miles SE of Cockermouth on the B5289

There is a yew tree, pride of Lorton Vale… wrote Wordsworth in his poem *Yew*

THE WHEATSHEAF INN

Low Lorton, Nr Cockermouth,
Cumbria CA13 9UW
Tel: 01900 85199/85268

Mark Cockbain and Jackie Williams are partners in **The Wheatsheaf**, a charming Jennings pub in a peaceful setting by the River Cocker. Behind the long white-painted frontage, the spotless interior has plenty of tables and chairs, a wood-burning stove and a good range of beers. Mark does the cooking, and his tasty dishes are served every session except Mondays in winter. Pool and darts are played in the bar, Wednesday is quiz night

and there's jazz on Sunday evenings starting about 8.30pm. The Wheatsheaf has a large rear garden and a children's play area, and a caravan/camping site with electric hook-ups.

THE ROYAL YEW

Dean, Nr Cockermouth, Cumbria,
CA14 4TJ
Tel: 01946 861342
e-mail: cam.train@btinternet.com

A quaint village four miles southwest of Cockermouth is the picturesque setting for **The Royal Yew**, a charming inn owned and run by a delightful local couple, Julie and Edward Fearon. Dating back to 1878, the inn takes its name from the splendid old yew that stands right outside. The main building, which was extended by the conversion of two

barns, has plenty of character, with sturdy stone walls and traditional decor and furnishings. An eye-catching feature is the stone stairway that leads up from the bar to nowhere - the upper floor at this point is no longer used.

The owners are lucky to have the services of an excellent manager/chef in Alan Saddleton, and between them they are building successfully on the already high reputation of the inn as a place to seek out for good food and drink. The bar stocks Jennings Cumberland Ale, Derwent Brewery of Silloth's State Controlled Bitter, Younger's Scotch and John Smith's Bitter, as well as lager, stout, cider and a developing selection of wines. Alan is constantly seeking to expand his repertoire, adding exciting new dishes to familiar favourites and thus offering something for everyone. Garlic prawns, salads and cold meat platters, pasta, pizza, chicken or vegetable Kiev, steak, mushroom and ale pie and very popular grills (bacon chop with Stilton, Cumberland sausage with a fried egg, steaks plain or sauced) are always on the menu, while the daily specials might include duck with black cherry sauce, vegetable curry, lamb hotpot with red cabbage, and chicken breast with sun-dried tomato sauce and couscous; for dessert, the choice is no less tempting, with the likes of Pavlova, sherry trifle and hot apple cobbler. Some of the eating areas are designated non-smoking. The Royal Yew is a great place to head for after a brisk walk along the shores of the local lakes or in the lovely surrounding countryside.

Dean itself is a very pleasant place for a stroll, with some handsome old farm buildings and private dwellings; the churchyard is entered through a lych gate, and just outside the church is an ancient preaching cross.

Trees, and astonishingly it's still there behind the village hall of High Lorton. It was in the shade of its branches that the Quaker George Fox preached to a large gathering under the watchful eye of Cromwell's soldiers. In its sister village, Low Lorton, set beside the River Cocker, is **Lorton Hall** (private) which is reputed to be home to the ghost of a woman who carries a lighted candle. Less spectral guests in the past have included King Malcolm III of Scotland, who stayed here with his queen while visiting the southern boundaries of his Kingdom of Strathclyde of which this area was a part.

Eaglesfield

2 miles SW of Cockermouth off the A5086

This small village was the birthplace of Robert Eaglesfield, who became confessor to Queen Philippa, Edward III's Queen. He was also the founder of Queen's College, Oxford where he was buried in 1349. Even more famous is **John Dalton**, who was born here in 1766. The son of Quaker parents, Dalton was teaching at the village school by the time he was 12. Despite having had no formal education himself, he became one of the most brilliant scientists, naturalists, and mathematicians of his age and was the originator of the theory that all matter is composed of small indestructible particles called atoms. He was also the first to recognise the existence of colour blindness. He suffered from it himself and in medical circles it is known as Daltonism. A memorial to this remarkable man now marks the house where he lived in Eaglesfield.

Workington

The largest town on the Cumbrian coast, Workington stands at the mouth of the River Derwent and on the site of the Roman fort of **Gabrosentum**. Its prosperity was founded on the three great Cumbrian industries - coal, iron and shipping. As early as 1650 coal was being mined here and, by the end of the 18th century, Workington was a major

THE TRAVELLERS REST

Whitehaven Road, Workington,
Cumbria CA14 4EU Tel: 01900 602064
e-mail: michael.littles@btopenworld.com

On the main Whitehaven Road out of Workington, the **Travellers Rest** presents an immaculate black and white frontage with spring flowers and picnic benches set well back from the road. Inside, all is equally neat and welcoming, with black beams and smart wooden tables and chairs. Michael Little's inn is open all day, every day for drinks, and appetising home cooking is served from 12 to 2 and from 6 to 8.30 seven days a week.

Steaks are a speciality, including sirloin, gammon and as part of a hearty mixed grill. The inn has off-road parking and a beer garden.

THE GREEN DRAGON HOTEL

Portland Square, Workington,
Cumbria CA14 4BJ
Tel: 01900 603803 Fax: 01900 68730
e-mail: paulrossall@tiscali.co.uk

The Green Dragon Hotel stands in one of the oldest parts of Workington, in Portland Square with its cobbled streets. A former coaching inn, it dates back to the mid-18th century, and subsequent modernisation has not detracted from its traditional appeal. Since March 2003 the hotel has been owned and run by Paul and Judith, who have various

for residents) two real ales from the Jennings Brewery are always on tap, and there's a good selection of draught and bottled beers, lagers, stout and cider.

Workington, the largest town on the Cumbrian coast, stands at the mouth of the River Derwent on the site of a substantial Roman fort. In its heyday it was a centre of the coal mining, shipbuilding and iron and steel industries, and visitors should take time to explore this legacy in the fascinating Helena Thompson Museum. The Green Dragon is open all year round and provides a first-class base for visiting

improvement plans that will come to fruition over the coming months.

The Green Dragon's primary role is as a very comfortable hotel, and the 11 guest bedrooms are well equipped to provide a very pleasant stay. Three rooms are on the first floor, the other eight on the floor above, and all the rooms have en suite facilities. Booking can be on either a Bed & Breakfast or a Dinner, Bed & Breakfast basis, and non-smoking rooms are available. In the restaurant (also non-smoking), printed menus and a daily changing specials board provide plenty of choice to cater for most appetites and tastes. In the public bar (open every lunchtime and evening and all day

the local sites, discovering the many delights of the North Cumbrian coast or heading eastwards towards the Lakes.

port exporting coal as well as smelting iron ore. Many of the underground coal seams extended far out to sea. In later years, Workington became famous for its fine quality steel, especially after Henry Bessemer developed his revolutionary steel making process here in 1850. The seat of the Curwen family for over 600 years, **Workington Hall** has an interesting history. Originally built around a 14th century pele tower, the hall was developed over the years with extensive alterations being made in the 18th century by the then lord of the manor, John Christian Curwen. Now a stabilised ruin, it has several commemorative plaques which give a taste of the hall's history. The most famous visitor was Mary, Queen of Scots who sought refuge here when she fled from Scotland in 1558. She stayed for a few days during which time she wrote the famous letter to her cousin Elizabeth I bemoaning her fate, "for I am in a pitiable condition....having nothing in the world but the clothes in which I escaped", and asking the Queen "to have compassion on my great misfortunes". The letter is now in the British Museum. Workington's **Church of St John the Evangelist** is a very grand affair built at enormous expense in 1823 to give thanks for the defeat of Napoleon at Waterloo. It is a copy of St Paul's, Covent Garden, and its walls were built with stones from the local Schoose and Hunday quarries. The interior was splendidly restored by Sir Ninian Comper in 1931. St Michael's is the

ancient parish church, restored after a fire in 1994.

The **Helena Thompson Museum** (see panel below), situated on Park End Road, is a fascinating place to visit with its displays telling the story of Workington's coal mining, ship-building, and iron and steel industries for which the town became internationally renowned. The Georgian Room gives an insight into the variety of decorative styles which were popular between 1714 and 1830, with displays of beautiful cut-glass tableware, porcelain from China,

HELENA THOMPSON MUSEUM

Park End Road, Workington,
Cumbria CA14 4DE.
Tel: 01900 326255 Fax: 01900 326256

Visit the **Helena Thompson Museum** and discover Workington's fascinating social and industrial heritage. The Museum is housed in a fine, listed mid Georgian building. It was bequeathed to the people of Workington in 1940 by local philanthropist Miss Helena Thompson. Displays in the museum include pottery, silver, glass and furniture, dating from Georgian, Regency and Victorian times; women's and childrens dresses from the 18th to the early 20th century, together with accessories and jewellery; the social and industrial history of Workington, the coal mining, ship building, iron and steel industry for which Workington became world renowned. Admission is free.

THE SAILORS RETURN

17 King Street, Maryport,
Cumbria CA15 6AJ
Tel: 01900 813124
e-mail: dave@stationst.freeserve.co.uk

Sailors are not the only visitors who return time and time again to Dave and Moree Weir's homely, welcoming old pub, which stands proudly in the redeveloped dock area of the town. Dave and Moree came to **The Sailors Return** towards the end of 2001,

bringing with them many years experience in the trade, and their genuine Northern hospitality and the guarantee of good food and drink have made their pub a popular port of call with the locals of Maryport and also with visitors to this fine old coastal town.

Built solidly and well in 1884, the pub has a bright, cheerful and traditional look, and in the bar a good selection of beers is on tap to enjoy with a chat, a game of pool or something to eat. Value for money is outstanding among the straightforward, appetising bar meals that Moree prepares and serves between 12 and 7

Monday to Saturday and from 12 to 4 on Sunday. Sandwiches are popular choices for a tasty quick snack, while main courses typically include roast beef, roast turkey, chicken curry, steak pie (home-made, of course, and a great favourite) and meat or vegetarian lasagne.

Some of the first visitors to Maryport were the Romans, who built a clifftop fort here, and their story is told in the Senhouse Roman Museum. Modern Maryport dates from the 18th century, when the harbour was built; it became a busy port and ship-building centre, and the restored Georgian quays are a tribute to its heyday. The Maritime Museum is another attraction not to be missed, and for visitors spending time in this interesting town the Sailors Return has two upstairs letting bedrooms providing good-value overnight accommodation, with a good hearty breakfast to start the day. Pub hours are 11am to 11pm (12 to 10.30 on Sunday).

and period pieces of furniture. Bequeathed to the town by the local philanthropist Miss Helena Thompson, MBE, JP, the museum was opened in 1949 and contains some of her own family heirlooms. One particularly interesting exhibit is the Clifton Dish, a

Maryport Harbour

locally produced 18th century piece of slipware pottery, while further displays demonstrate the links between this local industry and the famous Staffordshire pottery families. Fashion fiends will be interested in the display of women's and children's dresses from the 1700s to the early 1900s, together with accessories and jewellery. Workington is at the start of the C2C cycle route that runs to Sunderland and Newcastle. A short distance south of town is **Harrington Reservoir Nature Reserve**, a haven for wildlife with a rich variety of wild flowers, insects, butterflies, birds and animals.

North and East of Workington

Maryport

6 miles NE of Workington on the A596

Dramatically located on the Solway Firth, Maryport is a charming Cumbrian coastal town rich in interest and maritime history. The old part is full of narrow streets and neoclassical, Georgian architecture which contrast with sudden, surprising views of the sea. Some of the first visitors to Maryport were the Romans, who built a clifftop fort here, **Alauna**, which is now part of the Hadrian's Wall World Heritage Site. The award-winning **Senhouse Roman Museum** tells the story of life in this outpost of the empire. Housed in the striking Naval Reserve Battery, built in the 1880s, the museum holds the largest collection of Roman altars from a single site in Britain. Other highlights include a reconstruction of the shrine from the fort's headquarters and interpretive panels describing the fort, the Roman coastal defences and the Senhouse family - it was John Senhouse of Netherall who started the collection way back in the 1570s. Modern Maryport dates from the 18th century when another Senhouse, Humphrey, a local landowner, developed the harbour at what was then called Ellenport to export coal from his mines, and named the new port after his wife, Mary. Over the next century it became a busy port as well as a ship-building centre; boats had to be launched broadside because of the narrowness of the harbour channel. The town declined, along with the mining industry, from the 1930s onwards. It nevertheless attracted the artist LS Lowry, who was a frequent visitor and loved painting the harbour. Today, Maryport is enjoying a well-earned revival, with newly restored Georgian quaysides, clifftop paths, sandy beaches and a harbour with fishing boats.

The town's extensive maritime history is preserved in the vast array of objects, pictures and models on display at the **Maritime Museum** (see panel) overlooking the harbour. Housed in another of Maryport's more interesting and historic buildings, the former Queen's Head public house, the museum tells of the rise and fall of the harbour and docks. Other exhibits include a brass telescope from the *Cutty Sark* and the town's connections with the ill-fated liner, the *Titanic*, and with Fletcher Christian, instigator of the mutiny on the *Bounty*. The *Titanic* was part of the fleet of the White Star Line, which was founded by a Maryport man, Thomas Henry Ismay. Fletcher Christian was also more or less a local man, being born at nearby Cockermouth in 1764. The Tourist Information Centre is also located here.

Close by is the **Lake District Coast**

MARYPORT MARITIME MUSEUM

1 Senhouse Street, Maryport,
Cumbria CA13 6AB
Tel: 01900 813738 Fax: 01900 819496

Did you know that Maryport has connections with the ill fated 'Titanic', or Fletcher Christian of Mutiny on the Bounty fame? Visit **Maryport Maritime Museum** and discover the fascinating and proud maritime heritage of this delightful town. The building, formerly the Queens Head Public House, is built on one of the earliest plots of land developed by Humphrey Senhouse 11 when the town was built.

The Museum houses a wealth of objects, pictures, models and paintings that illustrate Maryport's proud maritime tradition; from a whale's tooth to a blunderbuss; from sailmakers' tools to telescopes;from a mutineer, Fletcher Christian, to a great shipowner, Thomas Henry Ismay of the great White Star Line, owners of the ill fated Titanic.

Aquarium where a series of spectacular living habitat re-creations introduce visitors to the profusion of marine life found in the Solway Firth - thornback rays (which can be touched), some small sharks, spider crabs and the comically ugly tompot blenny among them. Open all year, the Aquarium also has a gift shop and a quayside café that enjoys superb views of the harbour and the Solway.

Maryport's other attractions include a fresh fish shop, appropriately named The Catch, and an indoor Karting Centre.

Dearham

7 miles NE of Workington off the A594

Though this is not a particularly pretty village, it has a very beautiful church with open countryside on three sides. The chancel of **Dearham Church** is 13th century and the church has a fortress tower built for the protection of men and beasts during the Border raids. There are also some interesting relics within the church including the Adam Stone, dating from AD 900, which depicts the fall of man with Adam and Eve hand in hand above a serpent, an ancient font carved

with mythological beasts, a Kenneth Cross showing the legend of the 6th century hermit brought up by seagulls, and a magnificent wheel-head cross carved with Yggdrasil, the Norse Tree of the Universe.

Aspatria

14 miles NE of Workington on the A596

Lying above the shallow Ellen Valley, Aspatria's main interest for most visitors lies in the elaborate **Memorial Fountain** to 'Watery Wilfred', Sir Wilfred Lawson MP (1829-1906), a lifelong crusader for the Temperance Movement and International Peace. According to one writer, "No man in his day made more people laugh at Temperance meetings". Also worth a visit is the much restored **Norman Church** that is entered through a fine avenue of yew trees. Inside are several ancient relics including a 12th century font with intricate carvings, a Viking hogback tombstone, and a grave cover with a pagan swastika engraving. Like many other churches in the area,

THE GRAPES HOTEL

Market Square, Aspatria, Cumbria CA7 3HB
Tel: 01697 322550

On the A596 halfway between Maryport and Wigton, **The Grapes Hotel** is a welcoming place to pause for refreshment on a journey. Mine hostess Maureen Scott, whose family have owned the hotel for many years, has a cheerful greeting for all her customers, and in the bar the locals enjoy a great pint of real ale and a sandwich or light snack over a chat or a game of pool or darts or dominoes.

Five bedrooms with shared facilities are in a purpose-built extension.

THE MASONS ARMS

Gilcrux, Nr Wigton, Cumbria CA7 2QX
Tel: 016973 20765
e-mail: slapsgilcrux@aol.com

Once a busy little coal mining village, Gilcrux stands on a hillside overlooking the Ellen Valley commanding grand views across the Solway Firth to Scotland. When the mines were in their heyday, the village supported no fewer than seven licensed premises; now **The Masons Arms** is the only original one left. It's a charming old hostelry, with old beams and an open fire helping to create a wonderfully warm, welcoming and traditional

barbecue pork & bean casserole and an exotic mixed grill with wild boar, kangaroo and ostrich steak · exotic and exciting, and a treat not to be missed! For Sunday lunch, the evening menu is supplemented by traditional roasts. This family-friendly inn has a spacious beer garden and a games room; there's live entertainment on some Bank Holidays, and everyone is welcome for the quiz that's held every other Monday. The Masons Arms is about to add another string to its bow: three en suite guest rooms, including a family room, created in a converted barn

atmosphere. That welcoming feeling is strongly reinforced by Esther and Paul Bowness, a local couple who took over as tenants early in 2000 and became the owners in November 2001. They have established a fine reputation not only for hospitality but also for fine ales and excellent food. The inn is open every evening and Sunday lunchtime. Warm crusty baguettes, jacket potatoes and pizzas make tasty quick snacks, and the pub grub menu provides a good choice of classics from Cumberland sausage, steaks, scampi and battered cod to lasagne, curries and super home-made pies (chicken, leek & Stilton, steak in ale, turkey & ham). Everything is fresh, appetising and very moreish, but for many regulars the stars of the show are the specials, which run from crispy deep-fried mushrooms cooked in a cider batter and mini-onion bhajis to

next to the main building, are due to come on stream in the spring of 2004. The village of Gilcrux is particularly noted for its 12th century church and for the number of its springs · and of course for having one of the most delightful inns in the area.

THE HORSE & JOCKEY

Parsonby, Nr Wigton, Cumbria CA7 2DD
Tel: 016973 210482
e-mail: judanian@aol.com
website: www.horseandjockeypub.co.uk

The Horse & Jockey is a quaint, charming village pub dating from the middle of the 18th century. Ian and Judy Taylor, a delightful couple with a passion for Ireland and all things Irish, have created a very friendly, relaxed atmosphere in the bar, where open fires and massive old beams assist the homely, traditional look. Ian's home cooking brings in a loyal local clientele, and the

Sunday lunch is particularly popular. Parsonby is a quiet little village hidden down country lanes between the A595 and A596 about 8 miles northeast of Cockermouth.

the churchyard contains a holy well in which it is said St Kentigern baptised his converts.

Gilcrux
10 miles NE of Workington off the A596

From this village there are particularly good views across the Solway Firth to Scotland and it is well worth visiting for the 12th century **Church of St Mary** which is believed to be the oldest building in the district. Standing on a walled mound and with a buttressed exterior, it has a thick-walled chancel. The village is remarkable for the number of its springs, at least five of which have never failed even in the driest summers.

Allonby
11 miles N of Workington on the B5300

This traditional Solway village is backed by the Lake District fells and looks out across the Solway Firth to the Scottish hills. Popular with wind-surfers, the village has an attractive shingle and

sand beach which received a Seaside Award in 1998. The Allerdale Way and the Cumbrian Cycle Way both pass close by, and the village is also on the **Smuggler's Route** trail. Smuggling seems to have been a profitable occupation around here - a Government enquiry into contraband trade reported in 1730 that "the Solway people were the first working-class folk to drink tea regularly in Britain".

In the early 1800s, Allonby was a popular sea-bathing resort and the former seawater baths, built in 1835 and now Grade II listed buildings, still stand in the old **Market Square**. In those days, the upper floor was in popular use as a ballroom for the local nobility. Allonby still keeps much of its Georgian and early Victorian charm with cobbled lanes, alleyways, and some interesting old houses. It was also an important centre for herring fishing and some of the old kippering houses can still be seen. Allonby was the birthplace of Joseph Huddart, hydrographer and inventor of various ships' safety measures. He is buried at St Martin's in the Fields, London.

Holme St Cuthbert

14 miles N of Workington off the B5300

This inland hamlet is also known as Rowks because, in the Middle Ages, there was a chapel here dedicated to St Roche. The present church dates from 1845 but it contains an interesting torso of a medieval knight wearing chain mail. Found by schoolboys on a nearby farm, the hollowed-out centre of the torso was being used as a trough. It seems to be a 14th century piece and could be a representation of Robert the Bruce's father, who died at Holm Cultram Abbey.

Northeast of the hamlet, and enveloped among low hills, is a lovely 30-acre lake known as **Tarns Dub**, which is a haven for birdlife. A couple of miles to the southwest, the headland of **Dubmill Point** is popular with sea anglers. When the tide is high and driven by a fresh westerly wind, the sea covers the road with lashing waves.

Beckfoot

16 miles N of Workington on the B5300

At certain times and tides, the remains of a prehistoric forest can be seen on the sand beds here and, to the south of the village, is

the site of a 2nd century Roman fort known as **Bibra**. According to an inscribed stone found here, it was once occupied by an Auxiliary Cohort of 500 Pannonians (Spaniards) and surrounded by a large civilian settlement. The small stream flowing into the sea was used in World War I as a fresh water supply by German U-boats.

Silloth

18 miles N of Workington on the B5300

This charming old port and Victorian seaside resort is well worth exploring and its two-mile-long promenade provides wonderful views of the Solway Firth and the coast of Scotland. With the coming of the railways in the 1850s, Silloth developed as a port and railhead for Carlisle. The Railway Company helped to develop the town and had grey granite shipped over in its own vessels from Ireland to build the handsome church which is such a prominent landmark. The town's name is derived from Sea Lath -

Silloth

sea because of its position and lath being a grain store, used by monks from nearby Holm Cultram Abbey.

The region's bracing air and low rainfall helped to make Silloth a popular seaside resort. Visitors today will appreciate the invigorating but mild climate, the leisurely atmosphere, and the glorious sunsets over the sea that inspired Turner to record them for posterity. The town remains a delightful place to stroll, to admire the sunken rose garden and the pinewoods and two miles of promenades. Silloth's 18-hole golf course was the 'home course' where Miss Cecil Leitch (1891-1978), the most celebrated woman golfer of her day, used to play. Another keen woman golfer was the great contralto, Kathleen Ferrier, who stayed in the town for part of her tragically short life. The house on Eden Street where she lived is now a bank but a plaque on the wall records her stay here between 1936 and 1941. One of the most popular attractions is the **Solway Coast Discovery Centre**, where Auld

Michael the Monk and Oyk the Oystercatcher guide visitors through 10,000 years of Solway Coast history.

Wigton

The pleasant market town of Wigton has adopted the title 'The Throstle Nest of all England' - throstle being the northern term for a thrush. The story is that a Wigton man returning home from the trenches of the Great War crested the hill and on seeing the familiar cluster of houses, churches, farms and the maze of streets, yards and alleys, exclaimed "Awa' lads, it's the throstle's nest of England".

For centuries, Wigton has been the centre of the business and social life of the Solway coast and plain, its prosperity being based on the weaving of cotton and linen. It has enjoyed the benefits of a Royal Charter since 1262 and the market is still held on Tuesdays. Horse sales are held every April (riding horses and ponies) and October (Clydesdales, heavy horses and ponies). Today, most of

THE ROYAL OAK HOTEL

High Street, Wigton, Cumbria CA7 9NP
Tel: 016973 44334 Fax: 016973 45304

Owner George Deans and his family have given a new lease of life to the **Royal Oak Hotel**, an 18th century building on the main street of town. All aspects have been improved, and the homely bar provides a congenial meeting place, with the usual range of drinks on offer, along with fresh home-cooked food.

With the A595 running through the town and the A596 close by, the Royal Oak is a good stopover for drivers, and Bed & Breakfast accommodation is provided in ten letting bedrooms, five of them with en suite facilities. Thursday is quiz night.

the old town is a Conservation Area and, particularly along the **Main Street**, the upper storeys of the houses have survived in an almost unaltered state. On street corners, metal guards to prevent heavy horse-drawn wagons damaging the walls can also still be seen.

One feature of the town that should not be missed is the magnificent **Memorial Fountain** in the Market Place. Its gilded, floriate panels are set against Shap granite and surmounted with a golden cross. It was erected in 1872 by the philanthropist George Moore in memory of his wife, Eliza Flint Ray, with whom he fell in love when he was a penniless apprentice. Bronze reliefs show four of her favourite charities - giving clothes to the naked, feeding the hungry, instructing the ignorant, and sheltering the homeless. The bronzes were created by Thomas Woolner, the pre-Raphaelite sculptor.

Wigton boasts a couple of interesting literary connections. Charles Dickens and Wilkie Collins stayed at The King's Arms Hotel in 1857, during the trip described in *The Lazy Tour of Two Idle Apprentices*, and the author and broadcaster Melvyn Bragg (now Lord Bragg) was born here. The town, often disguised as Thurston, features in several of his novels, and sequences for *A Time to Dance* were set and filmed in Wigton.

One mile south of Wigton are the scant remains of the Roman fort of **Olenacum**; most of its stones were removed to rebuild Wigton in the 18th and 19th centuries.

Around Wigton

Skinburness
11 miles W of Wigton off the B5302

A lively market town, in the Middle Ages, Skinburness was used by Edward I in 1299 as a base for his navy when attacking the Scots. A few years later a terrible storm destroyed the town and what survived became a small fishing hamlet. From nearby **Grune Point**, the start of the **Allerdale Ramble**, there are some tremendous views over the Solway Firth and the beautiful, desolate expanse of marshland and sandbank. Grune Point, which was once the site of a Roman fort, now forms part of a designated Site of Special Scientific Interest notable for the variety of its birdlife and marsh plants.

Abbeytown
5 miles W of Wigton on the B5302

As its name suggests, Abbeytown grew up around the 12th century **Abbey of Holm Cultram** on the River Waver and many of the town's buildings are constructed of stone taken from the abbey when it fell into ruins. Founded by Cistercians in 1150, the abbey bore the brunt of the constant feuds between the English and the Scots. In times of peace the community prospered and soon became one of the largest suppliers of wool in the North. Edward I stayed here in 1300 and again, in 1307, when he made Abbot Robert De Keldsik a member of his Council. After Edward's death the Scots returned with a vengeance and in 1319 Robert the Bruce sacked the abbey, even though his own father, the Earl of Carrick, had been buried there 15 years earlier.

The final blow came in 1536 when Abbot Carter joined the Pilgrimage of Grace, the ill-fated rebellion against Henry VIII's seizure of Church lands and property. The rebellion was put down with ruthless brutality and the red sandstone **Church of St Mary** only survived because local people pointed out that the building was necessary to provide protection against Scottish raiders. It is still the parish church and was restored in 1883, a strange yet impressive building with the original nave shorn of its tower, transepts and chancel. The east and west walls are heavily buttressed and a porch with a new roof protects the original Norman arch of the west door. Within the church buildings is a room, opened by Princess Margaret in 1973, which contains the gravestones of Robert the Bruce's father and that of Mathias and Juliana De Keldsik, relations of Abbot Robert. Nearby, there are some lovely walks along the River Waver, which is especially rich in wildlife.

Newton Arlosh

5 miles NW of Wigton on the B5307

Situated on the **Solway marshes**, the village was first established by the monks of Holm Cultram Abbey in 1307 after the old port at Skinburness had been destroyed by the sea. The village's name means 'the new town on the marsh'. Work on the church did not begin until 1393, but the result is one of the most delightful examples of a Cumbrian fortified **Church**. In the Middle Ages, there was no castle nearby to protect the local population from the border raids and so a pele tower was added to the church. As an additional defensive measure, the builders created what is believed to be narrowest church doorway in the country, barely 2ft 7in across and a little over 5ft high. The 12-inch arrow-slot east window is also the smallest in England. After the Reformation, the church became derelict but was finally restored in the 19th century. Inside, there is a particularly fine eagle lectern carved out of bog oak.

THE BIRD IN HAND

Oulton, Cumbria CA7 0NR
Tel: 01697345166

On a quiet country road just outside Oulton, **The Bird in Hand** welcomes visitors all day, every day. The 18th century inn is the first venture for John and Carole Allan, and the place is looking immaculate after total refurbishment. Good wholesome food cooked by Carole is served throughout the day until 9 o'clock in the evening, either in the bar (which has a pool table) or in the lovely 28-cover

conservatory restaurant. The Bird in Hand has a beer garden and plenty of off-road parking.

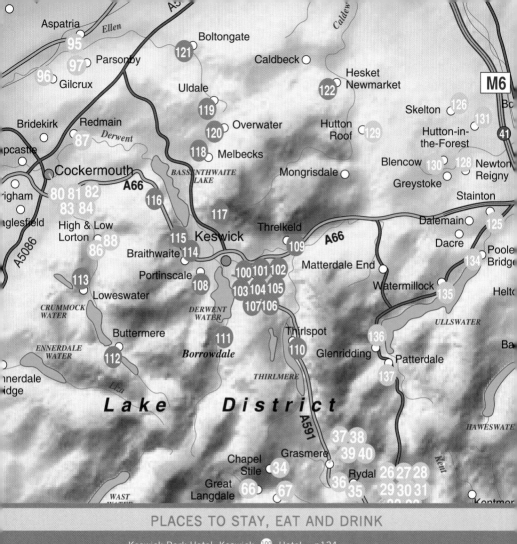

Aspatria
Ellen
95
97 Parsonby
96 Gilcrux
Bridekirk
Redmain
87 Derwent
pcastle
Cockermouth
A66
80 81 82
83 84
righam
High & Low
Lorton 88
aglesfield
86
A5086
113
Loweswater
CRUMMOCK
WATER
Buttermere
ENNERDALE
WATER
112
nnerdale
idge
Lea

Boltongate
121
Uldale
119
120 Overwater
118 Melbecks
BASSENTHWAITE
LAKE
116
117
115 Keswick
Braithwaite
114
Portinscale
108
100 101 102
103 104 105
107 106
DERWENT
WATER
111
Borrowdale

Caldew
Caldbeck
Hesket
122 Newmarket
Skelton 126
Hutton 129
Roof
Mongrisdale
Threlkeld
109 A66
Matterdale End
Thirlspot
110 Glenridding
THIRLMERE

M6
Bo
131
Hutton-in-
the-Forest
41
Blencow 130 128 Newton
Greystoke Reigny
Stainton
Dalemain
125
Dacre
Poole
134 Bridge
Watermillock
Helto
135
ULLSWATER
136
Patterdale
137
Ba

Lake District

Chapel
Stile 34
Great
Langdale 66
WAST
67

Grasmere
39 40
37 38
36
35
Rydal 26 27 28
29 30 31

A591

HAWESWATE

Kent
Kentmor

Denotes entries in other chapters

6 Keswick and the Northern Lakes

For many visitors this part of the county is classic Lakeland, the scenery dominated by the rounded, heather-clad slopes of the Skiddaw range to the north of Keswick, and the wild, craggy mountains of Borrowdale, to the south. Yet, despite this area's popularity, there are still many hidden places to discover and many opportunities to leave the beaten track.

The major town, Keswick, on the shores of Derwent Water, is a pleasant Lakeland town that has much to offer the visitor. The lake too, is interesting as, not only is it in a near

Ashness Bridge, Keswick

PLACES TO STAY, EAT AND DRINK

Denotes entries in other chapters

perfect setting, but it is unusual in having some islands - in this case four. It was the view over the lake, from Friar's Crag, that formed one of John Ruskin's early childhood memories.

However, there is much more to this part of Cumbria than scenic appeal. The area is rich in history and there is frequent and significant evidence of Roman occupation. Castlerigg Stone Circle can be found here. The industrial heritage is also important, and many of the villages in the region relied on coal mining and mineral extraction for their livelihood.

But it is the wonderful, dramatic scenery that makes this area of the Lake District so special. Not only are there several charming and isolated lakes within easy reach of Keswick, but Buttermere, considered by connoisseurs to be the best of all, lies only a few miles away. Not all the lakes, however, are what they first appear to be: Thirlmere, for example, is a 19th century reservoir constructed to supply Manchester's growing thirst.

The Lakeland Fells are home to Herdwick sheep, one of the country's hardiest breeds. Their coarse fleece cannot be dyed, but Herdwick sheep of various ages yield wool in a variety of subtle shades of grey and black which produces an unusual and very durable tweed-like weave.

Keswick

"Above it rises Skiddaw, majestic and famous, and at its door is Derwentwater, the lake beyond compare".

For generations, visitors to Keswick have been impressed by the town's stunningly beautiful setting, surrounded by the great fells of Saddleback, Helvellyn and Grizedale Pike.

Tourism, now the town's major industry, actually began in the mid-1700s and was given a huge boost by the Lakeland Poets in the early 1800s. The arrival of the railway in 1865 firmly established Keswick as the undisputed 'capital' of the Lake District with most of the area's notable attractions within easy reach.

Keswick Park Hotel

33 Station Road, Keswick, Cumbria CA12 4NA
Tel: 017687 72072 Fax: 017687 74816
e-mail: enquiries@keswickparkhotel.com
website: www.keswickparkhotel.com

The **Keswick Park Hotel** is an elegant Victorian building on a corner site a short stroll from the town centre. Resident owners Don and Tracey Rogers offer home-from-home comfort in a very pleasant, relaxed atmosphere, and the 16 well-appointed en suite bedrooms in various styles range from singles to family rooms. Breakfast in the dining room and conservatory includes both

buffet self service and table service, and a French-inspired dinner choice is served in the delightful wood-panelled restaurant. No smoking throughout.

Castlerigg Stone Circle

The grandeur of the lakeland scenery is of course the greatest draw but, among the man-made features, one not to be missed is the well-preserved **Castlerigg Stone Circle**. About a mile to the east

of the town, the 38 standing stones, some of them 8 feet high, form a circle 100 feet in diameter. They are believed to have been put in place some 4,000 years ago and occupy a hauntingly beautiful position. Beautiful, but forbidding, as evoked by Keats in his poem *Hyperion*:

A dismal cirque of Druid stones, upon a forlorn moor,
When the chill rain begins at shut of eve.
In dull November, and their chancel vault,
The Heaven itself, is blinded throughout night.

THE LAKELAND PEDLAR

Hendersons Yard, Bell Close, Keswick,
Cumbria CA12 5JD
Tel: 017687 74492
website: www.lakelandpedlar.co.uk

The Lakeland Pedlar is a delightful non-smoking, licensed café/restaurant serving an excellent range of natural, home-prepared vegetarian food. Owner Maggie Doron and her dedicated team produce a comprehensive menu of imaginative cuisine from around the world that includes sandwiches, soups, salads, pizzas, several breakfast options and Mediterranean and Tex-Mex specialities. The café, one of the most popular eating places in town, is open from 9 to 5 every day, and sometimes in the evening. The wittily named Lakeland

Pedlar is also a bicycle centre selling, repairing and hiring out bicycles.

SEVEN OAKS GUEST HOUSE

7 Acorn Street, Keswick, Cumbria CA12 4EA
Tel: 017687 72088
e-mail: info@sevenoaks-keswick.co.uk
website: www.sevenoaks-keswick.co.uk

Chris and Linda are the hands-on owners of **Seven Oaks** Guest House, a Victorian building near the centre of town. It's a particularly homely, welcoming place to stay, well decorated and furnished, and the seven comfortable bedrooms include a large family room. The tariff includes a hearty English breakfast, and evening meals are available by arrangement. Chris and Linda are keen

walkers and can point guests to the best local walks - they'll even drive them to the foot of local peaks and collect them later.

Keswick old town developed along the banks of the broad River Greta, with a wide main street leading up to the attractive **Moot Hall**. Built in 1813, the Hall has been at various times a buttermarket, courthouse and prison, Town Hall and now houses the Tourist Information Centre. A little further

Countryside around Keswick

south, in **St John's Street**, the church of that name was built in the very same year as the Moot Hall and its elegant spire provides a point of reference from all around the town. In the churchyard is the grave of Sir Hugh Walpole whose once hugely popular series of novels, *The Herries Chronicle* (1930-3), is set in this part of the Lake District.

In the riverside Fitz Park is the town's **Museum & Art Gallery** which is well worth a visit not just to see original manuscripts by Wordsworth and other lakeland poets but also for the astonishing 'Rock, Bell and Steel Band'

created by Joseph Richardson of Skiddaw in the 19th century. It's a kind of xylophone made of sixty stones (some a yard long), sixty steel bars and forty bells. Four 'musicians' are required to play this extraordinary instrument.

Surrounded by a loop of the River Greta to the northwest of the town is a museum which must be pencilled in on any visit to Keswick. This is the **Cumberland Pencil Museum**, which boasts the six feet long 'Largest Pencil in the World'. The 'lead' used in pencils (not lead at all but actually an allotrope of carbon) was accidentally discovered by a Borrowdale shepherd in the 16th

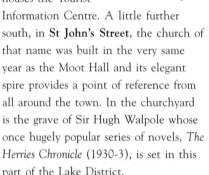

century and Keswick eventually became the world centre for the manufacture of lead pencils. The pencil mill here, established in 1832, is still operating here although the wadd, or lead, is now imported.

Other attractions in the town centre include the **Cars of the Stars Museum** (see panel on page 138), ideal for movie buffs since it contains such gems as Laurel and Hardy's Model T Ford, James Bond's Aston Martin, Chitty Chitty Bang Bang, Batman's Batmobile, Lady Penelope's pink Rolls-Royce FAB 1, the Mad Max car, and Mr Bean's Mini.

There are film set displays and vehicles from series such as *The Saint*, *Knightrider*, *Bergerac* and *Postman Pat*, and Del Boy's 3-wheel Reliant from *Only Fools and Horses* is there, too. **The Teapottery** makes and sells a bizarre range of practical teapots in the shape of anything from an upright piano to an Aga stove.

A short walk from the town centre, along Lake Road, leads visitors to the popular **Theatre by the Lake**, which hosts a year-round programme of plays, concerts, exhibitions, readings and talks. Close by is the pier from which there are

TWA DOGS INN

Penrith Road, Keswick, Cumbria CA12 4JU
Tel: 017687 72599

The **Twa Dogs** is a splendid 18th century country inn on the A591 just south of Keswick. It's very much a family affair, with leaseholders Peter and Marjorie Harding assisted by daughters Sharon and Zoe and their partners Alistair and Paul. Three real ales are always on tap in the bar, and excellent home cooking brings in the customers every lunchtime and evening. The beer garden is accessible to wheelchairs, and for guests staying overnight the inn has five pleasantly appointed en suite bedrooms. Pool

and darts are played in the games room, whose ceiling is adorned with football memorabilia.

WOODSIDE

Penrith Road, Keswick, Cumbria CA12 4LJ
Tel/Fax: 017687 73522
e-mail: ann@pretswell.freeserve.co.uk
website: www.woodside.uk.net

Very popular with walkers, cyclists and motorists touring this delightful part of the world, **Woodside** is an impressive 100-year-old property standing in an acre of attractive grounds. Ann and Norman Pretswell, here since May 2002, offer five good-quality en suite guest rooms located on two floors - a twin, three doubles and a family room. Bookings are on a Bed & Breakfast basis.

Woodside, a non-smoking establishment, is handily placed on the Penrith road out of Keswick, where the slip road off the A66 meets the A561 Windermere road.

CARS OF THE STARS MUSEUM

Standish Street, Town Centre, Keswick, Cumbria
Tel: 017687 73757

Located in the town centre, the **Cars of the Stars Museum** is definitely not to be missed by either movie buffs or devotees of vintage cars. This fascinating collection contains such gems as Laurel and Hardy's Model T Ford, James Bond's Aston Martin, Batman's Batmobile and Mr Bean's Mini.

There are film set displays and vehicles from series such as The Saint, The Prisoner, Bergerac, The Avengers, Noddy, Postman Pat and the A Team. Even Del Boy's shabby 3-wheeler Reliant van from Only Fools and Horses is here. This unique museum is open from 10am to 5pm, daily between Easter and the New Year, weekends in December, and during the February half term.

regular departures for cruises around Derwentwater and ferries across the lake to Nichol End where you can hire just about every kind of water craft, including your own private cruise boat. One trip is to the National Trust's **Derwent Island House**, an Italianate house of the 1840s on a wooded island.

Another short walk will bring the visitor to **Friar's Crag**. This famous view of Derwent Water and its islands, now National Trust property, formed one of John Ruskin's early childhood memories, inspiring in him "intense joy, mingled with awe". Inscribed on his memorial here are these words: "The first thing which I remember as an event in life was being taken by my nurse to the brow of Friar's Crag on Derwentwater." The Crag is dedicated to the memory of Canon Rawnsley, the local vicar, who was one of the founder members of the National Trust, which he helped to set up in 1895. Hardwicke Drummond Rawnsley, born at Shiplake, Oxfordshire in 1851, was a man of many parts -

THE FOUR IN HAND

Lake Road, Keswick, Cumbria CA12 5BZ
Tel: 018687 72069

The Four in Hand is a popular hostelry with a traditional appeal and a central location in Keswick. Tenants Debbie and Craig Howitt and manager Vicki brought many years accumulated experience when they arrived in September 2002, and visitors can always be sure of a friendly welcome. Five real ales head the list of drinks, and the excellent food choice runs from sandwiches and snacks to main courses that include local specialities (Cumberland sausage, Derwent game pie,

Borrowdale trout) as well as more far-flung choices such as goulash or chicken curry.

DERWENTWATER HOTEL & DERWENT MANOR

Portinscale, Nr Keswick, Cumbria CA12 5RE
Tel: 017687 72538 Fax: 017687 71002
e-mail:
info@derwentwater-hotel.co.uk
web: www.derwentwater-hotel.co.uk

Set in 16 acres of formal gardens and grounds leading down to the water's edge the **Derwentwater Hotel** is one of the best-known hotels in the Lake District, combining excellent service with great comfort and splendid food. The 48 individually styled en suite bedrooms include some with small sitting rooms and excellent views.

Local produce plays an important part in the modern British cuisine served in the non-smoking restaurant. Across from the main hotel, self-catering accommodation is available at Derwent Manor in apartments sleeping from two to six guests.

noted athlete at Balliol, writer, poet, traveller, vicar of Crosthwaite, Canon Carlisle, campaigner for the protection of footpaths. Keswick is host to several annual festivals, covering films, Cumbrian literature, jazz and beer. And on the first Sunday in December a colourful 'Christmassy' Fayre is held in the Market Place.

Around Keswick

Threlkeld

3 miles E of Keswick off the A66

From Keswick there's a delightful walk along the track bed of the old railway line to the charming village of Threlkeld, set in a plain at the foot of mighty **Blencathra**. The village is the ideal starting point for a number of mountain walks, including an ascent of Blencathra, one of the most exciting of all the Lake District mountains. Also known as Saddleback and a smaller sister

of Skiddaw to the west, the steep sides ensure that it looks every inch a mountain. Threlkeld is famous for its annual sheepdog trials though its economy was built up on the several mines in the area and the granite quarry to the south. At **Threlkeld Quarry & Mining Museum** (see panel on page 140) visitors can browse through the collection of vintage excavators, old quarry machinery and other mining artefacts, wander through the locomotive shed and machine shop, or join the 40-minute tour through a re-created mine. The museum has interpretive displays of Lakeland geology and quarrying and is used as a teaching facility by several university geology departments.

Matterdale End

8 miles E of Keswick on the A5091

This tiny hamlet lies at one end of Matterdale, a valley that an essential stop on any Wordsworth trail for it was here, on April 15th 1802, that he and his sister saw that immortal

host of golden daffodils,
Beside the lake,
beneath the trees,
Fluttering and dancing in the breeze.

Thirlmere

4 miles S of Keswick off the A591

This attractive, tree-lined lake, one of the few in the Lakes that can be driven around as well as walked around, was created in the 1890s by the Manchester Corporation. More than 100 miles of pipes and tunnels still supply the city with water from Thirlmere. At first, there was no public access to the lake shore but today these are being opened up for recreational use with car parks, walking trails and picnic places.

The creation of the huge **Thirlmere Reservoir**, five miles long, flooded the two hamlets of **Armboth** and **Wythburn** and all that remains of these places today is Wythburn chapel towards the southern end. Overlooking the narrow lake is **Helvellyn**, Wordsworth's favourite mountain and one that is also

THRELKELD MINING MUSEUM

Threlkeld Quarry, Keswick, Cumbria CA12 4TT
Tel: 017687 79747 / 01228 561883
e-mail: coppermaid@aol.com
website: www.golakes.co.uk

Entranced by the spectacular scenery of the Lake District, visitors are often unaware that in the past this was also a significant mining area. This industrial heritage is brought vividly to life at the **Threlkeld Quarry & Mining Museum** where visitors can browse through the collection of mining artefacts, wander through the locomotive shed and machine shop, or join the 40-minute tour through a re-created mine. At Threlkeld Quarry, men were employed from the 1870s until 1982 quarrying granite for railway ballast and road making, as well as producing granite setts and masonry stone. Several of the original buildings remain, including the locomotive

shed which now houses various industrial diesel locomotives which can be seen out on the track from time to time. A new acquisition to the museum is the steam locomotive Sir Thomas Callender which should be in use from June 2001.

On display in the Museum is probably the finest collection of small mining and quarrying artefacts in the North · everything from wedges, chisels and drills to candles, clogs and kibbles (large iron buckets used for conveying the ore and spoil to the surface). There's also an excellent mineral collection and in the Geology Room a fascinating table top relief map of the Lake District, enhanced by rock specimens. The Museum Shop stocks the largest selection of mining, geology and mineralogy books in the north of England, (including a second-hand section), beautiful minerals from around the world, along with gemstone jewellery and a complete range of mine exploration and caving gear.

THE KINGS HEAD HOTEL & INN

Thirlspot, Nr Keswick, Cumbria CA12 4TN
Tel: 017687 72393 Fax: 017687 72309
e-mail: stay@lakedistrictinns.co.uk
website: www.lakedistrictinns.co.uk

The Sweeney family are the long-established resident proprietors of the **Kings Head Hotel & Inn**, which enjoys a stunning location in the Lake District National Park. A coaching inn dating back some 300 years, it now offers comfortable modernised overnight accommodation in 17 single, twin and double bedrooms, all with en suite facilities. In the two dining areas (one non-smoking) a fine range of home-cooked dishes is served, from all-time favourites such as Cumberland sausage and bean casserole or Whitby scampi to chilli crab cakes, sea bass on a chive mash and grilled paprika chicken.

very popular with walkers and climbers today. At 3,116 feet, it is one of the four Lakeland fells over 3,000 feet high and the walk to the summit should not be undertaken lightly - but those reaching the summit will be rewarded with some spectacular views. The eastern aspect of the mountain is markedly different from the western as it was here that the Ice Age glaciers were sheltered from the mild, west winds.

Borrowdale

Runs S from Keswick via the B5289

"The Mountains of Borrowdale are perhaps as fine as anything we have seen" wrote John Keats in 1818. Six miles long, this brooding, mysterious valley, steep and narrow with towering crags and deep woods, is generally regarded as the most beautiful in the Lake District. Just to the south of Derwent Water are the **Lodore Falls**, where the Watendlath Beck drops some 120 feet before reaching the lake. Further along the dale, in woodland owned by the National Trust, lies the extraordinary **Bowder Stone** which provides an irresistible photo-opportunity for most visitors. A massive 50ft square and weighing almost 2,000 tons, it stands precariously on one corner apparently

Borrowdale Valley

defying gravity. A wooden staircase on one side provides easy access to the top. South of Grange village, the valley narrows into the 'Jaws of Borrowdale'. Castle Crag, the western mandible of the Jaws, has on its summit the remains of the defensive ditches of a Romano-British fort.

Just south of Rosthwaite the road turns westwards to the village of **Seatoller** where there's a National Park Information Centre and a minor road turns off to **Seathwaite**, which enjoys the unenviable reputation of being the wettest place in England with an average of 131 inches a year. Seathwaite is also the starting point for many fell walks and climbing expeditions, particularly to the Scafells and Great Gable.

From Seatoller, the B5289 slices through the spectacular **Honister Pass**, overlooked by dramatic 1,000ft high Honister Crag. At the top of the pass, the 18th century **Honister Slate Mine** has been re-opened and is once again producing the beautiful green slate that adorns so many Lakeland houses and is famous throughout the world. Buckingham Palace, The Ritz, New Scotland Yard and RAF Cranwell are among the prestigious buildings donned with this stone. Helmets and lights are provided for a guided tour through great caverns of the mine to show how a mixture of modern and traditional methods is still extracting the slate which was formed here some 400 million years ago. The monks of Furness Abbey

THE LEATHES HEAD COUNTRY HOUSE HOTEL

Borrowdale, Nr Keswick, Cumbria CA12 5UY
Tel: 017687 77247 Fax: 017687 77363
e-mail: enq@leatheshead.co.uk
website: www.leatheshead.co.uk

Standing back from the B5289 about three miles out of Keswick, the **Leathes Head Country House Hotel** is a handsome building in local slate, dating from 1908. The three acres of grounds in which it nestles make for a very peaceful and scenic ambience, and the spectacular views alone make a visit worthwhile. But the Leathes Head offers much more, and recent refurbishment by resident owners Janice and Roy Smith has enhanced the already high standards of comfort and amenity while sacrificing nothing of the Edwardian charm and elegance. The 11 guest bedrooms provide abundant space and comfort, and two on the ground floor are ideal for less mobile guests.

Another great attraction is the tremendous cooking of chef David Jackson; his daily changing menu features the very best of fresh local produce, and no diner should miss the pleasure of his wonderful desserts. Three spacious lounges and a bar are perfect spots to relax and plan trips with the guides and maps that are scattered throughout, and when the weather is fine a game of croquet or boules fills a happy hour or two. Children over 7 are welcome, but no pets please. The owners also offer self-catering accommodation in apartments in nearby Portinscale.

are thought to have been the first to avail themselves of the mine's resources, about 500 years ago. After the tour, complimentary tea or coffee is served in the Bait Cabin beside a warm fire, and the complex also has an informative Visitor Centre (honoured as the friendliest in the North of England) and a gift shop selling the ornamental green slate.

Buttermere
8 miles SW of Keswick on the B5289

Buttermere

Half the size of its neighbour, Crummock Water, Buttermere is a beautiful lake set in a dramatic landscape. To many connoisseurs of the Lake District landscape, this is the most splendid of them all. The walk around Buttermere gives superb views of the eastern towers of **Fleetwith Pike** and the great fell wall made up of High Crag, High Stile, and Red Pike.

In the early 1800s the village became involved in one of the great scandals of the age. Mary Robinson, the daughter of a local innkeeper, had been described as a maiden of surpassing beauty in J Budworth's book *A Fortnight's Ramble in the Lakes*. She became something of a local attraction with people flocking to the inn to admire her beauty, among

---

KESKADALE FARM

Newlands, Buttermere, Cumbria CA12 5TS
Tel: 017687 78544 Fax: 017687 78150
e-mail: keskadale.b.b@kencomp.net

A peaceful, relaxed holiday in a stunning Lakeland setting beckons at **Keskadale Farm**, a centuries-old farm raising beef cattle and Swaledale sheep. It has been in the Harryman family for generations, and Margaret Harryman offers Bed & Breakfast accommodation in three rooms in the oak-beamed farmhouse, and two self-catering holiday homes. A splendidly equipped apartment sleeps up to six guests, and a

luxury caravan for four stands in its own tranquil garden that commands magnificent views of the Newlands Valley and surrounding hills.

them Wordsworth and Coleridge. Another was a smooth-tongued gentleman who introduced himself as Alexander Augustus Colonel Hope, MP, brother of the Earl of Hopetoun. Mary fell for his charms and married him, only to discover that her husband was really John Hatfield, a bankrupt impostor and a bigamist to boot. Hatfield was tried at Carlisle for fraud, a capital offence in those days, and Coleridge supplemented his meagre income by reporting the sensational trial for the *Morning Post*. Hatfield was found guilty and was hanged at Carlisle gaol in 1802; Mary later married a local farmer and went on to live an uneventful and happy life. The author, broadcaster and great supporter of Cumbria, Melvyn (Lord) Bragg, tells her story in his novel, *The Maid of Buttermere*. Standing above the village is the small, picturesque **Church of St James**, where the special features of interest include an antique organ and a memorial to Alfred Wainwright.

Loweswater
10 miles W of Keswick off the B5289

Reached by narrow winding lanes, Loweswater is one of the smaller lakes, framed in an enchanting fellside and forest setting. The name, appropriately, means 'leafy lake', and eons ago it was just part of a vast body of water that

LOWESWATER HOLIDAY COTTAGES

Scale Hill, Loweswater, Nr Cockermouth, Cumbria CA13 9UX Tel/Fax: 01900 85232
e-mail:
   mike@loweswaterholidaycottages.co.uk
website: www.loweswaterholidaycottages.co.uk

Some 200 years ago, William Wordsworth stayed at the Scale Hill Inn near Loweswater and recommended it as "a roomy Inn with very good accommodation". A coaching inn dating back to 1620, Scale Hill continued to dispense hospitality to travellers through this spectacular corner of the Lake District until 1990 when its owners, the Thompson family, decided to change its role from a hotel to self-catering accommodation. They now live in the central part of the house while the wings have been converted into 2 luxurious holiday cottages, each providing every possible convenience and comfort.

   Just across the cobbled yard from the main building, the former Coach House, built in the colourful local stone, has

been imaginatively transformed into 4 beautifully furnished and decorated cottages. Two of them are on the ground floor with easy access for the disabled and all of them are well equipped with modern kitchens and colour TV. They sleep between 2 to 6 people and are available all year round. Scale Hill is ideally situated for exploring the peaceful western side of the Lake District.

   Walkers and anglers will be in their element here, so too will those who prefer just to "laze". Also available nearby are facilities for squash, tennis, sailing, paragliding and mountain biking, and there's also a trekking centre some 6 miles away and various golf courses of which the nearest is at Silloth, just 8 miles distant.

included what is now Crummock Water (see below) and Buttermere. Because it is so shallow, never more than 60 feet deep, Loweswater provides an ideal habitat for wildfowl, which also benefit from the fact that this is perhaps the

least visited lake in the whole of Cumbria. To the east of the lake lies the small village of the same name, while to the north stretches one of the quietest and least known parts of the National Park, a landscape of low fells through which there are few roads or even paths.

Crummock Water
9 miles SW of Keswick on the B5289

Fed by both Buttermere and Loweswater, this is by far the largest of the three lakes. In this less frequented part of western Cumbria, where there

Crummock Water

WHINLATTER FOREST PARK

Braithwaite, Keswick, Cumbria CA12 5TW
Tel: 017687 78469 Fax: 017687 78049
e-mail: Rangers@whinlatter.demon.co.uk

The only Mountain Forest in England, **Whinlatter Forest Park** is also one of the Forestry Commission's oldest woodlands, providing a whole range of outdoor activities. The best place to start is at the Visitor Centre which has a wealth of information about the work of the Lakes Forest District and staff who will be happy to help you plan your day in the forest. Visitors can also book a forest classroom or a forest discovery walk with the Rangers. There's a shop and tea room here, with a terrace overlooking the woodlands and valley, an adventure playground close

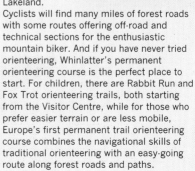

by and the Centre is also the starting point for several trails suitable for the whole family. The trails are clearly waymarked to provide easily followed routes taking in some spectacular views across the fells and forests of North Lakeland.

Cyclists will find many miles of forest roads with some routes offering off-road and technical sections for the enthusiastic mountain biker. And if you have never tried orienteering, Whinlatter's permanent orienteering course is the perfect place to start. For children, there are Rabbit Run and Fox Trot orienteering trails, both starting from the Visitor Centre, while for those who prefer easier terrain or are less mobile, Europe's first permanent trail orienteering course combines the navigational skills of traditional orienteering with an easy-going route along forest roads and paths.

are few roads, the attractions of Crummock Water can usually be enjoyed in solitude. Best seen from the top of Rannerdale Knotts, to the east, the lake has a footpath running around it though, in places, the going gets a little strenuous.

Braithwaite

3 miles W of Keswick on the B5292

This small village lies at the foot of the **Whinlatter Pass**, another of Cumbria's dramatic routes. The summit of this steep road, the B5292, is some 1043 feet above sea level and, on the westerly descent, there are magnificent views over Bassenthwaite Lake. The road runs through the **Whinlatter Forest Park** (see panel on page 145), one of the Forestry Commission's oldest woodlands, which has a Visitor Centre, trails and walks for all ages and abilities, an orienteering course, adventure playground, viewpoints, gift shop and a tearoom with a terrace overlooking the woodlands and valley. Many of the record numbers who visited the centre in 2002 came to see live footage of the Lake District ospreys beamed to a viewing

THE COTTAGE IN THE WOOD

Whinlatter Forest, Braithwaite, Nr Keswick, Cumbria CA12 5TW
Tel: 017687 78409 Fax: 017687 78064
e-mail: enquiries@thecottageinthewood.co.uk
website: www.thecottageinthewood.co.uk

'A tranquil gem in an area of outstanding natural beauty' is how the owners describe **The Cottage in the Wood**. Liam and Kath Berney, who came here in June 2002, are justly proud of their 17th century former coaching inn, which stands by the B5292 Braithwaite to Cockermouth road in Whinlatter Pass.

Ten excellent en suite bedrooms, two of them on the ground floor, are decorated and furnished with style and taste, and all make the most of the stunning views. Another asset is the fine cooking of professional chef Liam. There's a single sitting (7 o'clock in the winter, 7.30 in the summer) every evening except Monday, and Liam's four-course menu is based on regional and continental dishes using fresh seasonal produce. Vegetarian and special diets can be catered for, and the meals are accompanied by well-chosen wines; non-residents are welcome.

The Cottage in the Wood offers almost instant access to the many attractions of

Whinlatter Forest, the only mountain forest in Britain. And in the hotel's own garden a wide variety of wildlife can be spotted, including red squirrels and numerous species of birds. Viewing points for the famous Bassenthwaite ospreys are nearby.

facility or to see the birds through high-powered telescopes at the Dodd Wood viewing point. **The Lake District Osprey Project** is a partnership of the Forestry Commission, the Lake District National Park Authority and the RSPB whose aim is to protect the nesting ospreys and to encourage others to settle and breed in other suitable locations.

Bassenthwaite Lake

Bassenthwaite Lake
4 miles NW of Keswick on the A66

Here's one for the Pub Quiz: Which is the only lake in the Lake District? Answer: Bassenthwaite, because all the others are either Waters or Meres. Only 70 feet deep and with borders rich in vegetation, Bassenthwaite provides an ideal habitat for birds - more than 70 species have been recorded around the lake. Successful breeding is encouraged by the fact that no power boats are allowed on the lake and some areas are off limits to boats of any kind. Also, most of the shoreline is privately owned, with public access restricted mostly to the eastern shore where the Allerdale Ramble follows the lakeside for a couple of miles or so.

At the northern end of the lake, at Coalbeck Farm, **Trotters World of Animals** is home to many hundreds of animals - rare breeds, traditional farm favourites, endangered species, birds of prey and reptiles. In addition to the ring-tailed lemurs, wallabies, racoons and gibbons, 2002 saw the arrival of rough-coated lemurs, lechwe antelope, red, fallow and sika deer and guanaco. Visitors to the 25-acre site can bottle-feed baby animals, cuddle bunnies, meet Monty the python, take a tractor trailer ride, watch the birds of prey demonstrations, find a quiet picnic spot or sample the fare on offer in Trotters Tea Room. And for the smaller children there's an indoor soft play climbing centre. Trotters was the winner of the Good Britain Guide 2002 Cumbria Family Attraction of the Year. As a member of the National Association of Farms for Schools, the farm can cater for school groups either for an informal day out or for a structured programme based on National Curriculum requirements.

Rising grandly above Bassenthwaite's eastern shore is **Skiddaw** which, ever since the Lake District was opened up to tourists by the arrival of the railway in

THE PHEASANT

Bassenthwaite Lake, Nr Cockermouth,
Cumbria CA13 9YE
Tel: 017687 76234 Fax: 017687 76002
e-mail: info@the-pheasant.co.uk
website: www.the-pheasant.co.uk

Visitors from all over the world come to stay at **The Pheasant**, which enjoys a truly magnificent setting in 40 acres of formal gardens and woodland. The buildings date back more than 500 years, and the timeless elegance and understated luxury have gained a reputation that is second to none. Top-class accommodation is provided in 13 individually decorated bedrooms which have been sympathetically refurbished to the

highest standard. Beautiful fabrics and antique furniture create a unique atmosphere, and all the rooms have private bathrooms with both bath and shower; tea tray facilities and telephones are provided, and portable televisions can be supplied on request. Adjacent to the main hotel building are three Garden Lodge rooms where guests can bring their dogs.

The reputation of The Pheasant does not rest solely on its accommodation, as it has also established an enviable name for outstanding hospitality. The bar, where the renowned huntsman John Peel enjoyed many a pint, is one of the best known in the Lake District, and the panelled walls, the exposed beams, the oak settles and the polished parquet floors create a wonderfully welcoming ambience in which to enjoy a convivial glass or two of real ale from Bass,

Theakston or the local Jennings Brewery. The local artist Edward Thompson was a man with a large thirst but a small pocket, and a licensee of the time took payment in the form of two watercolours which still hang in the bar. Light lunches can be taken in the bar and lounges (also the setting for a traditional afternoon tea), while full lunches and dinners are served in the non-smoking dining room. A typical dinner menu of three or four courses brings skill and imagination to the finest fresh produce, much of it local, in such main courses as seared canon of lamb with a Jerusalem artichoke and garlic confit, or poached lemon sole on buttered spinach with a fennel and chervil cream and truffle cappuccino. Coffee and petits fours are served in the lounge.

The Pheasant, which is signposted on the A66 midway between Keswick and Cockermouth, is owned and run by Matthew and Barbara Wylie, who spent many years working in the Scottish Highlands before taking over the reins of this outstanding hostelry. Hogmanay and Burns Night call for special celebrations at The Pheasant, but for any lucky guest staying here any day is special.

the 19th century, has been one of the most popular peaks to climb. Although it rises to some 3,054 feet, the climb is both safe and manageable, if a little unattractive lower down, and typically takes around two hours. From the summit, on a clear day, there are spectacular views to Scotland in the north, the Isle of Man in the west, the Pennines to the east, and to the south the greater part of the Lake District.

Also on the eastern shore is the secluded, originally Norman, **Church of St Bridget & St Bega** which Tennyson had in mind when, in his poem *Morte d'Arthur*, he describes Sir Bedivere carrying the dead King Arthur:

"to a chapel in the fields,
A broken chancel with a broken cross,
That stood on a dark strait of barren land".

This then would make Bassenthwaite Lake the resting place of Excalibur but, as yet, no one has reported seeing a lady's arm, "clothed in white samite, mystic, wonderful", rising from the waters and holding aloft the legendary sword.

Set back from the lakeside, **Mirehouse** is a 17th century building which has been home to the Spedding family since 1688. Literary visitors to the house included Tennyson, Thomas Carlyle, and Edward Fitzgerald, the poet and translator of *The Rubaiyat of Omar Khayyam*. As well as some manuscripts by these family friends, there is also a fine collection of furniture and visitors can wander around the wildflower meadow, the walled garden and the lakeside walk. The gardens are open daily from April to October but the house, because it is still a family home, is only open on Sunday and Wednesday afternoons during the season, and also on Friday afternoons during August.

Uldale
11 miles N of Keswick off the A591

To the northeast of Bassenthwaite Lake stretches the area known locally as the 'Land Back of Skidda', a crescent of fells and valleys constituting the most northerly part of the Lake District

BROADWATER HOUSE

Under Skiddaw, Nr Keswick, Cumbria
CA12 4PZ
Tel: 017687 72084

Jean and Emyr Green, both formerly professional singers, have lived at **Broadwater House** since the early 1980s, and from the summer of 2003 they will have two rooms available for Bed & Breakfast guests. One room is en suite, the other has a private bathroom, and both make the most of the stunning location overlooking the Derwent Valley. The breakfast room and lounge also command superb views, and the house, which

was built in 1937 in the style of a Californian ranch house, stands in six acres of lovely grounds. No smoking in the house.

MELBECKS COTTAGES

Melbecks, Bassenthwaite, Nr Keswick,
Cumbria CA12 4OX
Tel: 017687 76065 Fax: 017687 76869
e-mail: info@lakelandcottages.co.uk
website: www.lakelandcottages.co.uk

Melbeck Cottages enjoy a superb setting commanding panoramic views of Bassenthwaite Lake and the surrounding fells, with Skiddaw and Ullock Pike providing a spectacular backdrop. The self-catering cottages have been stylishly and imaginatively converted from a large Grade II listed barn and are fitted and furnished to a very high standard.

All the cottages have fully equipped kitchens, tv, video recorders and access to a large video library. They share a large garden

ample space for ball games and for exercising well-behaved dogs. The cottages sleep from 2 to 7 guests and can be booked throughout the year. Some of them accept children, and dogs can be accommodated by arrangement. The smallest cottage, with an open-plan studio bedroom, is 'Randel', a converted byre detached from the main barn. It takes its name from a crag high on the side

and a games room with table tennis, table football, a pool table and several board games. Each cottage has its own parking space, and a small copse frequented by red squirrels provides a safe and exciting place for children to play.

A meadow in front of the cottages gives

of Skiddaw. 'Dodd', 'Dash' and 'Skiddaw' each sleep four, while the most recent conversion, 'Uldale', has three bedrooms - a double with en suite bathroom, a double with a four-poster bed and a twin with an additional single bed should it be required.

The setting is beautifully secluded, and in this prime walking country many trails are right on the doorstep. The village pub is only a short walk away; Dash Falls are a little further, the forest trails in Dodd Wood a three-mile drive, and the lovely town of Keswick is 7 miles distant. In addition to the Melbecks Cottages, the owners Jo and David Burton run an agency that takes bookings for another 50 or so cottages within the Northern Lakes region, mainly in the Borrowdale and Newlands areas. The smallest are cosy retreats for two, the largest have space for up to ten.

THE SNOOTY FOX

Uldale, Cumbria CA7 1HA
Tel: 01697 371479 Fax: 01697 371910

A pretty village in the heart of John Peel country is the charming setting of the **Snooty Fox**, whose name and decor reflect the local hunting traditions. This popular inn, which dates back to before 1700, is the first venture into the licensed trade for John and Pat Barker, who are expanding both the local and the tourist trade.

Fresh meat and fish are the basis of the daily changing menus, and the excellent food is complemented by super real ales and a good wine selection. For overnight guests the inn has three attractive en suite bedrooms.

National Park. This peaceful region is well off the tourist track and offers visitors a delightful landscape of gently undulating bare-backed fells and valleys sheltering unspoilt villages such as Uldale. Horace Walpole featured Uldale and its moorland surroundings in two of his *Herries Chronicle* novels, *Judith Paris* and *The Fortress*. The village boasts a friendly traditional pub, The Snooty Fox, and a Victorian school which now houses the **Northern Fells Gallery** where a wide range of work by Cumbrian artists - watercolours, jewellery, copperwork, ceramics, knitwear and woodcarvings - can be seen, all available

to buy. This tranquil village has one small claim to fame: it was the daughter of an Uldale farmer who eloped with and married the legendary huntsman John Peel (see Caldbeck).

Caldbeck
13 miles N of Keswick on the B5299

Caldbeck is perhaps the best-known village in the northern Lakes because of its associations with **John Peel**, the famous huntsman who died in 1854 after falling from his horse and is buried in the churchyard here. His ornate tombstone is decorated with depictions

OVERWATER HALL HOTEL

Overwater, Ireby, Nr Keswick,
Cumbria CA7 1HH
Tel/Fax: 017687 76566
e-mail: welcome@overwaterhall.co.uk
website: www.overwaterhall.co.uk

Overwater Hall is a distinguished 18th century country mansion in a beautiful, peaceful location two miles from Bassenthwaite Lake. Hosts Angela and Adrian Hyde and Stephen Bore welcome guests in the most civilised of surroundings, and the 11 individually furnished en suite bedrooms offer every comfort; top of the range are two Superior rooms, new for 2003, with luxurious bathrooms, plus two splendid Turret rooms.

The morning starts with a full Cumbrian breakfast, and a day spent walking and exploring the local sights will build up an appetite for afternoon tea, a drink in the Piano Bar and Adrian's superb five-course dinners.

BOLTONGATE OLD RECTORY

Boltongate, Cumbria CA7 1DA
Tel: 01697 371647
e-mail: boltongate@talk21.com
website: boltongateoldrectory.com

A 14th century pele tower is the oldest part of **Boltongate Old Rectory**, which sits among mature, rambling gardens with a little pond and stream a short drive from the A595 Cockermouth-Carlisle road. David and Gill Taylor offer comfortable, characterful guest accommodation in three delightful bedrooms with en suite or private facilities, and residents have the use of two lounges, one with tv, the other with views of the garden and beyond. Breakfast provides plenty of choice, and evening meals are available by arrangement. The rectory is a non-smoking establishment.

of hunting horns and his favourite hound. Also buried here are John Peel's wife Mary and their four children. John Peel was Master of Hounds for over 50 years and was immortalised by his friend John Woodcutt Graves, who worked in a Caldbeck mill making the grey woollen cloth mentioned in the song, "D'ye ken John Peel with his coat so grey?" The tune itself is based on an old Cumbrian folk song adapted by William Metcalfe, a chorister and organist at Carlisle Cathedral.

A few paces from Peel's tomb lies 'The Fair Maid of Buttermere', mentioned earlier, whose grave bears her married name, Mary Harrison. With its picturesque church, village green, cricket pitch, pond and blacksmith's forge, Caldbeck has all the ingredients of a picture postcard village. There has been a **Church** here since the 12th century, one of only eight in England to be dedicated to St Kentigern. The other seven are also to be found in the north of Cumbria, where Kentigern, a bishop in the Strathclyde area of Scotland who was also known as Mungo, spent his time in exile.

Some 200 years ago Caldbeck was an industrial village, with corn mills, woollen mills, and a paper mill all powered by the fast-flowing 'cold stream' - the Caldbeck. **Priest's Mill**, built in 1702 by the Rector of Caldbeck, next to his church, was a stone grinding corn mill, powered by a waterwheel which has now been restored to working order. It is open to the public and has an accompanying Mining Museum and a collection of old rural implements. The mill buildings are also home to a gift shop and craft workshops.

About a quarter of a mile outside the village is the limestone gorge known as **The Howk**, a popular beauty spot where the Caldbeck rushes past the restored ruins of one of the old bobbin mills.

Hesket Newmarket

13 miles N of Keswick off the B5305

Set around a well-kept village green, this pleasing little village used to have

DENTON HOUSE

Hesket Newmarket, Nr Caldbeck,
Cumbria CA7 8JG Tel: 016974 78415
e-mail: dentonhnm@aol.com

In the heart of the unspoilt village of Hesket Newmarket, **Denton House** is an ideal base for touring the Lakes or Borders, or for an energetic holiday in the stunning surrounding countryside. The family run business, here for more than 30 years, has added up-to-date amenities to their spacious 17th century end-of-terrace house and guests do not lack for comfort in the seven letting bedrooms (all with en suite or private facilities) or the sitting

room. Appetising home cooking and packed lunches can be provided. There is a Real Ale pub next door and the beer is brewed right behind Denton House.

its own market, as the name suggests, and much earlier there was probably also a racecourse here since that is what Hesket meant in Old Scandinavian. It could well be the reason why the village's main street is so wide. Although the market is no longer held, Hesket hosts two important agricultural events each year: an Agricultural Show and Sheepdog Trials. There's also a vintage motor cycle rally in May. Charles Dickens and Wilkie Collins stayed at Hesket Newmarket in the 1850s and wrote about it in their *Lazy Tour of Two Idle Apprentices*. In a converted barn at the back of the Old Crown pub, **Hesket Newmarket Brewery** was set up in 1988, and beer sales, which at first limited to the pub, soon spread across Cumbria. Many awards have come the way of Hesket Newmarket beers, which include Skiddaw Special Bitter, the nearly black Great Cockup Porter and the pale but potent Catbells Pale Ale. On Wednesday and Thursday evenings brewery tours, followed by a meal at the Old Crown, can (must) be booked in advance - Tel: 016974 78288.

Mungrisdale

7 miles NE of Keswick off the A66

The name of the village comes from Mungo, the name by which St Kentigern was known by those close to him, and the village church, not surprisingly, is dedicated to him. Though **St Kentigern's Church** is believed to have been established here as early as AD552, the present building dates from 1756 and contains a fine example of a 17th century triple-decker pulpit. A memorial on the church wall reveals an intriguing connection with Wordsworth. The tablet commemorates Raisley Calvert whose son, also called Raisley, was "nursed by Wordsworth". The younger Raisley was a sculptor and friend of the poet but fell ill of consumption (tuberculosis). Wordsworth spent many hours by his bedside in Penrith hospital but Raisley passed away in 1795, leaving in his will the huge sum of £900 to his friend. The bequest was timely and enabled the poet to complete with his friend Coleridge the seminal poems that were published in 1798 as the *Lyrical Ballads*.

Keswick and the Northern Lakes

PLACES TO STAY, EAT AND DRINK

The Purple Sage Restaurant, Penrith	123	Restaurant	p156
Station Hotel, Penrith	124	Hotel	p158
Rheged Discovery Centre, Stainton, Penrith	125	Discovery Centre	p159
The Dog & Gun Inn, Skelton, Penrith	126	Pub with Food	p160
The Stoneybeck Inn, Bowscar, Penrith	127	Pub with Restaurant	p161
The Sun Inn, Newton Reigny, Penrith	128	Pub, Restaurant and Accommodation	p161
Carrock Cottages, Hutton Roof, Penrith	129	Self Catering	p162
Little Blencowe Farm, Blencowe, Penrith	130	B&B	p163
Upfront Gallery & Coffee Shop, Hutton-in-the-Forest	131	Gallery and Coffee Shop	p163
The Crown Hotel, Eamont Bridge, Penrith	132	Hotel	p164

Denotes entries in other chapters

7 In and Around Penrith

Penrith is the most historic of Lakeland towns and was almost certainly settled long before the Romans arrived. They quickly appreciated its strategic position on the main west coast artery linking England and Scotland and built a fort nearby, although nothing visible of it remains today. Most of the town's oldest buildings have also disappeared, victims of the incessant Border conflicts down the centuries. Penrith today is a busy place, its location close to the M6 and within easy reach not only of the Lakes but also the Border Country and the Yorkshire Dales making it a hub of this northwestern corner of England.

Only a few miles from the town, Ullswater, eight miles long and the

Ullswater Lake

PLACES TO STAY, EAT AND DRINK

● Denotes entries in other chapters

THE PURPLE SAGE RESTAURANT

8 St Andrew's Church Yard, Penrith,
Cumbria CA11 9QT
Tel: 01768 895555
website: www.purplesage.info

The Purple Sage Restaurant is located in a charming 300-year-old house by the splendid Church of St Andrew. Since taking over as owners in 2002, Martin and Jan Strand have made it one of the region's most popular eating places, highly praised by both local residents and visitors to the town, and warmly

recommended by many of the local guest houses and Bed & Breakfast establishments. Martin is an experienced and very talented chef and his menus make mouthwatering reading. Results on the plate fully live up to expectations, whether it's a simple daytime snack or a three- or four-course evening meal. The daytime choice runs from toasted teacakes, sandwiches (made with white, wholemeal, granary, treacle or cheese bread), jacket potatoes and salads to bacon & egg pie, pasta carbonara, chicken with Bury black pudding and baked salmon with lemon mayonnaise. Typical dishes on the main evening menu might be gratin of natural smoked haddock, seared fillet of sea bass with green beans and a vanilla-infused sauce, and a chef's daily recommendation such as roast loin of rabbit with spinach, Parma ham, dauphinoise potatoes and rich game juices. Delicious home-made desserts set the seal on a truly memorable meal. The Purple Sage is a very cosy and characterful spot, with 20 covers downstairs (used mainly during the day) and 40 upstairs, which is a non-smoking area. Such is the popularity of the Purple Sage that booking is necessary at the weekend and also for the themed food evenings, which take place about six times a year, and for the bargain three-course menu served every Wednesday evening. This really top-grade restaurant is open Tuesday to Saturday, from 10 to 2.15 for coffees, light snacks and bar meals, and from 6.30 to 8.45 for evening meals. Outside catering and private functions can also be arranged. The neighbouring Church of St Andrew is well worth a visit, both for the treasures inside and for the churchyard with the strange group of gravestones known as Giant's Grave.

second longest lake in Cumbria, is also one of its most beautiful. The area around Penrith has some interesting old buildings, notably Shap Abbey and Brougham Castle, as well as two outstanding stately homes, Hutton-in-the-Forest where the Inglewood family have lived since 1605, and Dalemain, a fine mixture of medieval, Tudor and Georgian architecture which has also been inhabited by the same family for more than 300 years. Sadly, Greystoke Castle, which according to Edgar Rice Burroughs was the ancestral home of Tarzan, is not open to the public.

Penrith Castle

Penrith

In Saxon times Penrith was the capital of the Kingdom of Cumbria but after the Normans arrived the town seems to have been rather neglected - it was sacked several times by the Scots before **Penrith Castle** was finally built in the 1390s. The much-maligned Richard, Duke of Gloucester (later Richard III), strengthened the castle's defences when he was Lord Warden of the Western Marches and was responsible for keeping the peace along the border with Scotland. By the time of the Civil War, however, the castle was in a state of ruin. The Cromwellian General Lambert demolished much of what was left and the townspeople helped themselves to the fallen stones to build their own houses. Nevertheless, the ruins remain impressive, standing high above a steep-sided moat.

A short walk from the castle leads to the centre of this lively town with its charming mixture of narrow streets and wide-open spaces, such as **Great Dockray** and **Sandgate**, into which cattle were herded during the raids. Later they became market places and a market is still held every Tuesday.

Penrith has a splendid Georgian church in a very attractive churchyard, surrounded by a number of interesting buildings. The oldest part of **St Andrew's Church** dates from Norman times but the most recent part, the nave, was rebuilt between 1719 and 1772, possibly to a design by Nicholas Hawksmoor. Pevsner described it as "the stateliest church of its time in the county". Of particular interest is the three-sided gallery and the two chandeliers which were a gift from the Duke of Portland in 1745 - a reward for the town's loyalty during the Jacobite

Market Square, Penrith

high, and four 10th century hogback tombstones which have arched tops and sharply sloping sides. They have clearly been deliberately arranged but their original purpose is no longer known. According to a local legend the stones mark the burial place of a 5th century King of Cumbria, Owen Caesarius. Also buried somewhere in the churchyard is Wordsworth's mother, but her grave is not marked.

Overlooking the churchyard is a splendid Tudor house, bearing the date 1563, which is now a restaurant but was, at one time, Dame Birkett's School. The school's most illustrious pupils were William Wordsworth, his sister Dorothy, and his future wife, Mary Hutchinson. William is also commemorated by a plaque on the wall of the Robin Hood Inn stating that he was a guest there in 1794 and again in 1795.

Rising. A tablet on the wall records the deaths of 2,260 citizens of Penrith in the plague of 1597.

The church's most interesting feature however, is to be found in the churchyard, in the curious group of gravestones known as **Giant's Grave** - two ancient cross-shafts, each 11 feet

Other notable buildings in the town include the **Town Hall**; this is the result of a 1905 conversion of two former Adam-style houses, one of which was known as Wordsworth House as it was the home of the poet's cousin, Captain

STATION HOTEL

Castlegate, Penrith, Cumbria CA11 7JB
Tel: 01768 866714

The **Station Hotel** is an impressively large red sandstone building that has been a familiar landmark near the station in the town centre since 1898. Inside, there's a huge amount of space and a very traditional Northern feel, and owners David and Karen Reynolds welcome a wide cross-section of locals to enjoy their hospitality, a convivial drink (food planned soon) and perhaps a game of pool or darts.

For guests from further afield the Station Hotel has nine good letting bedrooms, all with en suite facilities.

John Wordsworth. Penrith's latest and most spectacular visitor attraction, **Rheged Discovery Centre** (see panel below), opened in Easter 2000 and dedicates itself to "a celebration of 2000 years of Cumbria's history, mystery and magic - as never seen before". Named after Cumbria's Celtic Kingdom, this extraordinary grass-covered building is also home to Britain's only exhibition dedicated to mountains and mountain adventure. It also has a giant cinema screen, speciality shops, pottery demonstrations, an artists' exhibition, restaurants and a children's play area.

The town is dominated by **Beacon Hill Pike**, which stands amidst wooded slopes high above Penrith. The tower was built in 1719 and marks the place where, from 1296, beacons were lit to warn the townsfolk of an impending attack. The beacon was last lit during the Napoleonic wars in 1804 and was seen by the author Sir Walter Scott who was visiting Cumberland at the time. Seeing it prompted Scott to hasten home to rejoin his local volunteer regiment. It is well worth the climb from the Beacon Edge, along the footpath to the summit, to enjoy a magnificent view of the Lakeland fells. It was on top of this hill, in 1767, that Thomas Nicholson, a murderer, was hanged. The gibbet was left on the summit and so was Nicholson's ghost, seen in the form of a skeleton hanging from the noose. The

RHEGED DISCOVERY CENTRE

Redhills, Stainton, Penrith,
Cumbria CA11 0DX
Tel: 01539 441164

Penrith's latest and most spectacular visitor attraction, **Rheged Discovery Centre,** opened in Easter 2000 and dedicates itself to "a celebration of 2000 years of Cumbria's history, mystery and magic - as never seen before". Open all year round, the Centre is housed in the largest earth-covered building in Britain, and is carefully designed to blend harmoniously with the surrounding fells. Although it is built on 7 levels, from the outside Rheged looks like just another Lakeland hill. Inside, babbling

brooks and massive limestone crags replicate the Cumbrian landscape but the centrepiece is a 6-storey high, giant cinema screen, 60ft wide and 48ft high, on which is shown a specially commissioned film, *The Lost Kingdom*, which relates the story of the ancient Kingdom of Cumbria which once extended from Strathclyde in Scotland to Cheshire. Only a couple of minutes drive from Exit 40 of the M6, Rheged also offers visitors a retail shopping street, a useful information centre, special exhibitions, and restaurants and coffee shops which specialise in local delicacies and also provide panoramic mountain views.

THE DOG & GUN INN

Skelton, Nr Penrith, Cumbria CA11 9SE
Tel: 017684 84301

The very popular **Dog & Gun Inn** stands at the crossroads in the attractive village of Skelton, its immaculate cream-and-green

supplemented by daily specials listed on the blackboards, which also show the day's desserts and the choice of wines by the bottle. The menu changes regularly, combining classic pub favourites with more unusual dishes that take their inspiration from around the world. Traditional roasts are the centrepiece of Sunday lunch, with the regular menu taking over in the evening. An excellent meal could finish with home-made desserts or a tempting selection of ice cream creations, then perhaps a special liqueur coffee to round things off in style.

Skelton is located off the B5305 (Junction 41 of the M6), a few miles northwest of Penrith. The Dog & Gun is well worth

frontage giving way to a delightfully traditional and welcoming interior. Dating back at least 300 years, it was originally called the Drovers Inn, as it stood beside a drovers road and provided rest and refreshment for drovers taking their flocks to sell at the market in Carlisle.

Today, owned and run by Ashleigh Hunt and her mother-in-law Patricia, it remains very much at the heart of village life, open Saturday, Sunday and Monday lunchtimes and every evening for the sale of drinks and food. The family, who brought many years' experience in the food and beverage industry when they took over in May 2002, do all the cooking, and their printed menus are

the short detour for motorway drivers and an excellent place for tourists to pause for refreshment. This is good walking country, and there are several places of interest in the village itself or within a short drive. Ashleigh and Patricia are ready to take care of the thirstiest and hungriest of visitors.

red sandstone from which many of Penrith's Victorian houses were built was quarried along the escarpments of Beacon Edge, and one of the old quarries, at **Cowraik**, is now a local nature reserve. In addition to the interesting variety of wildlife established down the years, it is a Site of Special Scientific Interest for the geological interest of the quarry faces. The rocks are the remnants of sand dunes formed 250 million years ago when the Eden Valley was part of a dry, sandy desert that started just north of the Equator.

Around Penrith

Hutton-in-the-Forest
6 miles N of Penrith on the B5305

The home of the Inglewood family since 1605, Hutton-in-the-Forest was originally a medieval stronghold and the **Pele Tower** still exists. The house has been added to and altered by successive generations, with the result that an unusual number of architectural and decorative styles can be seen. Among the notable features are the 17th century Gallery, the Hall dominated by a Cupid

THE STONEYBECK INN

Bowscar, Nr Penrith, Cumbria CA11 8RP
Tel: 01768 862369

Arriving as licensees in March 2003, Cameron Miller and Tracey Issolt have quickly found their feet at **The Stoneybeck Inn**. Dating from the early 18th century and once a well-known posthouse on a coaching route, it is now a splendid free house open every session and all day on Saturday and Sunday for the service of two real ales and a good range of other drinks. In the two spacious dining rooms (one is non-smoking) Cameron's home cooking covers an across-the-board menu supplemented by a daily specials list. The inn

has a small caravan/camping site with showers, toilets and electric hook-ups.

THE SUN INN

Newton Reigny, Nr Penrith, Cumbria CA11 0AP
Tel: 01768 867055
e-mail: dixond@tinyworld.co.uk

In a picture postcard village a few miles northwest of Penrith, **The Sun Inn** is a popular, traditional free house owned and run by Dennis Dixon. A fine selection of real ales will please anyone who loves a good pint, and in the 60-cover non-smoking restaurant Audrey Walker produces a good choice of appetising dishes on an à la carte menu that is supplemented by daily specials. The Sun also boasts five quality en suite letting

bedrooms that are open throughout the year. The inn has a large off-road car park and a beer garden leading down to the River Petteril.

CARROCK COTTAGES

How Hill, Hutton Roof, Nr Penrith,
Cumbria CA11 0XY
Tel: 017684 84111 Fax: 017684 88850
e-mail: info@carrockcottages.co.uk
website: www.carrockcottages.co.uk

In a tranquil, scenic setting among the Lakeland Fells, **Carrock Cottages** offer an ideal choice for a holiday, whether it's a relaxing break, a tour of the Lake District or an energetic few days walking or cycling. The owners, Malcolm and Gill Iredale, are the designers, the builders and the hands-on resident hosts at the cottages, which they have brilliantly converted from stables and

byres dating back to Tudor times. Each of the properties provides all the modern home comforts, including underfloor heating, a fully fitted kitchen and sitting room with tv and DVD player. yet they still retain their original rustic character with exposed oak beams, stone window frames and wood-burning stoves. 'Kirsty Cottage' has a double bedroom with en suite bathroom; 'Hannah Cottage' has three double bedrooms and a well-equipped tiled bathroom; 'Kyla Cottage' also has three double bedrooms, while the largest, 'Great Carrock', has no fewer than six double bedrooms, two full bathrooms, two separate living rooms and two fully equipped kitchens. This is an ideal choice for large families or for two families or groups of friends. Outside the cottages is a grassed area for soft ball games or other recreational activities.

Full week accommodation is available from Easter to the end of October, and short breaks are available all year. There's ample space for parking cars or even small boats, secure storage for bikes and stabling for guests who want to bring their horse or pony. A wet weather games room to include pool and table tennis will be available along side a games console, barbecue equipment and an extensive library of DVDs. The owners also offer a unique food service, with traditional farmhouse cooking delivered to the cottage door. The choice includes soup, pâté, main courses such as salmon with dill sauce, chicken & gammon pie, beef lasagne and vegetable cobbler, with sticky toffee pudding among the desserts. All the meals are fully prepared and in some cases partly cooked and come with full instructions for final preparation. Carrock Cottages are easily reached from either the M6 (leave at Junction 41) or the A66. On the approach to the properties, Carrock Fell provides a dramatic backdrop, and the owners' Highland cattle graze contentedly by the drive.

LITTLE BLENCOWE FARM

Blencowe, Nr Penrith, Cumbria CA11 0DG
Tel: 017684 83338 Fax: 017684 83054
e-mail: bart.fawcett@ukgateway.net

In a pleasant rural setting northwest of
Penrith, **Little Blencowe Farm**, a working
Dairy and Sheep farm recently restocked after
foot and mouth, offers homely Bed &
Breakfast accommodation in a friendly,
traditional ambience. Tom Fawcett, who was
born on the 270-acre farm, and his wife
Barbara have three letting rooms, one of them
with a private shower room, the other two
sharing facilities. Breakfast, with eggs from
the resident hens and excellent locally

sourced bacon and sausages, is a treat to look
forward to on the farm, which lies on the
Coast to Coast cycle route.

staircase, and a room decorated in the
Arts and Crafts style. The splendid
grounds include a beautiful walled
garden built in the 1730s, topiary
terraces that were originally laid out in
the 17th century, and fine specimen
trees and a 17th century dovecote that
form part of the Woodland Walk.

Greystoke
5 miles W of Penrith on the B5288

According to Edgar Rice Burroughs,
Greystoke Castle was the ancestral
home of Tarzan, Lord of the Apes, a
fiction which was perpetuated in the
1984 film *Greystoke*. Tarzan's aristocratic

UPFRONT
GALLERY & COFFEE SHOP

Nr Hutton-in-the-Forest, Penrith,
Cumbria CA11 9TG
Tel: 017684 84538 Fax: 017684 84187
e-mail: john-f.parkinson@btinternet.com
website: www.upfront.co.uk

Upfront Gallery is the brainchild and
creation of the Parkinson family, Elaine, John
and their daughter Holly, who opened the
premises to the public in 1997. Set in 2½
acres of picturesque grounds, it occupies a
beautifully converted 17th century barn and
presents a changing programme of
exhibitions in
four
individual
gallery
spaces. The
themes of the
exhibitions,
which last
about six

weeks, cover a
wide cross-
section of the
arts.
The gallery has
a shop area
where a unique
range of goods
are for sale,
including
original works
by local
craftspeople. In
the Coffee Shop, a tempting selection of
vegetarian food and delicious cakes is served
throughout the day. Visitors can enjoy eating
either in the main gallery or in the
conservatory overlooking the garden
courtyard. The Gallery and the Coffee Shop
are open from 10am to 5pm and are closed
on Monday except for Bank Holidays.

The owners run a small, select adjacent
Caravan Club site with electric hook-ups for
up to five touring caravans; they also have
three well-equipped static holiday caravans
which are available for hire.

THE CROWN HOTEL

Eamont Bridge, Nr Penrith,
Cumbria CA10 2BX
Tel/Fax: 01768 892092
e-mail: thecrownhotel@msn.com

The Crown Hotel is a very handsome black and white painted building standing on the main A6 at Eamont Bridge, a mile south of Penrith town centre. Built in 1770 as a coaching inn, it offers today's visitors the very best in food, drink and accommodation, along with friendly hospitality from affable owner Wendy Graham-Weston and bar manager Richard. Wendy is a super cook,

(one per adult) eat free from their own special menu. Pride of place on display in the 50-seat non-smoking restaurant is a 126lb blue marlin which Wendy caught off the Kenyan coast.

Overnight accommodation at this deservedly popular inn consists of 13 upstairs rooms ranging from singles to family rooms; six have en suite facilities. All are available throughout the year and can be booked on a Bed & Breakfast or Dinner, Bed & Breakfast basis. The Crown has a games and children's room, a beer garden and a capacious car park. Its position on the A6, with the M6 just a short drive away, makes it an ideal base for a touring holiday. But there's plenty of interest virtually on the doorstep: a delightful walk along the River Eamont leads to the prehistoric Mayburgh Earthwork and to the imposing remains of Brougham Castle. Also on the banks of the river is Giant's Cave, the supposed lair of a man-eating giant called Isir.

and with the help of an excellent team in the kitchen she produces an appetising choice of home-cooked dishes.

The main menu includes steaks, Cumberland sausage, battered cod, haddock with a prawn and mushroom filling, spare ribs, the very popular lamb Henry (marinated in mint) and giant Yorkshire pudding filled with beef, turkey or sausage. Lovers of chicken dishes are particularly well catered for with a choice of roast, Kiev, curry, korma, tikka masala and sweet & sour. Baguettes, burgers, pizzas and jacket potatoes make up the snack menu, and food is available daily from 11am to 3pm and from 6pm to 10pm, and all day at the weekend and on Bank Holidays. Over-60s enjoy a 50% discount on main meals at lunchtime Monday to Saturday, when children

credentials would have come as something of a surprise to the dignified Barons of Greystoke whose effigies are preserved in **St Andrew's Church**. As imposing and spacious as a cathedral, St Andrew's boasts a wonderful east window with much 13th century glass and, in the Lady Chapel, a figure of the Madonna and Child carved by a German prisoner-of-war.

About 100 yards from the church stands the **Plague Stone** where, during medieval times, coins were left in vinegar in exchange for food for the plague victims. An ancient **Sanctuary Stone**, now concealed behind a grille, marks the point beyond which fugitives could claim sanctuary.

Around the time of the American War of Independence, Greystoke Castle was bought by the 11th Duke of Norfolk, a staunch Whig who delighted in annoying his dyed-in-the-wool Tory neighbour, the Duke of Portland. Portland of course detested the American rebels, so Norfolk built two curious castle/farmhouses close to Portland's estate, and named them Fort Putnam and Bunkers Hill after the two battles in which the British had been trounced. Norfolk displayed a similarly elegant disdain for one of his tenants, a religious bore who maintained that church buildings were an abomination. The Duke built a medieval-looking farmhouse for him and crowned it with a very ecclesiastical spire. The Greystoke Castle Estate is open throughout the year, offering a wide variety of outdoor activities, from falconry and fly casting to clay target shooting, off-road driving and quad bike safaris.

Greystoke village itself is a gem, its attractive houses grouped around a trimly maintained village green. Nearby are the stables where Gordon Richards trained his two Grand National winners, Lucius and Hello Dandy.

Brougham
1 mile SE of Penrith off the A66

About a mile southeast of Penrith, the substantial and imposing remains of **Brougham Castle** (English Heritage) stand on the foundations of a Roman fort. The castle was inherited in the 1640s by the redoubtable and immensely rich Lady Anne Clifford, whose patrimony as Countess of Pembroke, Dorset and Montgomery also included another six northern castles. She spent a fortune restoring them all in medieval style and when told that Cromwell had threatened to destroy them replied "As often as he destroys them I will rebuild them while he leaves me a shilling in my pocket". Brougham was her favourite castle and she died here in 1676 at the age of 86. From the castle there's a delightful riverside walk to **Eamont Bridge** and the circular **Mayburgh Earthwork**, which dates from prehistoric times. On the huge embankment, more than 100 yards across, stands a single, large stone about 10 feet high. Close to the village, on the

HORNBY HALL

Brougham, Nr Penrith, Cumbria CA10 2AR
Tel: 01768 891114
e-mail: enquire@hornbyhall.co.uk
website: www.hornbyhall.co.uk

Hornby Hall is a beautiful Grade II listed country house built of local red sandstone in about 1550. The decor and furnishings are exceptional, and many period features distinguish the day rooms and bedrooms. The latter comprise five main rooms, with two smaller single rooms reached up a spiral stone staircase in the tower. The tariff includes a very generous breakfast, and packed lunches and evening meals can be provided with notice. Dry fly trout fishing can be arranged, and owner Ros Sanders can make the whole house available for private house parties and shooting parties.

banks of the River Eamont, is **Giant's Cave**, the supposed lair of a man-eating giant called Isir. This local tale is linked with the legend of Tarquin, a giant knight who imprisoned 64 men in his cave and was eventually killed by Sir Lancelot. Some people also claim that Uther Pendragon, King Arthur's father, lived here and that he too ate human flesh. A nearby prehistoric earthwork has been known as **King Arthur's Round Table** for many centuries. Lady Anne also rebuilt the chapel that stands on a hill above the castle, next to Brougham Hall. The Hall's colourful history goes back 500 years and its fame reached its height in the Victorian age, when, with its splendid appearance and its royal associations, it was dubbed the 'Windsor of the North'. The Hall today is home to a number of shops, craft workshops and even a brewery. The chapel, dedicated to St Wilfred, contains a remarkable collection of items acquired by William Brougham, later the 2nd Baron Brougham and Vaux; notable

among them are French and Flemish stalls from the 16th and 17th centuries. The old parish church of Brougham is the remotely located **St Ninian's**, also known as Ninekirks, which contains some family box pews that are screened so that they look almost like cages.

Stainton
2 miles W of Penrith off the A66 or A592

At Stainton, off the A592, **The Alpaca Centre** was set up in 1997 and has become a focal point for the development and expanding knowledge of the alpaca. The Centre is a working farm, breeding, rearing and selling alpacas and welcomes visits at any time of the year. Visitors can see the alpacas in their paddocks, and browse through the goods in the Spirit of the Andes shop, mostly made from the exceptional alpaca fibre. Also at the centre are a tea room and a gallery with a collection of furniture and ornamental pieces in wood.

Tirril

2 miles SW of Penrith on the B5320

Like its neighbour, Yanwath, Tirril has connections with the Quaker Movement. At Tirril there is an old **Quaker Meeting House** (now in private ownership), while **Yanwath Hall**, reputed to be the finest manorial hall in England, was the birthplace of the Quaker Thomas Wilkinson. Modern Yanwath also boasts an interesting gallery, located in a cottage garden setting. **Laburnum Ceramics** is dedicated to contemporary ceramics and glass, and, small though it is, over the course of a year exhibits the work of some 100 different artists. In addition to the ceramics, there are displays of original paintings, prints, textiles and turned wood.

Dalemain

3 miles SW of Penrith off the A592

Dalemain House is one of the area's most popular attractions - an impressive house with a medieval and Tudor core fronted by an imposing Georgian façade. The house has been home to the same family since 1679 - Sir Edward Hasell bought the property in that year - and over the years they have accumulated fine collections of china, furniture and family portraits. The grand drawing rooms boast some very fine

oak panelling and in the Chinese Room is some beautifully preserved 18th century Chinese wallpaper and a rococo chimneypiece by Nathaniel Hedges in Chinese Chippendale style; visitors also have access to the Nursery (furnished with toys from all ages) and Housekeeper's Room. The Norman pele tower houses the regimental collection of the Westmorland and Cumberland Yeomanry, a troop of mounted infantry which the Hasell family usually led, while the 16th century Great Barn contains an interesting assortment of agricultural bygones. The extensive grounds include a medieval herb garden, a Tudor-walled knot garden with a fine early Roman fountain, a wild garden alongside Dacre Beck, a deer park, and woodland and riverside walks.

Dacre

4 miles SW of Penrith off the A66

There is much of historic interest in this village. The **Church** occupies a site of a former monastery which was mentioned by the Venerable Bede in his accounts of

Dacre Castle

Cumberland in the 8th century. A later reference shows that in 926 the Peace of Dacre was signed between Athelstan of England and Constantine of Scotland. Fragments of masonry are reputed to have come from the monastery and the four weather-beaten carvings of bears in the churchyard are probably of Anglo-Viking origin. The bears are shown, respectively, sleeping, being attacked by a cat, shaking off the cat and eating the cat.

A 14th century pele tower, **Dacre Castle** (in private hands) is a typical example of the fortified house or small castle that was common in northern England during the Middle Ages. This was the seat of the Dacre family, Catholic Earls of Cumberland, and its turrets and battlements have walls which are 8 feet thick. Leonard Dacre took part in the ill-fated Rising of the North in 1589 and, some time later, the estate passed to the Earls of Sussex who restored the castle in 1675 and whose coat of arms can still be seen.

Pooley Bridge
5 miles SW of Penrith on the B5320

In Wordsworth's opinion Ullswater provides "the happiest combination of beauty and grandeur, which any of the Lakes affords", an opinion with which most visitors concur. The poet also noted the curious fact that the lake creates a sextuple echo, a natural phenomenon that the Duke of Portland exploited in the mid-1700s by keeping a boat on the lake equipped "with brass guns, for the purpose of exciting echoes".

The charming village of Pooley Bridge stands at the northern tip of **Ullswater**, and there are regular cruise departures from here during the season, stopping at Glenridding and Howton. Rowing and powered boats are available for hire, and since Ullswater is in effect a public highway, private boats can also be launched. A speed limit of 10mph applies over the whole of the 8-mile-long serpentine lake. Also, the greater part of the shoreline is privately owned and landing is not permitted.

The oldest building in Pooley Bridge is part of **Holly House**, which dates back to 1691, while the Bridge of the

Ullswater Lake

THE SUN INN

Pooley Bridge, Nr Penrith,
Cumbria CA10 2NN
Tel: 017684 86205 Fax: 017684 86913
e-mail: michaeljane66@btopenworld.com

Developed from a row of cottages dating from the early 18th century, the **Sun Inn** is a favourite local meeting place and a very pleasant place for tourists to visit. The inn fully lives up to its name, being one of the most friendly and cheerful hostelries in the region, and in owner-chef Mike Long it has one of the most popular landlords. For overnight guests, it has nine en suite bedrooms (all non-smoking) ranging from singles to a family room. A fine selection of

Jennings ales is served in the characterful bars, and Mike makes excellent use of fresh local produce in his bar and restaurant meals, which are available every lunchtime and evening.

village's name dates from 1763 when the elegant structure over the River Eamont was built at a cost of £400. At that time, a regular fresh fish market was held in the village square. Before Bridge was added, the name Pooley meant 'pool by the hill' and was derived from the pond which existed behind **Dunmallard**, the cone-shaped hill on the other side of the River Eamont. Above the village, on the summit of Dunmallard, are the remains of an Iron Age fort and, of course, splendid views, southwards over Ullswater.

Watermillock

7 miles SW of Penrith on the A592

This small village, perfectly situated on the shores of Ullswater, is hidden amongst the woodland which occupies much of the lake's western shores. About 4 miles southwest of the village, there are a series of waterfalls which tumble down through a wooded gorge and then into Ullswater. The name of the largest fall is **Aira Force** (70 feet high) and the second largest is **High Force**. They can easily be reached on foot through the

MELLFELL HOUSE FARM COTTAGES AND B&B

Watermillock-on-Ullswater, Cumbria CA11 0LS
Tel/Fax: 017684 86295
e-mail: ben@mellfell.co.uk
website: www.mellfell.co.uk

Traditional barns next to a 17th century farmhouse have been converted to provide high-quality self-catering accommodation in six cottages sleeping from 4 to 8 guests. **Mellfell House Farm** sits high on the slopes of Little Mellfell overlooking Ullswater, and though no longer a working farm, the grounds

are home to a variety of farm and domestic animals. The area offers walking both gentle and strenuous and many other activities. Ben and Diane Goddard can provide en-suite Bed & Breakfast accommodation in the farmhouse. They also have a cottage sleeping six people in the nearby village of Dacre.

woodlands of **Gowbarrow Estate**, which is owned by the National Trust. This famous waterfall, which can be viewed from stone bridges at top and bottom, was the setting for the romantic and tragic story of Emma, who fell in love with a renowned knight called Sir Eglamore. He had to leave her to follow the Crusades. As the months lengthened into years and he had not returned, Emma became so distraught that she started to sleepwalk to Aira Force where she eventually met her tragic death. On his return, the grief-stricken Sir Eglamore became a hermit and lived by the waterfall for the rest of his days.

Brothers Water, Patterdale

Glenridding
14 miles SW of Penrith on the A592

A popular base for walkers about to tackle the daunting challenge of **Helvellyn** (3,115ft), Glenridding is the largest and busiest of Ullswater's lakeside villages. Lake cruises depart from here, rowing boats are available for hire and there's plenty of room for waterside picnics.

Patterdale
15 miles SW of Penrith on the A592

It is this village's magnificent setting that makes it such a popular tourist destination. Close to the head of

---

GREYSTONES COFFEE HOUSE

Glenridding, Penrith, Cumbria CA11 0PA
Tel: 017684 82392 Fax: 017684 82122
e-mail: info@greystonescoffeehouse.com
web: www.greystonescoffeehouse.com

By a fast-moving stream that runs through the heart of the village, **Greystones Coffee House** serves a day-long selection of quality baking and tasty hot and cold lunches. The recently renovated 100-year-old building incorporates a contemporary art gallery featuring the work of local artists, Greystones also offers wireless broadband Internet access. Owners Julian and

Nicola Sharman also run a well-stocked general store in the village and offer self-catering accommodation. Greystones lies on the A592 Penrith-Windermere road.

THE WHITE LION INN

Patterdale, Nr Penrith, Cumbria CA11 0NW
Tel: 017684 82214

Dating back to the first decade of the 19th century, the **White Lion Inn** enjoys a spectacular location a short drive up from Kirkstone Pass at the southern end of Ullswater. In those early years stagecoach horses were changed and passengers took rest and refreshment before the long pull through the rugged countryside to Windermere, and that tradition of hospitality is carried on in fine style by leaseholders Mac and Rita. In the handsomely appointed bar, with its black beams, flagstones and brass counter rails, Marston Pedigree and Castle Eden head an excellent choice of beers, and Mac prepares a good selection of appetising dishes for the printed menu and specials board.

Among the favourites are sizzling steaks, chicken curry, traditional fish & chips and lamb Henry cooked in a mint marinade; desserts include a scrumptious home-made fruit pie. For a quick snack, the inn serves a variety of made-to-order sandwiches. The surrounding area is one of great natural beauty, and the White Lion is a very pleasant base for a walking or touring holiday. Five attractive en suite double or twin bedrooms are available throughout the year, along with two smaller single rooms.

Ullswater and with a series of fells framing the views, the scenery is indeed splendid. On the north side of the village is **St Patrick's Well**, which was thought to have healing properties, and the medieval chapel dedicated to the saint was rebuilt in the 1850s.

Clifton

3 miles S of Penrith on the A6

One of the last battles to be fought on English soil took place at nearby **Clifton Moor** in December 1745. Bonnie Prince Charlie was in retreat and his exhausted troops were easily routed by the English forces. Eleven soldiers were killed and are buried in Clifton churchyard, but some of the wounded Highlanders were hanged from the Rebels' Tree on the outskirts of the village. The tree is a sorry sight nowadays with its gaunt, dead branches but it is still a place of pilgrimage for the Scots.

To the southeast of the village is **Wetheriggs Country Pottery**, which was founded in 1855. Visitors can try their hand at the often messy business of throwing a pot, paint a pot, paint on glass and make a candle, and also take a conducted tour of the steam-powered pottery, the only one of its kind in the UK. The pottery was scheduled as an Industrial Monument in 1973, and its steam engine was restored by none other than Fred Dibnah, the famous steeplejack. The pottery has a tearoom, several shops and a pond that is home to three types of newt.

BECKFOOT HOUSE

Helton, Nr Penrith, Cumbria CA10 2QB
Tel: 01931 713241 Fax: 01931 713391
e-mail: info@beckfoot.co.uk
website: www.beckfoot.co.uk

Dating from Victorian times, **Beckfoot House** once stood at the heart of a working farm. For 25 years it has been the home of Lesley and David White, who offer spacious, well-appointed guest accommodation in seven en suite bedrooms that include a four-poster room. The drawing room is a perfect spot to unwind, and there's a separate room with tv and games, and an oak-panelled dining room where breakfast and suppers are served. The house is set in three acres of lovely grounds surrounded by superb walking country.

Askham

3 miles S of Penrith off the A6

Askham is a pleasant village set around two greens. In the centre of the village is one of its most interesting shops, the **Toy Works**, which combines a traditional toy shop with a toymaker's workshop. Special services include advice on restoring rocking horses and a repair service 'for ailing and worn old teddy bears'. **Askham Fell**, which rises to the west, is dotted with prehistoric monuments including one known as the Copt (or Cop) Stone which is said to mark the burial site of a Celtic chieftain. On the edge of the village is **Askham Hall** (private), now the home of the head of the Lonsdale family, who abandoned Lowther Castle in 1936 and moved here.

Lowther

4 miles S of Penrith off the A6

Lowther Castle is now only a shell, most of it having been demolished in 1957, but it was clearly once a grand place; after one visit Queen Victoria is reputed to have said that she would not return to the castle as it was too grand for her. The ancestral owners of the castle were the illustrious Earls of Lonsdale, a family of statesmen and sportsmen. The most famous is perhaps the 5th Earl (1857-1944), known as the Yellow Earl because

Askham Church and Mausoleum

LOWTHER HORSE DRIVING TRIALS AND COUNTRY FAIR

Lowther Estate Office, Penrith,
Cumbria CA10 2HG
Tel: 01931712378
e-mail: drivingtrials@lowther.co.uk
website: www.lowther drivingtrials.co.uk

Carriage drivers and up to 60,000 spectators from across the country and abroad converge at Lowther, near Penrith in the Lake District to compete in this prestigious three day celebration of the countryside, every year. Running annually over three days, the Friday, Saturday and Sunday of the first full weekend in August, the Lowther Horse Driving Trials and Country Fair promises visitors a spectacular programme of events. Gripping

competitions, main arena attractions, interactive displays and entertaining shows combine to offer something for the whole family.

The acclaimed Country Fair provides exhibitions and demonstrations from every country pursuit, including falconry, poultry shows, horse shoeing, carving, ferret racing, fox hound and terrier shows, hunter pony competitions, hound trails, archery and fly

casting. The much acclaimed and over subscribed Shopping Village, where many people actually come to buy Christmas presents as the choice and quality is so high, boasts the very best in country and fashion wear, local food and produce, guns, fishing rods, cars and country vehicles. For those who need to sit and soak up the Lowther Experience, the various popular Band's will serenade you while you enjoy a drink, food or ice cream!

However, it is the elegance and excitement of the horse driving trials that makes Lowther the show it has grown to be today. Following the pattern of horse eventing, and with courses that are among the most challenging on the driving calendar, there are three days of skill and daring by the very top drivers from Europe. Friday's Dressage is held in the Main Area that utilises the natural amphitheatre below the façade of Lowther Castle by the River Lowther, whilst the Saturday Cross Country takes place in the spectacular estate of the Earl of Lonsdale, much of which boasts breathtaking views over Ullswater. The Sunday Obstacle Driving finale returns to the Main Arena. Here, with drivers and carriages turned out in immaculate style, they re-create the splendour of a past age and what must have been a daily occurrence when the famous Yellow Earl was resident in Lowther Castle.

In and Around Penrith

of the colour of the livery used on his private carriage. He was the first President of the Automobile Association and permitted his family colours to be used by that organisation. The Earl was also a patron of amateur boxing and the Lonsdale Belt emerged from his interest. The yellow flag of the Lonsdales can be

seen in Lowther Church.

Lowther village itself was built in the 1680s by Sir John Lowther, who moved his tenants here to improve the view from the new house he was building. He also built **St Michael's Church** where several generations of the Lowthers are buried in a series of magnificent tombs

LAKELAND BIRD OF PREY CENTRE

Lowther, Nr Penrith, Cumbria CA10 2HH
Tel: 01931 712746

The centre is a sanctuary for birds of prey, set in the walled garden and parkland of Lowther Castle. Visitors can see a large collection of eagles, hawks, falcons and owls from around the world. The aim of the centre is to conserve birds of prey through education, breeding and caring for injured and orphaned birds before releasing them back to the wild. There is also a tearoom as well as regular courses and lectures.

beginning with a medieval style alabaster monument to Sir Richard who died in 1608. Fashions in funerary sculpture continue through the obligatory skull of the late-17th century to the grandiose representation of the 1st Viscount Lonsdale who sits nonchalantly nursing his viscount's coronet. Later monuments show a moustachioed Henry, Earl of Lonsdale, in military garb, and a charming Pre-Raphaelite plaque to Emily, wife of the 3rd Earl, who is depicted with her favourite dog at her feet.

Bampton
8 miles S of Penrith off the A6

For several hundred years this small village was well known for its **Grammar School**, two of whose pupils rose swiftly in the church hierarchy. One was Hugh Curwen, who as a Protestant became Chaplain to Henry VIII, as a Catholic under Queen Mary was elevated to the Archbishopric of Dublin, and then prudently re-embraced Protestantism when Elizabeth succeeded to the throne. Another Bampton boy was less pliable: Edmund Gibson was baptised in the church here in 1669 and later became a fiery Bishop of London who repeatedly denounced the degenerate morals of the age - with little apparent effect.

A couple of miles south of Bampton, **Haweswater** is the most easterly of the lakes. It is actually a reservoir, created in the late 1930s to supply the growing needs of industrial Manchester. Beneath the water lies the village of **Mardale** and several dairy farms for which Haweswater Valley was once famous. By 1940, the lake had reached its present extent of 4 miles and Manchester Corporation set about planting its shores with conifers and today the area is managed as a nature reserve. Walkers have a good chance of seeing woodpeckers and sparrowhawks, buzzards and peregrine falcons, and with luck may even catch sight of golden eagles gliding on the thermals rising above Riggindale. An observation is manned throughout the breeding season if the eagles are nesting.

Haweswater Beck

The Abbey stands about a mile to the west of the village, just inside the National Park, and it's well worth seeking it out to see the imposing remains of the only abbey founded in Westmorland; the only one in the Lake District mountains; the last abbey to be consecrated in England (around 1199) and the last to be dissolved, in 1540. Henry VIII's Commissioners seem to have been especially thorough in their demolition of the Abbey and local builders continued the depredations. But the mighty west tower and some of the walls

Above Haweswater runs the **High Street**, actually a Roman road, which is now one of the most popular fell walks in the Lake District. It overlooks the remote and lovely Blea Tarn and the lonely valley of Martindale, a cul-de-sac valley to the south of Ullswater, where England's last remaining herd of wild red deer can often be seen.

Shap
10 miles S of Penrith on the A6

This small village on the once congested A6 enjoys some grand views of the hills. In coaching days Shap was an important staging post for the coaches before they tackled the daunting climb up **Shap Fell** to its summit some 850 feet above sea level. Much earlier, in medieval times, the village was even more significant because of nearby **Shap Abbey**, constructed in the local Shap granite which has been used in many well-known buildings, St Pancras Station and the Albert Memorial in London among them.

Shap Abbey

remain, and they enjoy a lovely setting - secluded, tranquil and timeless.

From the Abbey there's a pleasant walk of well under a mile to **Keld**, a tiny village of just 17 houses. So quiet today, in medieval times Keld was a busy little place servicing the monks of Shap Abbey nearby. It was the monks of Shap Abbey who built the village's oldest building, the early-16th century **Keld Chapel** (National Trust). After the closure of the Abbey, the chapel fell on hard times and for two hundred years was used as a dwelling house - that's when the incongruous chimney was added. In 1860 it was 'serving as a cow-house' but was saved from this ignominious role in 1918 by the National Trust. A service is held in the tiny chapel once a year in August; at other times, a notice on the chapel door tells you where you can obtain the key.

Maulds Meaburn
11 miles SE of Penrith off the A6

This charming village in the Lyvennet Valley has a large green through which the river flows, crossed by footbridges and stepping stones. As well as a fine collection of 17th and 18th century cottages, there is also an early 17th century Hall.

Orton
15 miles S of Penrith on the B6260

By far the best approach to Orton is along the B6290 from Appleby to Tebay. This scenic route climbs up onto the

CRAKE TREES MANOR

Maulds Meaburn, Nr Penrith,
Cumbria CA10 3JG
Tel: 01931 715205 Mob: 017968 744305
e-mail: ruth@craketreesmanor.co.uk
website: www.craketreesmanor.co.uk

Crake Trees Manor is a beautifully restored 18th century barn conversion halfway between the lovely villages of Maulds Meaburn and Crosby Ravensworth. It's a spectacular setting for a holiday, with meadows and pasture all around and views of the Eden Valley and the Pennines beyond. Local materials and local skills were used in the creation of the five superb bedroom suites, two of them on the ground floor and all with en suite facilities, central heating, drinks trays, locally made toiletries, tv, radio/cd player and information

about the locality. Stylishly decorated and furnished, they all enjoy wonderful views.

The owners Mike and Ruth Tuer and their children Laura, William and India run a traditional mixed farm here, and guests are welcome to watch the activities of the changing seasons. A hearty farmhouse breakfast gets the day off to a fine start, and an excellent supper is served at 7 o'clock each evening. Both meals are prepared by Ruth and can be served in the dining room or in the bedrooms. The surrounding villages and countryside are well worth exploring, and there's splendid walking on the paths and byways of this very lovely part of Cumbria.

moors, passing **Thunder Stone**, some mighty limestone bluffs and the pavements of **Great Asby Scar**, the setting for BBC-TV's *The Tenant of Wildfell Hall*. As motorists descend the side of Orton Scar, grand views open up of the Howgills and the Lune Gorge with the Shap Fells looming on the horizon.

A village now ("one of the prettiest in Westmorland" according to one writer), for centuries Orton was a market town of some consequence with a charter granted in the 13th century by Edward I and a licence to hold fairs accorded by the puritan Oliver Cromwell. There are reminders of Orton's former importance in the noble church tower, completed in 1504; in the attractive proportions of **Petty Hall**, an Elizabethan house at the lower end of the village, (a private residence, incidentally); and the grandeur of **Orton Hall**, built in 1662 and now converted into holiday apartments.

Orton's most famous visitor was Bonnie Prince Charlie, on his way northwards after the crushing defeat of his troops at Derby. He was followed soon afterwards by the Duke of Cumberland, 'Butcher' Cumberland, the victor of the Battle of Culloden. The Duke may have stayed in the village at an inn which was later re-named the Cumberland Hotel. The Inn, dating from 1632, still stands in the centre of the village although it is now a private house.

To the north there is some superb limestone scenery and the village stands below **Orton Scar**, on which a beacon was lit to warn people to seek safety from advancing Scottish raiders. The village church, in common with many in the Eden Valley, has a massive 16th century tower that was built for defensive purposes and, presumably, was one place that the villagers sought shelter. Its features include an ancient oak parish chest and a stained glass window by Beatrice Whistler, wife of the American artist James McNeill Whistler. Orton was the birthplace of George Whitehead (1636-1723) who, along with George Fox, was one of the founders of the Quaker Movement.

Tebay
17 miles S of Penrith, by Exit 38 of the M6

At one time a sheep farming area and a railway settlement, this long rambling village now owes its importance to the arrival of the M6 motorway, Cumbria's main thoroughfare. The village was the home of Mary Baynes, the **Witch of Tebay**, who died in 1811 at the age of 90. She is said to have foretold the coming of fiery horseless carriages speeding across Loups Fell where, today, the London to Glasgow railway line runs. Greatly feared by the people of Tebay, she is said to have withered and died at the same time as some eggs on which she had put a curse were fried in boiling fat.

PLACES TO STAY, EAT AND DRINK

● Denotes entries in other chapters

8 The Eden Valley and East Cumbria

The River Eden is entirely Cumbrian and is one of the few large rivers in England that flows northwards. The source of the river is on the high limestone fells above Mallerstang Common, near the North Yorkshire border, and it runs to the outskirts of Carlisle where it turns sharply east and flows into the Solway Firth. For much of its course, the river is accompanied by the famous Settle to Carlisle Railway, a spectacularly scenic route saved from extinction in the 1960s by the efforts of local enthusiasts.

Carved through boulder clay and red sandstone and sandwiched between the Lakeland fells and the northern Pennines, the Eden Valley is green and fertile - in every sense another Eden. But the valley was vulnerable to Scottish raids in medieval times and the number of pele towers and castles in the area are testament to a turbulent and often violent past.

This, too, is farming country and many of the ancient towns and villages have a market place.

Appleby-in-Westmorland, the old county town of Westmorland, had an important market and also an annual horse fair which continues today and has gained a large following.

An attractive man-made feature of the valley is the collection of specially commissioned stone sculptures known as Eden Benchmarks dotted along its length. Each created by a different sculptor, they have been located beside public paths and, since they also function as seats, provide the perfect setting in which to enjoy the valley's unspoilt scenery. There are 10 of them in all, beginning with Mary Bourne's *Water Cut*, an intriguing limestone sculpture, shaped rather like a

Eden Valley

tombstone riven from top to bottom by a serpentine space representing the river. It stands on Lady Anne's Way, a public path along the eastern ridge of the Mallerstang Fells.

Kirkby Stephen

Surrounded by spectacular scenery, the old market town of Kirkby Stephen lies at the head of the beautiful Eden Valley. It was the Vikings who first established a village here and they named it 'Kirke and Bye'. Although essentially part of the Eden Valley, Kirkby Stephen has a strong Yorkshire Dales feel about it. Indeed, the church, with its long, elegant nave, has been called the Cathedral of the Dales.

Dating from Saxon times, rebuilt in 1220 and with a 16th century tower, **St Stephen's Church** is one of the finest in the eastern fells, dominating the northern end of the town from its elevated position. Until the last century the **Trupp Stone** in the churchyard received money from local people every Easter Monday in payment of church tithes and, at eight o'clock, the curfew is still sounded by the **Taggy Bell**, once regarded by local children as a demon. Inside the church are a number of pre-Conquest stones, some of which show Norse influence. The most remarkable is the 10th century **Loki Stone**, one of only two such carvings in Europe to have survived. Loki was a Norse God and presumably Viking settlers brought their belief in Loki to Kirkby Stephen. The carving of Loki shows a figure resembling the Devil with sheep's horns, whose legs and arms are bound by heavy irons, an image symbolising the overpowering of paganism by Christian beliefs. For many years the stone lay undiscovered, reused as a building stone. The church also boasts some interesting memorials, among them the Elizabethan tomb of Thomas, Lord Wharton and his two wives, and the earlier memorial to Sir Richard de Musgrave of Hartley Castle who died in the early 1400s. Sir Richard was the man reputed to have killed that last boar upon Wild Boar Fell, and the story was given credence

THE PENNINE HOTEL

Market Square, Kirkby Stephen,
Cumbria CA17 4QT
Tel: 017683 71382 Fax: 017683 72686
e-mail: kirkbyjohn7354@aol.com

For nearly 300 years the handsome building that houses the **Pennine Hotel** has been a familiar landmark in the heart of Kirkby Stephen, and since the autumn of 2002 it has been in the very capable hands of John and Jean Redmond. Bright, spotless and very welcoming, it serves as a comfortable hotel, a fine restaurant and a popular place to meet for a drink and a chat. Blackboards list an impressive choice of traditional dishes cooked by Jean, and in summer food is served from breakfast onwards. Guest accommodation comprises seven bedrooms, some with en suite facilities.

Kirkby Stephen

most important product of the town and a restored spinning gallery reflects the importance of the woollen industry.

There are many delightful walks from the town, to **Croglam Earthworks** for example, a prehistoric fort, or to nearby Stenkrith Park where the second of the **Eden Benchmarks** can be found. Created by Laura White in Ancaster limestone and titled *Passage*, the sculpture is deceptively simple, suggesting perhaps the course of a river bed. There are also some pleasant strolls along the riverside to a fine waterfall where the River Eden cascades into Coop Karnel Hole. Look out for the unusual shapes of the weathered limestone rock. For more strenuous exercise, walkers could tackle a stretch of the **Coast to Coast** long distance footpath, which passes through the town.

when, some years ago, the tomb was opened to reveal the bones of a man and woman alongside two tusks from a boar. The splendid pulpit, given by the town in memory of a much-loved vicar, is made of Shap granite and Italian marble.

Between the church and the market square stand the cloisters, which served for a long time as a butter market. The **Market Square** is surrounded by an ancient collar of cobblestones which marked out an area used for bull-baiting - a 'sport' that ceased here in 1820 after a disaster when a bull broke loose. The market, still held every Monday, has existed since 1351 and has always been a commercial focus for the surrounding countryside. In the 18th century, knitting - mostly of stockings - was the

Around Kirkby Stephen

Outhgill

5 miles S of Kirkby Stephen on the B6259

This remote village has close links with the Clifford family of Skipton Castle, North Yorkshire. The village **Church of St Mary**, first built in 1311, was repaired by Lady Anne Clifford who, from 1643 when she finally obtained possession of the Clifford estates, devoted her life to restoring her many properties and lived in each of them for varying periods of time. Her estates included six castles - Skipton and Barden in Yorkshire; Appleby, Brough, Brougham and Pendragon in Westmorland. Lady Anne's zeal for restoration didn't stop at castles: she also repaired the Roman road between Wensleydale and the Eden Valley, a route she often travelled (along with a huge retinue) between her castles and her birthplace at Skipton. The route is now known as Lady Anne's Way but in times past it was aptly called the **High Way** since it was a regular place of employment for highwaymen such as Dick Turpin and William 'Swift' Nevison.

The landscape around Outhgill is remote and beautiful. To the south is **Wild Boar Fell**, a brooding, flat-topped peak where the last wild boar in England was reputedly killed, while tucked down in the valley are the romantic ruins of Lammerside and Pendragon Castles.

Pendragon Castle, about a mile north of the village, is shrouded in legend but there are claims that it was the fortress of Uther Pendragon, father of King Arthur. If so, nothing remains of that 6th century wooden castle. The present structure dates from the 1100s and was built by Hugh de Morville, one of the four knights who murdered Thomas à Becket, to guard the narrow pass of **Mallerstang**. Twice it was burned by the Scots and twice restored, on the latter occasion by the formidable Lady Anne Clifford in 1660. Another mile or so downstream, **Lammerside Castle** dates from the 12th century but only the remains of the keep survive. They can be found along a bridle path between Pendragon and Wharton Hall.

Ravenstonedale
5 miles SW of Kirkby Stephen on the A685

Known locally as Rissendale, this pretty village of stone-built cottages clustered along the banks of **Scandal Beck** lies on the edge of the Howgill Fells. The parish **Church of St Oswald** is especially interesting: built in 1738, it is one of

---

THE KINGS HEAD

Ravenstonedale, Cumbria CA17 4NH
Tel: 015396 23284
e-mail: enquiries@kings-head.net
website: www.kings-head.net

Three 17th century cottages have been converted into a popular picture postcard pub in a lovely village on the edge of the Howgill Fells. **The Kings Head** is owned and run by Gary and Susan Kirby, and along with Spot the dog and three amiable ghosts they have a friendly welcome for all their customers. The four public rooms are a charming and convivial setting for enjoying a drink, and in the non-smoking restaurant traditional English

home cooking is served every lunchtime and evening. For guests staying overnight the inn, once the local courthouse, has three comfortable bedrooms.

MOSS COTTAGES

The Moss, Newbiggin-on-Lune, Nr Kirkby Stephen, Cumbria CA17 4NB
Tel: 015396 23316
e-mail: shallmoss@aol.com

Nestling at the base of the Howgill Fells, **Moss Cottages** enjoy a gloriously scenic and peaceful setting. Converted from a handsome stone barn attached to a 17th century farmhouse, the three cottages are self-contained, self-catering holiday homes, comfortable and full of character, and sleeping two or four guests. All have living rooms with tv, books and games, and fully equipped kitchen areas. Resident owners Bob and Bunny Shallcross make their large garden available to guests, and also provide a utility room with washing machine and dryer. The cottages lie just off the A685 five miles east of the M6 (J38).

the few Georgian churches in Cumbria. An earlier church, built on the same site, had a separate bell tower which rested on pillars and at its centre hung a refuge bell. Anyone guilty of a capital offence who managed to escaped to Ravenstonedale and sound the bell was free from arrest by the King's officials. This useful custom was finally abolished in the reign of James I.

The present church, surrounded by yew trees, is well worth a visit with its bow pews facing one another and its three-decker pulpit complete with a sounding board and, at the back of the third deck, a seat for the parson's wife. The window at the east end commemorates the last woman in England to be put to death for her Protestant faith. Elizabeth Gaunt was sentenced in 1685 by the notorious Judge Jeffreys to be burnt at the stake for sheltering a fugitive rebel. She met her end at Tyburn in London.

Nateby

2 miles S of Kirkby Stephen on the B6269

Now a quiet hamlet of houses standing alongside a beck, for centuries Nateby was dominated by **Hartley Castle**. Believed to have been built in the 13th century, the castle was the home of Sir Andrew de Harcala, a renowned soldier during the reign of Edward II. Harcala was one of the first men to fight on a pony and he was made Earl of Carlisle in recognition of his service to the Crown. However, his

Mallerstang

failure to prevent Robert the Bruce invading the north of England led him to be accused of treason and he was executed in 1325. His castle was finally demolished by the Musgrave family who used the stone to build their manor house at Edenhall near Penrith.

Crosby Garrett
4 miles W of Kirkby Stephen off the A685

Local legend has it that the Devil, seeing all the stones lying ready to build **Crosby Garrett Church**, carried them in his leather apron to the top of a nearby hill. He reasoned that, as people grew old, they would be unable to climb the hill and attend church and thus would come to him rather than go to Heaven. Such tales apart, the church itself is said to be of Anglo-Saxon origin though the visible fabric is 12th century. Inside there are some superb carvings, particularly near the font. The church is also famous for its hagioscope, cut through the wall to allow people in the north aisle to see the altar. Near the church gates is a tithe barn, built in the 18th century to store farm produce given to the church as a religious tax. To the west of the village runs the **Settle-Carlisle Railway** whose splendid viaduct dominates Crosby Garrett.

Winton
3 miles N of Kirkby Stephen off the A685

This a quiet and picturesque hamlet whose name, in old English, means

pasture farmland. It is built on a spring line and, like many other Cumbrian villages of medieval origin, once followed the runrig, or two-field system of agriculture. The evidence is still visible in long, thin fields to the north of the village. These would have been individual strips in medieval times: the open fields were enclosed in the 17th and 18th centuries.

In the centre of the village is the manor house, built in 1726, and Winton's only three-storey building. It was formerly a boys' school where, apparently, the boys were treated like prisoners and not allowed to return home until the end of their education in case they told of their life at the school. The oldest building is **Winton Hall**, built of stone and dated 1665, but looking older with its stone buttresses and mullion windows with iron bars.

Those taking a walk on **Winton Fell** are likely to see red grouse lifting off from the large tracts of heather on the fellside. Indeed, the wildlife is much more prolific around this area where the limestone provides more plentiful food than on the fells around the lakes.

Kaber
4 miles N of Kirkby Stephen off the A685

In 1663, this small village was the improbable focus of the **Kaber Rigg Plot**, a rebellion against Charles II led by Captain Robert Atkinson of Watergate Farm in Mallerstang. The rising failed and Atkinson was hanged, drawn, and quartered at Appleby; tragically, a messenger carrying his reprieve was delayed on Stainmore and arrived too late to save Atkinson from his gruesome fate.

Appleby-in-Westmorland

The old county town of Westmorland, Appleby is one of the most delightful small towns in England. It was originally built by the Norman, Ranulph de Meschines, who set it within a broad loop of the River Eden which protects it on three sides. The fourth side is guarded by **Castle Hill**. The town's uniquely attractive main street, **Boroughgate**, has been described as the finest in England. A broad, tree-lined avenue, it slopes down the hillside to the river, its sides lined with a pleasing variety of buildings, some dating back to the 17th century. At its foot stands the 16th century **Moot Hall** (still used for council meetings and also housing the Tourist Information Centre); at its head rises the great Norman Keep of **Appleby Castle** which is protected by one of the most impressive curtain walls in northern England. Attractions here include the dramatic view from the top of the five-storey keep and the attractive grounds which are home to a wide variety of animals and include a **Rare Breeds Survival Centre**.

During the mid-1600s, Appleby Castle was the home of Lady Anne Clifford, the remarkable woman who has already been mentioned several times and to

River Eden and Mill Weir

whom Appleby has good cause to be grateful. The last of the Clifford line, the diminutive Lady Anne (she was just 4ft 10in tall) inherited vast wealth and estates, among them no fewer than six northern castles. She lavished her fortune on rebuilding or restoring them all. Churches and chapels in the area also benefited from her munificence and at Appleby, in 1651, she also founded the almshouses known as the Hospital of St Anne, for '12 sisters and a Mother'. Set around a cobbled square, the picturesque cottages and minuscule chapel still serve their original function, maintained by the trust endowed by Lady Anne; visitors are welcome.

Lady Anne died in 1676 in her 87th year and was buried with her mother, Margaret Countess of Cumberland, in **St**

THE KINGS HEAD HOTEL

3 Bridge Street, Appleby-in-Westmorland,
Cumbria CA16 6QH
Tel: 017683 51168

The Kings Head Hotel enjoys a prominent position in the delightful town of Appleby, the old county town of Westmorland. The part-brick, part-stone property dates back to the early 18th century and was once an important staging post on a coaching route. It no longer offers overnight accommodation, but it remains a popular spot both as a meeting place for locals and as a first-class stopping place for motorists and visitors to Appleby.

The inn has been run by Kim Denby and family since 1996, and everyone passing through the doors can look forward to a friendly greeting and a selection of well-kept draught ales. Bar snacks and meals, both hot and cold, are served throughout opening hours, which are

every lunchtime and evening and all day in the summer months; the inn is closed on Mondays in winter. The courtyard behind the inn runs down to the River Eden. Once a month on a Saturday the Kings Head hosts an evening of entertainment, which could be live music, a disco or a themed night. In Appleby, the Castle, St Lawrence's Church and the Moot Hall are all well worth taking time to visit, and the Gypsy Horse Fair is a popular annual attraction.

Lawrence's Church. The church is well worth visiting to see their magnificent tombs and also the historic organ, purchased from Carlisle Cathedral in 1684, which is said to be oldest still in use in Britain.

Just a few years after Lady Anne's death, James II granted the town the right to hold a Fair during the week leading to the second Wednesday in June. More than three hundred years later, the **Gypsy Horse Fair** is still thriving with hundreds of gypsies flooding into the little town (population 1,800) with their caravans and horse-drawn carts. The trade, principally in horses, and the trotting races provide a picturesque and colourful spectacle.

Around Appleby-in-Westmorland

Brough

8 miles SE of Appleby-in-Westmorland on the A66/A685

This small town, standing at the point where the **Stainmore Pass** opens into the Vale of Eden, is, in fact, two settlements: **Church Brough** and **Market Brough**. Church Brough is a group of neat houses and cottages clustered around a little market square in which a maypole stands on the site of the former market cross. **Brough Castle**, built within the ramparts of the Roman camp of Verterae, was constructed to protect the Roman road over Stainmore

Pass. The building of this Norman castle was begun by William Rufus in 1095 but it was largely destroyed in 1174 by William the Lion of Scotland. Many times Scottish raiders laid siege to Brough Castle and fierce battles were fought. An ancient ballad tells of the legendary bravery of one knight from the town who defended the tower alone after his comrades had fallen. He was finally vanquished when the Scottish army set fire to his hiding place but the incident was so dramatic that it became a part of local folklore and was remembered in the ballad of the Valiant Knight of Brough. Another fortification restored by the remarkable Lady Anne Clifford, the castle, with its tall keep 60 feet high is well worth visiting, if only for the superb panorama of the surrounding fells seen from the battlements.

Market Brough is also an ancient settlement and was particularly important in the 18th and 19th centuries when it became a major coaching town on the stagecoach routes between England and Scotland. It was on the junction of several routes and boasted more than 10 inns. The width and breadth of its High Street also indicates its importance as a market town. Brough was granted a charter in 1330 enabling it to hold a weekly market as well as four cattle markets and an annual fair. One custom still celebrated in Brough is the Twelfth Night Holly Burning, a unique festival with pagan origins.

The distinctive, low hills that lie to the west of Brough are drumlins - heaps of material deposited by Ice Age glaciers. In this area many drumlins are marked by broad, grassy ridges, remains of ancient lynchets or ploughing strips.

North Stainmore
10 miles SE of Appleby-in-Westmorland on the A66

The village lies on the Stainmore Pass which carries the old Roman road, now the A66, through a remote area of the North Pennines which David Bellamy described as "England's last wilderness". Near Stainmore summit are the foundations of **Maiden Castle**, a Roman fort built to guard the pass against marauders. A few yards over the Cumbrian border, into County Durham, is the stump of the ancient **Rey Cross** which was erected before AD946 and which, until 1092, marked the boundary between England and Scotland. It is thought to be the site of the battle at which the last Viking King of York and North England, Eric Bloodaxe, was killed following his expulsion from the city.

Warcop
5 miles SE of Appleby-in-Westmorland on the B6259

The largest village in this part of the Eden Valley, Warcop grew up as a crossing point of the river. The bridge, the oldest to cross the river, dates from the 16th century and the red sandstone buildings surrounding the village green, with its central maypole, make this a charming place to visit.

THE NEW INN

Hoff, Nr Appleby-in-Westmorland,
Cumbria CA16 6TA
Tel: 01768351317
e-mail: des@newinnhoff.fsnet.co.uk

The New Inn has a history going back to the early 17th century, when it was part of a farmstead. It started brewing its own beer towards the end of the 18th century and its status later changed from alehouse to fully fledged public house. In that role it has

become a very popular and welcoming free house, and its reputation has been further enhanced under Derek and Sue, who have been at the helm together since January 2003.

The inn is open all day, every day, for drinks, and real ale fans will always find a minimum of three brews; there's also a good selection of lagers, plus two German beers. The bar area is delightfully traditional, with horse brasses hinging from black beams, period prints and other objects and ornaments appropriate to the inn's age. Sue is an excellent cook and is reinforcing the New Inn's position as one of the leading food pubs in the region. Her dishes are served between 12 and 3 at lunchtime and from 6 to 9 in the evenings (no food

Monday or Tuesday except Bank Holidays).

The lunch menu offers a good choice of familiar favourites ranging from ploughman's platters and salads to Cumberland sausage, lasagne and meat pies, while in the evening the choice extends to a wide variety of dishes that could include steaks, lamb Henry and always a number of fish dishes. Everything is fresh, tasty and appetising, and many of those in the know choose from the specials board, which changes day by day to reflect what's best from the local suppliers. Such is the popularity of the inn that booking is necessary at the weekend.

The atmosphere is always very friendly and congenial here, and many visitors would like to stay longer; their wishes may soon be answered, as the owners are planning to make some rooms available for Bed & Breakfast accommodation. The inn has plenty of off-road parking and some outside seating, and its elevated position commands exceptional views. When the accommodation comes on stream, the inn will be an excellent base for a holiday in this most appealing part of the world. It is situated in the quiet village of Hoff on the B6260 a couple of miles southwest of Appleby, and is within easy reach of many places of interest, both scenic and historic.

The **Church of St Columba** is built outside the village on the site of a Roman camp. An interesting building in its own right, it is particularly famous for the rush-bearing ceremony which takes place in late June each year. Warcop is surrounded by Ministry of Defence tank firing ranges from which the public are understandably excluded but on the hills above the village are stones, cairns, and the remains of what is claimed to be a **Druid Temple**.

River Eden

Great Ormside
2 miles SE of Appleby-in-Westmorland off the B6260

This was once an important fort guarded by a pele tower, and the ancient **Church of St James**, which dates from the 11th century, occupies a site on the steep-sided defence mound. Relics of pre-Christian burials have been found in the mound, as well as a Viking sword (now in the Tullie Museum in Carlisle). A silver gilt and enamel bowl from the 7th century has also been found and is regarded as one of the most important pieces of Anglo-Saxon metalware to survive. A particularly beautiful piece, richly decorated with vine scrolls, birds, and animals, it is now on permanent display in the Yorkshire Museum in York.

From the village a path leads across fields to the village of **Little Ormside**, with its large cedar tree said to have been brought back from Lebanon as a sapling by General Whitehead. On the voyage home he grew it in his hat and shared with it his daily ration of one pint of water.

Great Asby
4 miles S of Appleby-in-Westmorland off the B6260

This pretty village is set in a wooded hollow, its houses separated by **Hoff Beck**. Alongside the beck is **St Helen's Well** which is said never to run dry or freeze and nearby are the splendid almshouses of St Helen's, built between 1811 and 1820. Across a footbridge is **Asby Hall** (in private hands), built in 1670. It was once the home of the Musgrave family of Edenhall, whose crest and coat of arms can still be seen above the door.

Brampton
2 miles N of Appleby-in-Westmorland off the A66

This village, along with the surrounding area, was said to be haunted by the ghost

THE NEW INN

Brampton, Nr Appleby-in-Westmorland,
Cumbria CA16 6JS
Tel: 01768351231

Like many other establishments with the same name, **The New Inn** is in fact very old, with a history going back more than 300 years. Records show that part of the premises, where the restaurant is now located, was originally a private dwelling, where refurbishment was carried out in the first decades of the 18th century.

Behind the attractive black and white frontage, it's delightfully traditional, with flagstone floors, beamed ceilings, real fires

and a variety of ornaments, including horse brasses, firearms, plates and prints. Always a focal point of local life, the inn has won even greater popularity both locally and with visitors since it was taken over by the present owner in the autumn of 2000.

Open every lunchtime and evening and all day at peak tourist times, the inn serves a full range of drinks, including Black Sheep and Bombardier real ales, and often a third, guest ale. Its reputation for good beer is matched by its popularity as one of the best places in the region to fine good home cooking at very reasonable prices.

Food is served every lunchtime

from 12 to 2 and every evening from 7 to 9, and diners can eat in the 35-seat dining room, in the bar or, if the weather permits, in the capacious beer garden at the back of the inn. The printed menu is supplemented by a daily specials board, and booking is strongly recommended to be sure of a table on Saturday evening, when from time to time live entertainment is laid on.

The New Inn has firmly established itself as a delightful place to visit for a drink and a meal, and the owners hope soon to widen its scope by offering Bed & Breakfast accommodation. When that happens, it will be a splendid base for exploring the numerous local places of interest, among which are Appleby itself, one of the most delightful small towns in England, and the peaks and forests of the Pennines.

of Elizabeth Sleddall, the wife of a 17th century owner of nearby Crackenthorpe Hall. Elizabeth died believing that she had been cheated out of her share of the estate, so to shame the false inheritors her spirit was seen being driven around the countryside in a coach drawn by four black horses. Her ghost became so troublesome that the local people exhumed her body and reburied the remains under a larger boulder. Her ghost, while no longer troubling the local people, is said still to visit the hall.

Dufton
3 miles N of Appleby-in-Westmorland off the A66

Behind this delightful hamlet lies **Dufton Gill**, a beautiful, secluded wooded valley through which runs a footpath. Also from Dufton there is a track carrying the Pennine Way up to High Cup Nick, a great horseshoe precipice at the edge of the northern Pennine escarpment that was formed by a glacial lake during the Ice Age.

Long Marton
3 miles N of Appleby-in-Westmorland off the A66

Visitors to this village can experience two very different forms of architecture, both of them equally impressive. The village church, with its carvings of knights and monsters over the doorway, is remarkably unspoilt and Norman, while nearby the Settle to Carlisle Railway sweeps across a grand viaduct.

Temple Sowerby
7 miles NW of Appleby-in-Westmorland on the A66

Temple Sowerby prides itself on the title 'Queen of Westmorland villages', an accolade justified by its lovely setting in the Eden valley. (Here's a bonus: the average rainfall here is half that recorded in the Lake District National Park to the west.) To the north, the massive bulk of **Cross Fell**, the highest point in the Pennines, swells skywards to provide a spectacular backdrop. The

CROFT HOUSE SELF CATERING COTTAGES

Bolton, Nr Appleby-in-Westmorland, Cumbria CA16 6AW
Tel: 017683 61264
e-mail: stay@crofthouse-cottages.co.uk
website: www.crofthouse-cottages.co.uk

In the pretty Eden Valley village of Bolton, Edith Stockdale and her brother-in-law Des offer exceptional holiday accommodation in **Croft House Self Catering Cottages**. Croft Farm House sleeps up to 11 guests, the Hayloft 2 or 4, Granary Cottage 4 or 6. The interlinked Old Barn and Stable Cottage can be let separately or as a unit with

accommodation for up to 10. Most of the buildings date back to the 17th century and all have been carefully modernised to provide everything for a comfortable stay in scenic, civilised surroundings

The Eden Valley and East Cumbria

The Eden Valley and East Cumbria

THE STAG INN

Gullom, Milburn, Nr Penrith,
Cumbria CA10 1TL
Tel/Fax: 01768361401
e-mail: gullonpub@ktdinternet.com

New owners Ken and Sharon Bland have greatly enhanced the appeal of the 18th century **Stag Inn** by retaining the period charm while carefully restoring and upgrading the premises. Tucked away off the A66 on the Scotch Corner road east of Penrith, it's a great place to seek out to enjoy a warm, genuine welcome, a drink and Sharon's appetising home cooking. Everything is freshly

cooked, and her dishes are served every lunchtime in summer (only on Sunday in winter) and every evening except winter Mondays.

village itself, picturesquely grouped around a sloping green and an 18th century red sandstone church, takes its name from the medieval Knights Templar who owned the manor of Sowerby until their Order was suppressed in 1308. But the little community long outdates those predatory Knights: evidence of a Stone Age settlement has been found and a Roman milestone just outside the village marks the route of the old Imperial highway, now the A66.

From Temple Sowerby there are delightful walks through the Eden valley or, if you prefer a gentle stroll, it's only a mile to the National Trust gardens at **Acorn Bank** where **Crowdundle Beck** splashes beneath an elegant 18th century bridge. The 16th century manor house is now a Sue Ryder Home and not open to the public, but visitors are welcome to explore the attractive gardens planted with a collection of some 250 medicinal and culinary herbs. A circular woodland walk runs along the beck to a watermill that was first

mentioned on the site as far back as the 14th century. At different times it has been a saw mill, a corn mill and a source of power for the local gypsum mines; now restored, it is open for visits.

North East of Penrith

Edenhall

3 miles NE of Penrith off the A686

An old tradition asserts that in the 8th century the monks of Jarrow, fleeing from Viking invaders with the body of St Cuthbert, stopped here briefly. As a result the village church is dedicated to the saint. Part of the **Church of St Cuthbert** appears to be pre-Norman but most of the structure dates from the 1100s. Close to the church is the **Plague Cross** which stands where there was once a basin filled with vinegar. This acted as a disinfectant into which plague victims put their money to pay for food from the people of Penrith. The plague of the 16th century killed a quarter of the village's inhabitants.

Edenhall is particularly famous for the story of the 'Luck of Eden Hall', a priceless glass cup which, according to legend, was stolen from some fairies dancing round the garden wall by a butler in the service of the Musgrave family back in the 15th century. Despite the fairies' entreaties, the butler refused to return the 6-inch high glass to them. As he departed with the precious goblet, the fairies laid a curse upon it: "If ever this cup shall break or fall, Farewell the luck of Eden Hall". On inspection, the glass was identified as a 13th century chalice of enamelled and gilded glass that is thought to have come from Syria and may well have been brought back by a Crusader. It was a treasured heirloom of the Musgraves for many generations and is now in the Victoria & Albert Museum in London. The goblet is still intact but Eden Hall has long since disappeared.

Langwathby
4 miles NE of Penrith on the A686

Located on the opposite bank of the River Eden from Edenhall, Langwathby's name means 'the settlement by the long ford' and, though there are two prehistoric pathways crossing here, the name of the village and of its neighbouring settlements suggests a Viking past. Langwathby has a huge village green which still hosts maypole dancing on the third Saturday in May. The green is medieval in origin and would once have been surrounded by wood and mud houses, perhaps to protect cattle but also for defence against border raids. After the Civil War and the growth in prosperity in the late 17th century, these wattle and daub cottages were replaced by stone buildings. The drovers from Scotland passed through here to the market towns of England. West of the village, at Langwathby Hall Farm, **Eden Ostrich World** offers visitors the chance to see these splendid birds in a farm setting in the heart of the Eden Valley. The farm is also home to rare breed sheep, cattle and pigs, donkeys, deer, wallabies, alpacas and many other creatures from around the world. A giant maze was opened in 2001, and the farm has a tea room, gift shop, picnic areas and adventure play areas.

Little Salkeld
6 miles NE of Penrith off the A686

A lane from the village leads to **Long Meg** and her Daughters, a most impressive prehistoric site and second only to Stonehenge in size. Local legend claims that Long Meg was a witch who, with her daughters, was turned to stone for profaning the Sabbath, as they danced wildly on the moor. The circle is supposedly endowed with magic so that it is impossible to count the same number of stones twice. Another superstition is that Long Meg will bleed if the stone is chipped or broken. The actual name, Long Meg, has been the subject of debate. It has been suggested that Meg may be a corruption of the word 'magus' meaning a magician.

There are more than 60 stones in the Circle (actually an oval), which is approximately 300 feet across. The tallest, Long Meg, is a 15ft column of Penrith sandstone, the corners of which face the four points of the compass. Cup and ring symbols and spirals are carved on this stone which is over 3,500 years old. The circle is now known to belong to the Bronze Age but no one is certain of its purpose. It may have been used for rituals connected with the changing seasons since the midwinter sun sets in alignment with the centre of the circle and Long Meg herself. The brooding majesty of the site was perfectly evoked by Wordsworth:

A weight of awe, not easy to be borne,
Fell suddenly upon my spirit - cast
From the dread bosom of the unknown
past,
When first I saw that family forlorn.

In 1725 an attempt was made by Colonel Samuel Lacy of Salkeld Hall to use the stones for mileposts. However, as work began, a great storm blew up and the workmen fled in terror believing that the Druids were angry at the desecration of their temple.

It was the same Colonel Lacy who gave his name to the **Lacy Caves**, a mile or so downstream from Little Salkeld. The Colonel had the five chambers carved out of the soft red sandstone, possibly as a copy of St Constantine's Caves further down the river at Wetheral. At that time it was fashionable to have romantic ruins and grottoes on large estates and Colonel Lacy is said to have employed a man to live in his caves acting the part of a hermit. Alternatively, the caves may have been intended to provide a wine store; Colonel Lacy used to entertain his guests here, and there were probably gardens around the caves. The rhododendrons and laburnums still flower every spring.

Great Salkeld

6 miles NE of Penrith on the B6412

The River Eden formed the boundary between the two old counties of

THE HIGHLAND DROVE INN

Great Salkeld, Nr Penrith, Cumbria CA11 9NR
Tel: 01768 898349
e-mail: highlanddroveinn@btinternet.com
website: www.highland-drove.co.uk

The father and son team of Donald and Paul Newton welcome visitors to the **Highland Drove Inn**, which has been providing hospitality for over 200 years. They are maintaining that tradition in the best possible style by offering top-quality food in Kyloes restaurant, where interesting dishes range from fish, charcuterie and meze plates to Peking duck pancakes, snapper with a risotto cake and Moroccan-style chicken. The inn is

also a very comfortable port of call for an overnight stay, with five en suite guest bedrooms. A balcony in the bar overlooks a paved rear garden.

Westmorland and Cumberland so while Little Salkeld was in Westmorland its larger namesake stood in Cumberland. The village is a picturesque collection of 18th century cottages and farmhouses built in red sandstone which are typical of this area. Great Salkeld is best known for the impressive **Church** with its massive, battlemented pele tower built in the 14th century and complete with a dungeon. The Norman doorway in the porch is less than a yard wide and its arch has three rows of deeply cut zig-zags with five heads, one with a crown.

Kirkoswald

8 miles NE of Penrith on the B6413

The village derives its name from the **Church of St Oswald**: Oswald was the King of Northumbria who, according to legend, toured the pagan north with St Aidan in the 7th century. The church is unusual in having a detached bell tower standing on top of a grassy hill some 200 yards from the main building (this is in a valley, so the bells could not be heard

by the villagers).

This once thriving market town still retains its small cobbled market place and some very fine Georgian buildings. There's also a striking ruined 12th century **Castle**, formerly the home of the Featherstonehaugh family which, although not open to the public, can be seen from the road and footpath. In 1210 a licence was received from King John to fortify the original structure and enclose the extensive park. The castle was later destroyed by Robert the Bruce in 1314 but was rebuilt and extended in the late 15th century. The whole site covered three acres with the courtyard surrounded by a massive wall and a main gate with a drawbridge over the moat. The castle's splendour was due to the efforts of Thomas, Lord Dacre but, after his death in 1525, the panelling, stained glass, and beamed ceilings were transferred to Naworth and the castle became a quarry. Today, it is still protected by a wide moat and the great turreted tower rises 65 feet above the remains of the vaulted dungeons.

MIDLAND HOTEL

Lazonby, Nr Penrith, Cumbria CA10 1BY
Tel: 01768 898901

The **Midland Hotel** is an 18th century country pub sitting in the shadow of the railway bridge in the tiny village of Lazonby, off the A686 Penrith-Alston road. Behind the smart black and white frontage, the interior is very neat and cosy, and landlords David and Jenny Ousby have built up a strong local following.

Jenny does the cooking, producing appetising, unpretentious pub dishes served both lunchtime and evening during the week and all day at the weekend. The Midland lies

on the scenic cycle route from Land's End to John O'Groats.

One of Kirkoswald's most splendid buildings is the **College**, its name recalling the days when St Oswald's was a collegiate church. The two-storey house with its sloping-ended roof was originally built as a pele tower and converted into the college for priests in the 1520s. The manor house opposite has a particularly attractive entrance front in sandstone, which was added in 1696.

Just to the northwest of Kirkoswald are the **Nunnery Walks** which start at a Georgian house built in 1715 on the site of a Benedictine Nunnery founded during the reign of William Rufus. Narrow footpaths have been cut into the sandstone cliffs along the deep gorge of **Croglin Beck** and they pass through beautiful woodland to reveal exciting waterfalls. The walks are open to the public during the summer months.

Armathwaite
10 miles NE of Penrith off the A6

Set on the western bank of the River Eden, the village has a particularly fine sandstone bridge from which there is a lovely view of **Armathwaite Castle** (private), the home of the Skelton family, one of whose forebears was Poet Laureate to Henry VIII. Close by, visitors to the **Eden Valley Woollen Mill** can see traditional looms rattling away and browse through a huge range of knitwear produced from the finest wools and mohair. The Mill offers an inexpensive making-up service and accepts commissions for pile and rag

rugs. It is open daily during the season but times vary during the winter months. Also worth seeking out in **Coombs Wood** to the south is another of the Eden Benchmarks. Entitled *Vista* and created by Graeme Mitchison, this remarkable sculpture seems to make the Lazenby Sandstone flow into liquid shapes. North of Armathwaite, the River Eden approaches Carlisle and the Solway Firth; these lower stretches of the river are surveyed in the next chapter.

Melmerby
9 miles NE of Penrith on the A686

Melmerby nestles at the foot of **Hartside Pass**, its spacious village green dissected by three becks. Even today, every householder in Melmerby has grazing rights on the green. Horses are grazed more commonly now, but in the past it would have been more usual to see flocks of geese - indeed, there was once a cottage industry here making pillows and mattresses from goose feathers. Overlooking the 13-acre village green is **Melmerby Hall**, a defensive tower that was extended in the 17th and 18th centuries. The village church, with its tower, is a Victorian building, but the first known rector of the church on the site came here in 1332.

A curious meteorological feature here is what is known as the **Helm Winds**, localised gusts which sweep through the valley with the force of a gale while the surrounding countryside is perfectly calm.

From Melmerby the main road climbs out of the Eden Valley to the east and

THE SHEPHERDS INN

Melmerby, Nr Penrith, Cumbria CA10 1HF
Tel: 01768 881217
e-mail: theshepherdsinn@btopenworld.com

2002 saw the arrival of Garry and Marcia Parkin at the **Shepherds Inn**, which stands on the A686 Penrith-Alston road at Melmerby. The stone-built pub dates from the 18th century, and behind the long façade overlooking the village green the spacious bars and restaurant combine period and modern elements to pleasing effect - thanks to the great pride the Parkins take in the place. Marcia's home cooking provides plenty of choice and can be enjoyed every session. Everything on her menu is worth trying, and one of her specialities is Chicken Leoni cooked with cheese and garlic.

the landscape changes suddenly. The road passes Fiend's Fell, close to the highest point in the Pennine Chain, the summit of Cross Fell. Early Christians erected a cross on the highest point of the fell to protect travellers from the demons who haunted the moors. Today, a cairn marks the spot where the cross once stood.

Alston

18 miles NE of Penrith on the A689/A686

For a few weeks in 1999 the small town of Alston, 1,000 feet up in the Pennines, became transformed into Bruntmarsh, the fishing village in which the fictional Oliver Twist spent his early years. To re-create the squalid conditions of the poor in early 19th century England, production designers 'dressed down' the town, so much so that anxious visitors noticing the soot-blackened buildings inquired whether there had been a major fire.

Alan Bleasdale's re-working of the Dickens classic was for many the television highlight of 1999 and one of its many strengths was the authenticity of the locations. Alston proved to be ideal since the town centre has changed little since the late 1700s when the story is set and there are many even older buildings.

Alston Village

The town has a cobbled main street and, from the picturesque **Market Cross**, narrow lanes radiating out with courtyards enclosing old houses. Many of the older buildings still have the outside staircase leading to the first floor - a relic from the days when animals were kept below while the family's living accommodation was upstairs. This ancient part of Alston is known as **The Butts**, a title acquired by the need of the townspeople to be proficient in archery during the times of the border raids.

An unusual feature of Alston was the number of watermills in and around the town and the mill race was once the central artery of the old town. The tall spire of **St Augustine's Church** is a well known local landmark and its churchyard contains a number of interesting epitaphs, as well as affording wonderful views of the South Tyne Valley.

Considering its small population, Alston supports an astonishing diversity of shops and pubs. In addition, the town is home to a wide variety of craftspeople, ranging from blacksmiths to candlemakers, wood turners to potters, and also boasts an outstanding art and crafts centre in the **Gossipgate Gallery**. Housed in a converted congregational church built 200 years ago and with its original gas lights still intact, this gallery is the premier centre in the North Pennines for contemporary art and craft. A programme of exhibitions runs non-stop from February to December, and in the gallery shop a huge range of artefacts is for sale, including original watercolours and prints, jewellery, glass, ceramics, sculpture and striking turned wooden bowls made from native woods.

Another popular attraction in Alston is the **South Tynedale Railway**. This narrow gauge (2ft) steam railway runs regular services during the summer months and at the northern terminus of the 2½-mile long track travellers can join a stretch of the Pennine Way that

THE CUMBERLAND HOTEL

Townfoot, Alston, Cumbria CA9 3HX
Tel/Fax: 01434 381875
e-mail: helenguyh@aol.com
website: www.cumberlandalston.co.uk

Standing by the A686 at the foot of Alston's main street, the **Cumberland Hotel** is run with flair and enthusiasm by Helen and Guy Harmer, who previously owned and operated a Narrowboat Hotel business. Behind the smart white exterior the hotel is delightfully cosy and comfortable, and five well-equipped en suite bedrooms provide an ideal base for touring the area, starting with the many places of interest in Alston itself. With well kept Real Ales, and good value appetising Home Cooking, Helen and Guy offer a warm family welcome to all their guests.

runs alongside the River South Tyne. In between the station and the A686, is the **HUB Exhibition** of historic vehicles, a wealth of local images and the stories that bring them alive.

Alston Moor, to the south of the town, was once the centre of an extremely important lead mining region, one of the richest in Britain. Lead and silver were probably mined on the moor by the Romans, but the industry reached its peak in the early 19th century when vast quantities of iron, silver, copper, and zinc were extracted by the London Lead Company. A Quaker company, it was a pioneer of industrial welfare and also built the model village of Nenthead to house the miners. Here, not only were the workers and their families provided with a home, but education was compulsory and there were some public baths. **Nenthead Mines Heritage Centre** (see panel) is a 200-acre site high in the hills that tells the story of the lead and zinc mining industry. One of the main visitor attractions is 'The Power of Water', an impressive interactive area that looks at the technology used, including three working water wheels that drive model machinery. Another is the Brewery Shaft with its 328 feet drop and amazing virtual stone feature.

NORTH PENNINES HERITAGE TRUST

Nenthead House, Nenthead, Alston, Cumbria CA9 3PD
Tel: 01434 382037

Welcome to **Nent Valley**. Visit the 200-acre centre at Nenthead, in the North Pennines, an Area of Outstanding Natural Beauty. It offers a unique insight into the lives of the miners who transformed these fells. Visitors have the chance to experience the underground world through guided trips in Carr's Mine, last commercially worked for lead in 1920. There is the huge "Power of Water" interactive area, where visitors can open sluice gates to operate water wheels and drive machinery. **Brewery Shaft** is an impressive 328 feet deep, with a viewing platform for visitors to gaze down into the depths and be amazed at the courage of anyone daring to descend.

Around the centre are various restored buildings, which contain exhibitions and interactive displays about the geology of the area, the local wildlife and social history of the area. The 200 acre site includes woodland walks, mountain streams and a waterfall, whilst the surrounding area is ideal for walkers of all ages and gives access to the spectacular scenery of the North Pennines. There is a café where you can rest your legs and take refreshments, and a well-stocked shop to purchase postcards, books and gifts.

The Eden Valley and East Cumbria

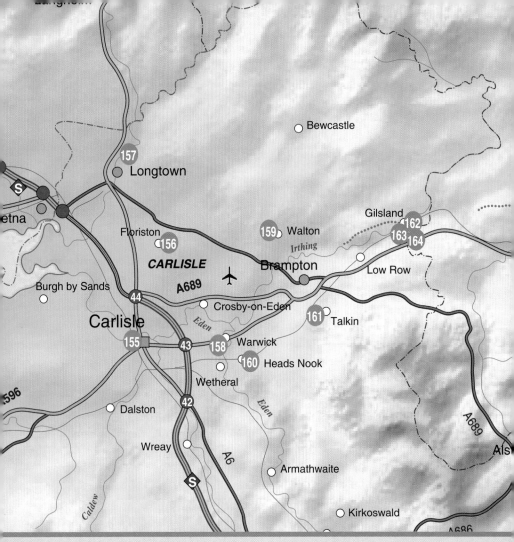

PLACES TO STAY, EAT AND DRINK

● Denotes entries in other chapters

9 Carlisle and the Scottish Borders

For more than 350 years the area around Carlisle was known as the Debatable Lands, a lawless region where the feared Border Reivers sacked and plundered at will. Every winter, when their own food stocks were almost depleted, armed gangs from across the border would ride southwards to seize the cattle and sheep of their more prosperous neighbours. Stealing and murdering, they wreaked havoc in this area and almost every village would have had a fortified structure, usually a pele tower, where the inhabitants and their animals could hide safely. There are some 77 names on record as belonging to these disreputable Reiver families - among them are the names Trotter and Maxwell - and anyone who wishes to find out if their family was involved should go to Carlisle's Tullie House Museum.

This is, too, the country of Hadrian's Wall, the most important monument built in Britain by the Romans; many stretches of the wall are still visible, and

Birdoswald and other centres give an excellent insight into Roman border life. The wall was built as a great military barrier across the narrowest part of Britain, from the mouth of the River Tyne, in the east, to Bowness-on-Solway, in the west. Guarded by forts at regular intervals, it was built between AD122 and 128 following a visit by the Emperor Hadrian, who saw the then military infrastructure as insufficient to withstand the combined attacks of northern barbarians. Originally, much of the western side was built from turf, but by AD163 this had been replaced by stone. The wall was finally abandoned in the late 4th century, and in later

Christmas in Carlisle

centuries many of the stones were used for local buildings and field walls. There are many ways of exploring the Wall (including the bus number AD122!), and for those with the energy to walk from end to end the newly opened Hadrian's Wall National Trail passes some of the country's greatest archaeological monuments.

Carlisle Castle

Carlisle

According to a recent survey, if you are born in Carlisle you are more likely to stay here than the inhabitants of any other place in England. Its castle, cathedral, many other historic buildings, parks, thriving traditional market, shopping centres and leisure facilities all combine to endow Carlisle with the true feel of a major city. Carlisle is the largest settlement in Cumbria, with a population of around 130,000, and is also its county town. The city stands at the junction of three rivers, the Eden, the Caldew and the Petteril, and was already fortified in Celtic times when it was named Caer Lue, the 'hill fort'. It became a major Roman centre: it was the military base for the Petriana regiment, Luguvallum, guarding the western end of Hadrian's Wall, and also an important civilian settlement with fountains, mosaics, statues and centrally-heated homes.

Today, the squat outline of **Carlisle Castle** (English Heritage) dominates the skyline of this fascinating city. There has been a castle at Carlisle since 1092 when William Rufus first built a palisaded fort. The Norman Castle was originally built of wood but, during the Scottish occupation in the 12th century, King David I laid out a new castle with stones taken from Hadrian's Wall. The 12th century keep can still be seen enclosed by massive inner and outer walls. Entry is through a great 14th century gatehouse, complete with portcullis, and with a maze of vaulted passages, chambers, staircases, towers, and dismal dungeons. Children, especially, enjoy the legendary 'licking stones' from which parched Jacobite prisoners tried to find enough moisture to stay alive. Archaeologists working outside the castle walls unearthed the remains of three Roman forts, and many of the finds are on display in a special exhibition at the castle. Carlisle Castle is everything a real castle should be and is still the headquarters of the King's

Own Royal Border Regiment, whose **Regimental Museum** is located within the castle walls. Two floors of displays include uniforms, weapons, medals, pictures, photographs and archives. During the Civil War, the castle was besieged for eight months by the Parliamentarians under General Leslie. When the Royalists finally capitulated, Leslie began repairing the castle and the city walls. The Puritans were no respecters of Britain's ecclesiastical heritage; stones from six of the eight bays of the cathedral were used for the repairs and the building of block-houses for the Puritan troops.

Partly for this reason, **Carlisle Cathedral** is now one of the smallest cathedrals in England but it has many interesting features, including an exquisite east window that is considered to be one of the finest in Europe. Below the beautifully painted wooden ceiling of the choir, with its gold star shimmering against deep blue, are the carved, canopied choir-stalls with their medieval misericords. These wonderful carved beasts and birds include two dragons joined by the ears, a fox killing a goose, pelicans feeding their young, and a mermaid with a looking glass. In St Wilfrid's Chapel is the superb 16th century Flemish Brougham Triptych which was originally in Cologne Cathedral. In the 19th century it was brought to Brougham Chapel near Penrith. The altar piece was later restored by the Victoria & Albert Museum in London and is now on permanent loan to Carlisle. It is a beautiful, intricate piece with delicately carved figures depicting scenes from the life of Christ.

It is hard to believe that it was here that Edward I solemnly used bell, book, and candle to excommunicate Robert the Bruce. It was here also that the church bells were rung to welcome Bonnie Prince Charlie in 1745. It is claimed that after the suppression of the Jacobite rebellion the bells were removed for their 'treason' and only

THE SPORTSMAN INN

Heads Lane, Carlisle, Cumbria CA3 8AQ
Tel: 01228 522387 Fax: 01228 543907

The Sportsman Inn, which dates from the 17th century, is an oasis of calm amid the hustle and bustle of the city. It stands next to St Cuthbert's Church, and outside seats overlook the church grounds. Tenants Anne and Keith Bignall have been at the helm since 1975, and two of their staff – Monica and Elsie – have each clocked up more than 20 years loyal service. The inn is open all day for a fine selection of draught ales and other drinks, and from 11.30 to 7 an excellent choice of home-cooked food is served, from baguettes with hot fillings to salads, baked potatoes and

classics such as lasagne, Cumberland sausage and a terrific steak & ale pie. Sunday lunch, served from 12 to 5, brings a choice of roasts with all the trimmings.

replaced in the 19th century.

Carlisle Cathedral is one of the few where visitors can enjoy refreshments actually within the precincts, in this case in the Prior's Kitchen Restaurant situated in the Fratry Undercroft. Seated beneath superb fan vaulting, customers have a good choice of home made soups, cakes and pastries, as well as morning coffee, lunches and afternoon teas.

Although an appointment is usually necessary, a visit to the nearby **Prior's Tower** is a must. On the first floor of this 15th century pele tower is a wonderful 45 panel ceiling incorporating the popinjay crest and arms of the Prior Senhouse. The 16th century Prior's gatehouse leads to a narrow lane called Paternoster which is named after the monks reciting their offices.

Like many great medieval cities, Carlisle was surrounded by walls. Guided walks and tours are available and the best view is to be found in a little street called **West Walls** at the bottom of Sally Port Steps, near the Tithe Barn. The walls date from around the 11th century and they remained virtually intact until the 1800s.

When the castle was under siege, the **Sally Port** allowed an individual to 'sally forth'. It was later used for access to the **Tithe Barn** to avoid paying city tolls. It is unusual to find a Tithe Barn within a city wall but this exception was probably made because of the Border raids. The barn dates from the 15th century and was used to collect and store taxes, or tithes, destined for the priory.

Close by is **St Cuthbert's Church**, the official city church of Carlisle and where the Lord Mayor's pew can be found. Although the present building dates from 1778, there has been a church on this site since the 7th century and the dedication is obvious, since St Cuthbert was Bishop of Carlisle in AD680. It is a charming Georgian building with several interesting features including a moveable pulpit on rails.

The award winning **Tullie House Museum & Art Gallery**, in the centre of the city close to the cathedral, is certainly another place not to be missed. Through skilful and interpretive techniques the fascinating, and often dark, history of the Debatable Lands, as this border region was called, is told. The museum's centrepiece is its story of the Border Reivers who occupied the lands from the 14th to the 17th century. These lawless, unruly people raged interfamily warfare with each other, destroying or threatening the lives of the local people with their bloodthirsty raids. Their treacherous deeds have also added such words as 'bereave' and 'blackmail' to the English language.

The horrific stories of the Reivers have been passed down through the generations in the Border Ballads, and many of the Reivers family names are still known - the museum even offers a genealogy service, so that visitors find out if their ancestry goes back to these people. What is perhaps the definitive Reiving story has been told in *The Steel Bonnets* by George MacDonald Fraser,

Carlisle City Centre

Standing next to a 280ft high chimney built in 1836 as part of what was once one of the largest cotton mills in Britain, the Centre has displays of hand weaving on original looms, informative displays and a selection of world famous fabrics and designer knitwear for sale.

The **Old Town Hall**, now an excellent Tourist Information Centre, dates from the 17th century and once housed the Muckle Bell, an alarm bell which, it was claimed, could be heard 11 miles away. The bell is now housed in the Tullie House Museum.

author of the Flashman books. The city of Carlisle dates back far beyond those desperate days and Tullie House also has an extensive collection of Roman remains from both the city and the Cumbrian section of Hadrian's Wall. The Art Gallery features contemporary arts and crafts, and the spectacular underground Millennium Gallery has a stunning collection of local minerals, archaeological finds of wood and leather, artist-made glass and interactive exhibits. Old Tullie House showcases paintings and drawings by renowned Pre-Raphaelite artists, as well as other artworks and a selection of fine English porcelain.

A short walk from the Museum leads to the **Linton Visitor Centre** in Shaddongate which provides an insight into the city's industrial heritage.

The **Guildhall Museum** is housed in an unspoiled medieval building constructed by Richard of Redeness in 1407. Originally a town house, it provides an ideal setting for illustrating the history of both the Guilds and the City. Several rooms are devoted to creating the atmosphere of trade Guilds such as the shoemakers, the butchers, the weavers and the glovers. There is a splendid early 19th century banner of the Weavers Guild and an impressive collection of 17th and 18th century Guild silver. One of the silver bells on show is thought to be the earliest horse racing trophy in the country. Displays also feature other items relating to the history of Carlisle and include medieval stocks and a magnificent ironbound Muniment Chest dating from the 14th century. Conducted tours of this remarkable Guildhall are available.

Not far from the museum is the **Citadel**, which is often mistaken for the castle. In fact, this intimidating fortress with its well-preserved circular tower was built in 1543 on the orders of Henry VIII to strengthen the city's defences. Much of it was demolished in the early 1800s to improve access to the city centre but what remains is mightily impressive.

Across the road from the Citadel is the railway station. The first railway to Carlisle opened in July 1836 and Citadel Station, which opened in 1850, was built to serve seven different railway companies whose coats of arms are still displayed on the façade. So elegant was its interior - and much of it remains - that Carlisle was known as the 'top hat' station. Today it is still an important centre of communications; InterCity trains from Glasgow and London now link with lines to Dumfries, Tyneside, West Cumbria, and Yorkshire, and it is, of course, the northern terminus of the famous **Settle-Carlisle Railway** line.

One of the last great mainline railways to be built in Britain - it was completed in 1876 - the Settle to Carlisle line takes in some of the most dramatic scenery that the north of England has to offer. Scenic it may be but the terrain caused the Victorian engineers many problems and it is thanks to their ingenuity and skill that the line was ever finished. During the course of its 72 miles, the line crosses 20 viaducts and passes through 12 tunnels, each of which was constructed by an army of navvies who had little in the way of resources besides their strength and some dynamite to remove the rock.

Located on the northwestern edge of the city, **Kingmoor Nature Reserve** occupies an area of moorland given to the city in 1352 by Edward III. Citizens enjoyed the right to graze sheep on the moors and to cut peat for fuel. Later, Carlisle's first racecourse was established here with annual Guild races being held up until 1850. Then in 1913, Kingmoor became one of the first bird sanctuaries in England and today provides a peaceful retreat away from the bustle of the city. A half-mile circular path wanders through the woodland with gentle gradients of 1 in 20 making it fully accessible to wheelchairs and pushchairs, and with seats every 100 yards or so providing plenty of resting places. Another path links the reserve to **Kingmoor Sidings**, which since the old railway sheds closed has been colonised by a wide variety of wildlife.

Around Carlisle

Wreay
5 miles S of Carlisle off the A6

This little village is known for its extraordinary **Church of St Mary**, designed by a local woman, Sarah Losh, in memory of her sister and her parents. It was built in 1835 and incorporates many Italian Romanesque features. The church is full of beautiful touches, including the carvings, mostly by Sarah herself, on the font.

Dalston
4 miles SW of Carlisle on the B5299

Lying on the banks of the **River Caldew**, Dalston became a thriving centre of the cotton industry in the late 18th century, thanks to George Hodgson of Manchester, who used the river as a source of power for the flax mill and four cotton mills that were established here. The local economy was sustained still further by the creation of a forge and two corn mills.

At the eastern end of the village square stands **St Michael's Church**, believed to date back to Norman times, which can be approached via a memorial lychgate. One of the few red brick buildings to be found in the village is the **Victorian Chapel**, which stands somewhat hidden between several Georgian houses along the village green. From the car park near the bridge there's a pleasant 2-mile circular walk along the banks of the river.

Burgh by Sands
5 miles W of Carlisle off the B5307

On 7th July 1307, the body of King Edward I was laid out in the village church: he was already a dying man when he left Carlisle to march against his old enemy, Robert the Bruce. A monument to Edward was erected on the marshes and a later monument still

marks the spot. At the time of the king's death, the **Church of St Michael** was already well over a century old and is possibly the earliest surviving example of a fortified church. Dating from 1181 and constructed entirely of stones from a fort on the Roman wall, the church was designed for protection against Border raids, which is why its tower has walls seven feet thick. The tower can only be entered through a strong iron grille.

Port Carlisle
12 miles W of Carlisle off the B5307

At one time, sailing boats could make their way by canal from Port Carlisle to the heart of the city of Carlisle. Boats were towed there, a journey that took about 1 hour 40 minutes, enabling Carlisle to be reached within a day by sea from Liverpool. The canal was later replaced by a railway which brought many Scandinavian emigrants through the village on their way to the United States and Canada. But the building of the Bowness railway viaduct altered the deep water channels, causing Port Carlisle to silt up. The railway was eventually dismantled but its old course can still be traced and stretches of it form part of the Cumbrian Cycle Way.

This stretch of the Solway coastline provided the setting for Sir Walter Scott's novel *Redgauntlet*, and the fortified farmhouse by the roadside at nearby Drumburgh is said to be the 'White Ladies' of the novel.

Bowness-on-Solway

14 miles W of Carlisle off the B5307

Hadrian's Wall continues along the Solway coast to Bowness and many of the sandstone cottages around here contain stones from the Wall. Some of these stones can easily be identified, such as the small inscribed altar let into a barn near the King's Arms. The Roman fort of **Maia** once covered a 7-acre site, but today there is only a plaque explaining where it used to be. Bowness is sometimes said to be the end of the Wall but in fact it just turned a corner here and continued south along the coast for another 40 miles.

One local story tells that, in 1626, some Scotsmen crossed the Solway and stole the Bowness church bells. The thieves were spotted, chased, and forced to lighten their boats by throwing the bells overboard. Later, the men of Bowness crossed the Firth and, in retaliation seized the bells of Middlebie, Dumfries. Two miles south of the village lies **Glasson Moss National Nature Reserve**, a lowland raised mire extending to 93 hectares. Many species of sphagnum moss are to be found here, and the birdlife includes red grouse, curlew, sparrowhawk and snipe.

Longtown

9 miles N of Carlisle on the A7

Situated on the north side of **Hadrian's Wall**, only a couple of miles from the Scottish border, this is the last town in England. Its position on the River Esk so close to the border has influenced its history from earliest times. The Romans occupied this land and they were followed by other conquerors. The legendary King Arthur attempted to organise the Northern Britons against the pagan hordes who tried to settle and control this territory. In AD573 the mighty battle of Ardderyd was fought

CASTLETOWN FARM SHOP

Floriston, Nr Carlisle, Cumbria CA6 4HG
Tel: 01228 674400 Fax: 01228 672251
e-mail: enquiries@castletownfarmshop.co.uk
website: www.castletownfarmshop.co.uk

Castletown Farm Shop stands within a 5,000-acre working mixed farm either side of the A74 between Carlisle and Gretna. The shop sells a wide range of home-produced meat and vegetables, a large selection of cheeses, and it has an excellent delicatessen. The shop stocks a selection of organic produce but the emphasis is on locally produced or English foods. The Castletown Kitchen produces a large selection of home cooked frozen meals in varying sizes along with many different cakes and bakes. There is also The Coffee

Shop serving baguettes, baked potatoes, soup and cakes from the kitchen as well as a daily special, all made without artificial preservatives or additives. Open 7 days a week Mon-Sat 9.30am-5.00pm, Sunday 10.00am-4.00pm.

March Bank Hotel

Scotch Dyke, north of Longtown,
Cumbria CA6 7KP
Tel: 01228 791325 Fax: 01228 791216

In a glorious setting overlooking the lovely Esk Valley, the **March Bank Hotel** is a charming villa built in 1870. The house is owned and run by Richard and Clair Moore, who have made it not only one of the top places in the area to stay, but also a place to seek out for its superb food. Richard is a skilled and adventurous chef whose menus combine both traditional English cooking and dishes from around the world, and a meal in the **Sportsmans Restaurant** is definitely an

occasion to savour, with good wines accompanying the fine food. Guest accommodation comprises seven well-equipped en suite bedrooms.

here and, according to legend, 80,000 men were slain.

Until 1750 Longtown was a small hamlet of mud dwellings. Dr Robert Graham, an 18th century clergyman, proposed the building of the Esk bridge which was completed in 1756, and it was this venture that led to Longtown's establishment as a bustling border town. These days it has some fine individual buildings and broad, tree-lined terraces of colour-washed houses.

On the outskirts of Longtown is **Arthuret Church**. The earliest records of the church date from 1150 and it was originally served by the monks of Jedburgh. But it is thought that the earliest church here may have been founded by St Kentigern in the 6th century; recent research has led some to believe that King Arthur was actually interred here after his last battle, Camboglanna, was fought a few miles east of Longtown at Gilsland. The present church, dedicated to **St Michael and All Angels**, was built in 1609, financed by a general collection

throughout the realm which James I ordered after a report that the people of Arthuret Church were without faith or religion. The people that he referred to, of course, were the infamous Reivers, ungoverned by either English or Scottish laws.

Archie Armstrong, favourite Court Jester to James I and later to Charles I, is buried in the churchyard which also contains an unusual stone cross. It consists of two parts of an early medieval wheel-head cross clamped together onto a tapering shaft with 19th century decorations.

Bewcastle
14 miles NE of Carlisle off the B6318

Roman legionaries assigned to the fort at what is now Bewcastle must certainly have felt that they had drawn the short straw. The fort stood all on its own, about 9 miles north of Hadrian's Wall, guarding a crossing over the Kirk Beck. The site covered around six acres and most of it is now occupied by the ruins of a **Norman Castle**. Most of the south wall is still standing but little else remains and the castle is best admired for its setting rather than its architecture.

A much more impressive survival dominates the village churchyard. Here stands the **Bewcastle Cross**, erected around AD670 and one of the oldest and finest stone crosses in Europe. Standing over 13 feet in height, its intricate Celtic carvings have survived the centuries of weathering and much of the runic inscription can still be made out in the yellow sandstone. One of the carvings, a semicircle with 13 radiating lines, three of which have crossbars, is believed to be a sophisticated sundial which not only indicated the 12 hours of the Roman clock but also the three 'tides' of the Saxon day - morning, noon and eventide.

Wetheral
4 miles E of Carlisle off the A69

Wetheral stands above the **River Eden**, over which runs an impressive railway viaduct, carrying the **Tyne Valley Line**, which was built by Francis Giles in 1830. Wetheral **Parish Church** lies below the village beside the river and contains a poignant sculpture by Joseph Nollekens of the dying Lady Mary Howard clasping her dead baby. Nearby, occupying a lovely riverside setting, is another of the **Eden Benchmarks**, a sculptured bench in St Bee's sandstone by Tim Shutter, entitled *Flight of Fancy*.

St Constantine was the local patron

and the church is dedicated to the Holy Trinity, St Constantine and St Mary. Constantine is said to have lived in caves in what are now National Trust woodlands alongside the river, a location known as **Constantine's Caves**. (The caves were also used later by the nearby Priory to conceal their valuables during the Reiver raids.) Constantine died as a martyr in AD 657 and a life-sized statue of him can be seen in the grounds of **Corby Castle** to the south of the village. The castle, with its impressive 13th century keep and terraced gardens overlooking the Eden, is usually open during the summer months.

During the reign of William Rufus, one of his barons, Ranulph Meschin, founded a priory for Benedictine monks at Wetheral above a red-rock gorge of the River Eden. It was a dependency of the Abbey of St Mary at York and the prior and the monastery served the church and domestic chapel of Corby Castle. All that remains now is the imposing three-storey gatehouse.

Warwick
4 miles E of Carlisle on the A69

It is well worth visiting the village's remarkable Norman **Church of St Leonard**, which consists of a restored nave and chancel with a curiously buttressed apse and a splendid arch leading into a modern vestibule. Warwick's other church, St Paul's, is reputed to have been commissioned by a wealthy Carlisle man who took umbrage at a sermon preached at St Leonard's.

THE QUEEN'S ARMS INN

Warwick-on-Eden, Nr Carlisle,
Cumbria CA4 8PA
Tel: 01228 560699 Fax: 01228 562239
e-mail: evilema@hotmail.com
website: www.queensarms.uk.com

The Queen's Arms is a marvellous old hostelry located just off the A69 and only a mile or so from Junction 43 of the M6. Run in fine style by experienced tenants Emma Holt and her parents Elizabeth and Peter, the inn is a perfect base for touring a region of great historical interest or for doing business in Carlisle, but it's also an ideal spot for staying put, with a picturesque village setting and good walks in the neighbouring countryside and along the river banks.

The guest accommodation comprises six en suite bedrooms with tv and tea-makers; they include a honeymoon suite and a family room. Traditional ales, including excellent Thwaites brews, are served in the lounge bar, along with good bar food, while in the lovely restaurant Elizabeth and Emma produce classic pub dishes such as meat pies, battered haddock and the crowd-pulling Sunday roasts (the Sunday carvery operates from noon to 8 o'clock). When the weather is kind the beer garden and children's play area come into their own. Thursday is quiz night at this outstanding inn.

Crosby-on-Eden

4 miles NE of Carlisle off the A689

The tiny hamlet of **High Crosby** stands on the hillside overlooking the River Eden; the small village of **Low Crosby** sits beside the river, clustered around a Victorian sandstone church. Inside the church there's a modern square pulpit, intricately carved with pomegranates, wheat and vines. Apparently, it was carved from one half of a tree felled nearby; the other half was used to create a second pulpit which was installed in the newly-built Liverpool Cathedral.

A couple of miles east of Crosby, The **Solway Aviation Museum** is one of only a few museums located on a 'live' airfield, in this case Carlisle Airport.

Opened in 1997, the museum is home to several British jet aircraft of the 1950s and 1960s, among them the mighty Vulcan and the Canberra. Other exhibits include a wartime air raid shelter where a video presentation explains the story behind the museum, displays of the Blue Streak rocket programme, testing for which took place only a few miles from here, and a very impressive engine room which houses one of Frank Whittle's first development jet engines.

Brampton

Nestling in the heart of the lovely Irthing Valley, Brampton is a delightful little town where the Wednesday market has been held since 1252, authorised by a charter granted by Henry III. Overlooking the Market Place is the town's most striking building, the octagonal **Moot Hall** topped by a handsome clock tower. There has been a Moot Hall here since 1648 but the present Hall was built in 1817 by Lord Carlisle. The iron stocks at the foot of a double flight of external stairs were last used in 1836.

Just around the corner, in **High Cross Street**, is the house (now a shop) which once witnessed one of the high points in Bonnie Prince Charles' rebellion of 1745. It was here that the Prince stayed during the siege of Carlisle and it was here, on November 17, 1745 that the Mayor and Aldermen presented him with the keys to the city. A few months later, following the Prince's defeat, six of his supporters were hanged on the Capon Tree on the south side of the town and in sight of the Scottish hills. The tree survived until the last century and in its place there now stands a monument commemorating the event.

Just off the Market Place is **St Martin's Church**, which was built anew

LOW RIGG FARM

Walton, Nr Brampton, Cumbria CA8 2DX
Tel: 01697 73233
e-mail: lowrigg@tiscali.co.uk

Low Rigg is a 125-acre working dairy farm lying 3 miles north of Brampton off the A6071. At the heart of the farm is a lovely old farmhouse where owners Ann and Clifford Thompson welcome Bed & Breakfast guests in two pleasantly appointed bedrooms. The day starts with an excellent farmhouse breakfast which includes homemade bread and preserves, and guests can be supplied with a packed lunch to see them through a day's walking and exploring nearby Hadrian's Wall. Lanercost Priory and Bewcastle Cross are other local places of historic interest. Guests have their own lounge and are invited to look round the farm.

CROFTLANDS HOUSE

Heads Nook, Brampton, Cumbria CA8 9AF
Tel: 01228 560437 Mobile: 07778781061
Fax: 01228 561658
e-mail: playjumps@aol.com

Croftlands House is a large and distinguished country property with attached stables and an equestrian arena that reflects the main interest of the owners. Ann and Hugh Lawson open their home to Bed & Breakfast guests in three very comfortable twin bedrooms with en suite (2) or private facilities. A good choice is available for breakfast, and guest amenities include a full-size snooker table. The guest accommodation is geared mainly towards the week, as the Lawsons are engaged in eventing activities most summer weekends. Croftlands is situated off the A69 (Warwick Bridge) not far from J43 of the M6.

in 1874 and contains one of the undiscovered secrets of the area - some magnificent stained glass windows designed by one of the founder members of the pre-Raphaelite brotherhood, Edward Burne-Jones. It was his fellow-member of the brotherhood, Philip Webb, William Morris's associate, who designed the church and insisted that contemporary stained glass should be installed.

Around Brampton

Low Row
3 miles E of Brampton off the A69

Within easy reach of the town is **Hadrian's Wall**, just 3 miles to the north. If you've ever wondered where the Wall's missing masonry went to, look no further than the fabric of **Lanercost Priory** (English Heritage). An impressive red sandstone ruin set in secluded woodland, the priory was founded in 1166 by Robert de Vaux. In 1306, Edward I spent six months at the priory recuperating after his skirmishes with the Scots. Lanercost is well preserved and its scale is a reminder that it was a grand complex in its heyday. However, the priory suffered greatly in the border raids of the 13th and 14th centuries. One such raid is known to have been led by William Wallace, an early campaigner for Scottish independence from English rule. When the Priory was closed in 1536, the sandstone blocks were recycled once

again for houses in the town. But much of the Priory's great north aisle remains intact, set in a romantic and hauntingly beautiful position in the valley of the River Irthing. The Priory is well signposted and lies only 3 miles off the A69 (leave at Brampton).

Also most impressive is **Naworth Castle**, built around 1335 in its present form by Lord Dacre as an important border stronghold. The castle passed through the female line to the Howard family after the last Lord Dacre was killed as a child, improbable as it might seem, by falling off his rocking horse. Now owned by the Howard family, Earls of Carlisle, the Castle is private but there are good views from the minor road off the A69 that passes in front of it - the scene is particularly attractive in spring when the lawns are ablaze with daffodils. Pre-booked parties are welcome all year round and the Castle has become a popular venue for weddings and corporate events.

The Castle's supreme glory is the Great Hall, hung with French tapestries and guarded by four unique heraldic beasts holding aloft their family pennants. The Long Gallery extends for 116 feet and was used as a guardroom. It now houses an interesting collection of paintings, many brought together by the 9th Earl, George Howard. He entertained many pre-Raphaelite painters here, but the only surviving example of their work is Burne-Jones's *Battle of Flodden* - the rest were destroyed by a fire in 1844. In the courtyard there are some intriguing medieval latrines!

The area around Brampton had good reason to be grateful to the Dacres of Naworth, who as Wardens of the Northern Marches protected it against marauding Scots. However, the townspeople of Brampton in Victorian times must have had mixed feelings about a later descendant, Rosalind, wife of the 9th Earl of Carlisle. An enthusiastic supporter of total abstinence, she contrived to get most of the small town's 40 public houses and drinking rooms closed.

South of Brampton are **Gelt Woods**, lying in a deep sandstone ravine carved by the fast-flowing River Gelt. By the river is an inscribed rock called **Written Rock** which is thought to have been carved by a Roman standard bearer in AD207.

Talkin

2 miles S of Brampton off the B6413

Talkin Tarn, now the focus of a 120-acre country park, has been a popular place for watersports for over 100 years. Glacial in origin, the Tarn was formed some 10,000 years ago and is continually replenished by underground springs. Modern day visitors can sail, windsurf, canoe or hire one of the original wooden rowing boats. Talkin Tarn Rowing Club has been rowing on the tarn for 130 years and holds its annual regatta in July. Fishing licences are available, there's a nature trail and an orienteering course, a play area for children under 8, a tea room and a gift shop; guided walks with a warden are also available for organised groups. The park is a peaceful place but, according to legend, beneath the surface of the lake there is a submerged village destroyed by a wrathful god, the ruins of which can still be seen below the water surface in a certain light.

Gilsland

7 miles E of Brampton on the B6318

Located in one of the most picturesque settings along the whole length of Hadrian's Wall and overlooking the

THE BLACKSMITHS ARMS

Talkin Village, Nr Brampton,
Cumbria CA8 1LE
Tel: 01697 73452 Fax: 01697 73396

Three miles from Brampton in the beautiful village of Talkin, the 18th century **Blacksmiths Arms** welcomes visitors with a winning combination of charm, warm hospitality, fine food and drink and excellent accommodation. The restaurant menu tempts with a superb choice of meat, fish and vegetarian dishes, and at lunchtime lighter snacks are also available. The inn has five lovely bedrooms, all

with en suite facilities, that provide a perfect base for exploring an area rich in scenic and historic interest.

BIRDOSWALD ROMAN FORT

Gilsland, Carlisle, Cumbria CA8 7DD
Tel: 016977 47602 Fax: 016877 47605
e-mail: birdoswald@dial.pipex.com

Located in one of the most picturesque settings along the whole length of Hadrian's Wall and overlooking the River Irthing, **Birdoswald Roman Fort** is one of the best preserved mile-castles along the Wall and unique in that all the components of the Roman frontier system can be found here. This World Heritage Site is set high on a plateau with magnificent views over the surrounding countryside. The early turf wall, built in AD122, can be seen along with the fort, and a superb stretch of the Wall stretches from the fort for a third of a mile. Originally, this fort would have covered five acres and it may have been the base for up to 1000 soldiers. During its 300-year occupation, the fort underwent substantial alterations and the turf wall, the stone wall, Harrow's Scar Milecastle, and the fort itself are all visible reminders of the occupation.

Between April and October, history comes to life at Birdoswald with a wide variety of events - battle re-enactments, music and drama, and the site also has an interactive Visitor Centre, a gift and tea shop, and a picnic area. In 1999, a residential study centre with a range of excellent study facilities as well as accommodation was added to the site's amenities.

It is thanks to Henry Norman, a Victorian romantic and owner of the land on which the fort stands, that today's visitors can see these wonderful remains. An enthusiastic archaeologist, Norman extended the farmhouse, built the tower, and carried out the major excavation work to the fort, walls, and gates.

River Irthing, **Birdoswald Roman Fort** (see panel above) is one of the best preserved mile-castles along the Wall and unique in that all the components of the Roman frontier system can be found here. Set high on a plateau with magnificent views over the surrounding countryside, the early turf wall, built in AD122, can be seen along with the fort. Originally, this fort would have covered five acres and it may have been the base for up to 500 cavalry and 1,000 foot soldiers.

Gilsland village is also known for its

THE HILL ON THE WALL

Gilsland, Brampton, Cumbria CA8 7DA
Tel/Fax: 016977 47214
e-mail: info@hadrians-wallbedandbreakfast.com
web: www.hadrians-wallbedandbreakfast.com

A superb view over Hadrian's Wall and the Irthing Valley is just one of the many attractions that make **The Hill on the Wall** a really pleasant place to stay. The listed 16th century fortified farmhouse has stood the test of time in fine style, and guests of owners Elaine and Dick Packer soon feel like old friends. Three bedrooms with en suite or private facilities guarantee a quiet, comfortable stay, and a good English breakfast gets the day off to a fine start. Packed lunches and evening meals are available by arrangement.

THE STATION HOTEL

Gilsland, Nr Brampton, Cumbria CA8 7DS
Tel: 01697 747338
e-mail: thestationhotelgilsland@fsmail.net

Lynn and Brian McCubbin have undertaken a top-to-toe refurbishment at the **Station Hotel**, which stands between Brampton and Haltwhistle straddling the Northumberland border and close to Hadrian's Wall. The sturdy stone-built hotel provides a friendly, comfortable base for a touring holiday with five guest bedrooms (two en suite) available all year round. A good range of traditional pub dishes is served throughout the long opening

hours, and an adjacent tea room serves hot and cold snacks. Golfers can take advantage of discounts at local courses.

sulphur spring and there was once a convalescent home for miners and shipyard workers here. It is now owned by the Co-operative Society and people still drink the waters as a cure for arthritis and rheumatism. Near the spring is the **Popping Stone**, traditionally the place where a man 'popped the question' to his lover. It was here that Sir Walter Scott successfully popped to Charlotte Carpenter.

Hadrians Wall, Banks

TOURIST INFORMATION CENTRES

ALSTON MOOR

Town Hall
Front Street
Alston
Cumbria
CA9 3RF
Tel: 01434 382244
Fax: 01434 382255
e-mail: alston.tic@eden.gov.uk
website: www.visiteden.co.uk

AMBLESIDE

Central Buildings
Market Cross
Ambleside
Cumbria
LA22 9BS
Tel: 015394 32582
Fax: 015394 34901
e-mail: amblesidetic@southlakeland.gov.uk
website: www.amblesideonline.co.uk

APPLEBY-IN-WESTMORLAND

Moot Hall
Boroughgate
Appleby-in-Westmorland
Cumbria
CA16 6XD
Tel: 017683 51177
Fax: 017683 51090
e-mail: tic@applebytowncouncil.fsnet.co.uk

BARROW-IN-FURNESS

Forum 28
Duke Street
Barrow-in-Furness
Cumbria
LA14 1HU
Tel: 01229 894784
Fax: 01229 894703
e-mail: touristinfo@barrowbc.gov.uk
website: www.barrowtourism.co.uk

BOWNESS

Glebe Road
Bowness-on-Windermere
Cumbria
LA23 3HJ
Tel: 015394 42895
Fax: 015394 88005
e-mail: bownesstic@lakedistrict.gov.uk
website: www.lakedistrict.gov.uk
Seasonal Opening

BRAMPTON

Moot Hall
Market Place
Brampton
Cumbria
CA8 1RW
Tel: 016977 3433
Fax: 016977 3433
e-mail: ElisabethB@CarlisleCity.gov.uk
Seasonal Opening

BROUGHTON-IN-FURNESS

Town Hall
The Square
Broughton-in-Furness
Cumbria
LA20 6JF
Tel: 01229 716115
Fax: 01229 716115
e-mail: email@broughton-tic.fsnet.co.uk

CARLISLE

Old Town Hall
Green Market
Carlisle
Cumbria
CA3 8JH
Tel: 01228 625600
Fax: 01228 625604
e-mail: tourism@carlisle-city.gov.uk

COCKERMOUTH

Town Hall
Market Street
Cockermouth
Cumbria
CA13 9NP
Tel: 01900 822634
Fax: 01900 822603
e-mail: email@cockermouth-tic.fsnet.co.uk
website: www.gocumbria.co.uk

CONISTON

Ruskin Avenue
Coniston
Cumbria
LA21 8EH
Tel: 01539 441533
Fax: 01539 441802
e-mail: conistonic@lakedistrict.gov.uk
website: www.lakedistrict.gov.uk

EGREMONT
12 Main Street
Egremont
Cumbria CA22 2DW
Tel: 01946 820693
e-mail: email@egremont-tic.fsnet.co.uk
Seasonal opening

GRANGE-OVER-SANDS
Victoria Hall
Main Street
Grange-over-Sands
Cumbria
LA11 6DP
Tel: 015395 34026
Fax: 015395 34331
e-mail: grangetic@southlakeland.gov.uk
website: www.grange-over-sands.com

GRASMERE
Redbank Road
Grasmere
Cumbria
LA22 9SW
Tel: 01539 435245
Fax: 01539 435057
e-mail: Grasmeretic@lake-district.gov.uk
Seasonal opening

HAWKSHEAD
Main Car Park
Hawkshead
Cumbria
LA22 0NT
Tel: 01539 436525
Fax: 01539 436349
e-mail: hawksheadtic@lake-district.gov.uk
Seasonal opening

KENDAL
Tourist Information Centre
Town Hall
Highgate
Kendal
Cumbria LA9 4DL
Tel: 01539 725758
Fax: 01539 734457
e-mail: kendaltic@southlakeland.gov.uk
website: www.southlakeland.co.uk

KESWICK
Moot Hall
Market Square
Keswick
Cumbria
CA12 5JR
Tel: 01768 772645
Fax: 01768 775043
e-mail: keswicktic@lake-district.gov.uk
website: www.keswick.org

KILLINGTON LAKE
Killington Lake Services
M6 South
Nr Kendal
Cumbria
LA8 0NW
Tel: 01539 620138
Fax: 01539 621071
e-mail: killingtonlaketic@hotmail.com
Seasonal opening

KIRBY LONSDALE
Tourist Information Centre
24 Main Street
Kirby Lonsdale
Cumbria
LA6 2AE
Tel: 01524 271437
e-mail: kitic@southlakeland.gov.uk
www.kirkbylonsdale.co.uk

KIRKBY STEPHEN
Market Street
Kirkby Stephen
Cumbria
CA17 4QN
Tel: 01768 371199
Fax: 01768 372728
e-mail: ks.tic@eden.gov.uk
Seasonal opening

LONGTOWN
3 High Street
Longtown
Carlisle
Cumbria
CA6 5PU
Tel: 01228 792835
Fax: 01228 792835
e-mail: ElisabethB@Carlisle-City.gov.uk

MARYPORT
1 Senhouse Street
Maryport
Cumbria
CA15 6AB
Tel: 01900 813738
Fax: 01900 819496
e-mail: maryporttic@allerdale.gov.uk

PENRITH
Robinsons School
Middlegate
Penrith
Cumbria
CA11 7PT
Tel: 01768 867466
Fax: 01768 891754
e-mail: pen_tic@eden.gov.uk
website: www.visiteden.co.uk

POOLEY BRIDGE

Finkle Street
Pooley Bridge
Cumbria
CA10 2NW
Tel: 01768 486530
Fax: 01768 486530
Seasonal opening

SEATOLLER

Seatoller Barn
Borrowdale
Keswick
Cumbria
CA12 5XN
Tel: 01768 777294
Fax: 01768 777294
e-mail: Seatollertic@lake-district.gov.uk
website: www.lake-district.gov.uk

SEDBERGH

72 Main Street
Sedbergh
Cumbria
LA10 5AD
Tel: 01539 620125
Fax: 01539 621732
e-mail: sedbergh@yorkshiredales.org.uk
website: www.yorkshiredales.org.uk

SELLAFIELD

Sellafield Visitors Centre
Seascale
Cumbria
CA20 1PG
Tel: 01946 776510
Fax: 01946 727021
e-mail: julia.s.watson@bnfl.com

SILLOTH

Tourist Information Centre
10 Criffel Street
Silloth-on-Solway
Cumbria
CA5 4BT
Tel: 01697 331944
Fax: 01697 331944
e-mail: sillothtic@allerdale.gov.uk

SOUTHWAITE

M6 Service Area
"Southwaite, Carlisle"
Cumbria
CA4 0NS
Tel: 01697 473445
Fax: 01697 473445
e-mail: southwaite@scot-borders.co.uk

ULLSWATER

Main Car Park
Glenridding
Penrith
Cumbria
CA11 0PA
Tel: 01768 482414
Fax: 01768 482414

ULVERSTON

Coronation Hall
County Square
Ulverston
Cumbria
LA12 7LZ
Tel: 01229 587120
Fax: 01229 582626
e-mail: ulverstontic@southlakeland.gov.uk

WATERHEAD

Main Car Park
Waterhead
Ambleside
Cumbria
LA22 0EN
Tel: 01539 432729
Fax: 01539 431728
e-mail: waterheadtic@lake-district.gov.uk

WHITEHAVEN

Tourist Information Centre
Market Hall
Market Place
Whitehaven
Cumbria
CA28 7JG
Tel: 01946 852939
e-mail: tic@copelandbc.gov.uk

WINDERMERE

Tourist Information Centre
Victoria Street
Windermere
Cumbria
LA23 1AD
Tel: 01539 446499
Fax: 01539 447439
e-mail: windermeretic@southlakeland.gov.uk

WORKINGTON

Tourist Information Centre
21 Finkle Street
Workington
Cumbria
CA14 3BE
Tel: 01900 606699
Fax: 01900 606699
e-mail: workingtontic@allerdale.gov.uk

LIST OF ADVERTISERS

INDEX OF TOWNS, VILLAGES AND PLACES OF INTEREST

Travel Publishing

The Hidden Places

Regional and National guides to the less well-known places of interest and places to eat, stay and drink

Hidden Inns

Regional guides to traditional pubs and inns throughout the United Kingdom

Regional and National guides to 18 hole golf courses and local places to stay, eat and drink

Regional and National guides to the traditional countryside of Britain and Ireland with easy to read facts on places to visit, stay, eat, drink and shop

For more information:

Phone: 0118 981 7777   **Fax:** 0118 982 0077
e-mail: adam@travelpublishing.co.uk   **website:** www.travelpublishing.co.uk

Easy-to-use, Informative
Travel Guides on the British Isles

Travel Publishing Limited

7a Apollo House • Calleva Park • Aldermaston • Berkshire RG7 8TN

HIDDEN PLACES ORDER FORM

To order any of our publications just fill in the payment details below and complete the order form. For orders of less than 4 copies please add £1 per book for postage and packing. Orders over 4 copies are P & P free.

Please Complete Either:

I enclose a cheque for £ [＿＿＿＿＿] made payable to Travel Publishing Ltd

Or:

Card No: [＿＿＿＿＿＿＿＿＿] Expiry Date: [＿＿＿＿＿]

Signature: [＿＿＿＿＿＿＿＿＿]

Name: [＿＿＿＿＿＿＿＿＿]

Address: [＿＿＿＿＿＿＿＿＿]

Tel no: [＿＿＿＿＿＿＿＿＿]

Please either send, telephone, fax or e-mail your order to:

Travel Publishing Ltd, 7a Apollo House, Calleva Park, Aldermaston, Berkshire RG7 8TN
Tel: 0118 981 7777   Fax: 0118 982 0077   e-mail: karen@travelpublishing.co.uk

	PRICE	QUANTITY		PRICE	QUANTITY
HIDDEN PLACES REGIONAL TITLES			**HIDDEN INNS TITLES**		
Cambs & Lincolnshire	£8.99	....	East Anglia	£5.99	....
Chilterns	£8.99	....	Heart of England	£7.99	....
Cornwall	£8.99	....	Lancashire & Cheshire	£5.99	....
Derbyshire	£8.99	....	North of England	£5.99	....
Devon	£8.99	....	South	£5.99	....
Dorset, Hants & Isle of Wight	£8.99	....	South East	£7.99	....
East Anglia	£8.99	....	South and Central Scotland	£5.99	....
Gloucs, Wiltshire & Somerset	£8.99	....	Wales	£7.99	....
Heart of England	£8.99	....	Welsh Borders	£5.99	....
Hereford, Worcs & Shropshire	£8.99	....	West Country	£7.99	....
Highlands & Islands	£8.99	....	Yorkshire	£7.99	....
Lake District & Cumbria	£8.99	....			
Lancashire & Cheshire	£8.99	....	**COUNTRY LIVING RURAL GUIDES**		
Lincolnshire & Notts	£8.99	....	East Anglia	£9.99	....
Northumberland & Durham	£8.99	....	Heart of England	£9.99	....
Sussex	£8.99	....	Ireland	£10.99	....
Yorkshire	£8.99	....	North East	£9.99	....
			North West	£9.99	....
HIDDEN PLACES NATIONAL TITLES			Scotland	£10.99	....
England	£10.99	....	South of England	£9.99	....
Ireland	£10.99	....	South East of England	£9.99	....
Scotland	£10.99	....	Wales	£10.99	....
Wales	£9.99	....	West Country	£9.99	....

Total Quantity [＿＿＿＿＿]

Post & Packing [＿＿＿＿＿]   Total Value [＿＿＿＿＿]

READER REACTION FORM

The *Travel Publishing* research team would like to receive reader's comments on any visitor attractions or places reviewed in the book and also recommendations for suitable entries to be included in the next edition. This will help ensure that the *Hidden Places series of Guides* continues to provide its readers with useful information on the more interesting, unusual or unique features of each attraction or place ensuring that their visit to the local area is an enjoyable and stimulating experience. To provide your comments or recommendations would you please complete the forms below and overleaf as indicated and send to:

**The Research Department, Travel Publishing Ltd,
7a Apollo House, Calleva Park, Aldermaston, Reading, RG7 8TN.**

Your Name:

Your Address:

Your Telephone Number:

Please tick as appropriate:

Comments ☐   Recommendation ☐

Name of Establishment:

Address:

Telephone Number:

Name of Contact:

READER REACTION FORM

Comment or Reason for Recommendation:

....

....

....

....

....

....

....

....

....

....

....

READER REACTION FORM

The *Travel Publishing* research team would like to receive reader's comments on any visitor attractions or places reviewed in the book and also recommendations for suitable entries to be included in the next edition. This will help ensure that the *Hidden Places series of Guides* continues to provide its readers with useful information on the more interesting, unusual or unique features of each attraction or place ensuring that their visit to the local area is an enjoyable and stimulating experience. To provide your comments or recommendations would you please complete the forms below and overleaf as indicated and send to:

**The Research Department, Travel Publishing Ltd,
7a Apollo House, Calleva Park, Aldermaston, Reading, RG7 8TN.**

Your Name:

Your Address:

Your Telephone Number:

Please tick as appropriate:

Comments ☐   Recommendation ☐

Name of Establishment:

Address:

Telephone Number:

Name of Contact:

READER REACTION FORM

Comment or Reason for Recommendation:

READER REACTION FORM

The *Travel Publishing* research team would like to receive reader's comments on any visitor attractions or places reviewed in the book and also recommendations for suitable entries to be included in the next edition. This will help ensure that the *Hidden Places series of Guides* continues to provide its readers with useful information on the more interesting, unusual or unique features of each attraction or place ensuring that their visit to the local area is an enjoyable and stimulating experience. To provide your comments or recommendations would you please complete the forms below and overleaf as indicated and send to:

**The Research Department, Travel Publishing Ltd,
7a Apollo House, Calleva Park, Aldermaston, Reading, RG7 8TN.**

Your Name:

Your Address:

Your Telephone Number:

Please tick as appropriate:

Comments ☐   Recommendation ☐

Name of Establishment:

Address:

Telephone Number:

Name of Contact:

READER REACTION FORM

Comment or Reason for Recommendation:

READER REACTION FORM

The *Travel Publishing* research team would like to receive reader's comments on any visitor attractions or places reviewed in the book and also recommendations for suitable entries to be included in the next edition. This will help ensure that the *Hidden Places series of Guides* continues to provide its readers with useful information on the more interesting, unusual or unique features of each attraction or place ensuring that their visit to the local area is an enjoyable and stimulating experience. To provide your comments or recommendations would you please complete the forms below and overleaf as indicated and send to:

**The Research Department, Travel Publishing Ltd,
7a Apollo House, Calleva Park, Aldermaston, Reading, RG7 8TN.**

Your Name:

Your Address:

Your Telephone Number:

Please tick as appropriate:

Comments ☐   Recommendation ☐

Name of Establishment:

Address:

Telephone Number:

Name of Contact:

READER REACTION FORM

Comment or Reason for Recommendation:

READER REACTION FORM

The *Travel Publishing* research team would like to receive reader's comments on any visitor attractions or places reviewed in the book and also recommendations for suitable entries to be included in the next edition. This will help ensure that the *Hidden Places series of Guides* continues to provide its readers with useful information on the more interesting, unusual or unique features of each attraction or place ensuring that their visit to the local area is an enjoyable and stimulating experience. To provide your comments or recommendations would you please complete the forms below and overleaf as indicated and send to:

**The Research Department, Travel Publishing Ltd,
7a Apollo House, Calleva Park, Aldermaston, Reading, RG7 8TN.**

Your Name:

Your Address:

Your Telephone Number:

Please tick as appropriate:

Comments ☐   Recommendation ☐

Name of Establishment:

Address:

Telephone Number:

Name of Contact:

READER REACTION FORM

Comment or Reason for Recommendation:

(blank lined form)